75¢

Books by Orville Schell

The China Reader
Modern China
Starting Over
The Town That Fought to Save Itself
In the People's Republic
Brown

BROWN

Orville Schell

BROWN

RANDOM HOUSE
NEW YORK

Library of Congress Cataloging in Publication Data
Schell, Orville.
Brown.
1. Brown, Edmund Gerald, 1938-
2. California—Governors—Biography. I. Title.
F866.2.B732S33   979.4'05'0924   77-90246
ISBN 0-394-41043-2

Manufactured in the United States of America
2 4 6 8 9 7 5 3
First Edition

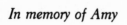
In memory of Amy

Acknowledgments

I would like to express my gratitude to Fred and Libby Miller for the kindness they showed in lending me their house while this book was being written.

I would also like to thank my friends Burr Heneman and Meredith Tromble, as well as my editors, Rob Cowley and Jason Epstein, and my copy editor, Cordelia Jason, for all their energy, insights and editorial help.

Orville Schell
California, 1978

CAMPAIGN

Presidential Candidate

"My announcement did catch some a little by surprise," Governor Edmund G. "Jerry" Brown is saying. He smiles wryly. The date is March 16, 1976, late in the primaries, and he has just announced that he will run for the Presidency of the United States.

Actually the word "announced" does not aptly describe the circumstances in which he imparted the information. It was during an otherwise-unmemorable spontaneous question-and-answer session with several reporters in the hallway that he nonchalantly dropped this piece of news. Even most of his staff were unaware of his decision.

"I know that the normal thing is to include a number of people prior to the announcement, but I just didn't do it that way."

"Can you be misled by your high popularity in this state?" asks a surprised reporter.

"That's not what I'm basing my decision on. I'm offering the benefit of my thinking and vision of where we're going as a people. I have the sense that the American people are a bit disillusioned with government, and that a lot of stock answers don't serve us very well. I can't give you ready-made recipes on how to solve each and every problem, but I have a lot of energy. I hope I can inspire some enthusiasm, and I think I can bring people together. If the people have the same kind of feelings, then what I'm doing will take hold. If not, then it will grind to a halt like other ventures of this type in the past."

The hallways around the Capitol here in Sacramento now

abound with rumors and speculation about Brown's late and unorthodox entry into national politics.

Why did he decide so precipitously to run for the Presidency?

"Because I really couldn't think of a good reason not to," he says. And then he adds sardonically, "A little vagueness goes a long way in this business."

Can vagueness be aggressively proffered to the voting public? Can this man, who seems to spar without ever taking a punch, electrify the nation? Time will tell. What Brown already knows is that he has an 85-percent favorability rating right now in his own state. And what the press knows—though many are skeptical—is that even if Brown loses, his campaign must be watched: as dry run for a future presidential assault if nothing else.

The Maryland Primary

Brown sits at a folding table laden with microphones at the Los Angeles International Airport. He is about to depart for his first presidential primary in Maryland.

He looks younger and smaller in person than one might expect from seeing him in photographs and on television.

He has handsome, almost delicate, facial features, although he is somewhat wide of girth. He has the white, unbruised hands of a surgeon, and skin that is pale, except for a slight ruddiness in his cheeks. He usually combs his hair for public occasions. And from up close one notices that a front tooth is slightly discolored and askew. His eyes are alert.

The press is gathered around him in an unruly group.

Several reporters are trying to blurt out questions to him at the same time.

"Okay, okay. Let's just take it easy," he says, raising both hands like a conductor trying to focus the attention of his musicians. "I'm not going anyplace."

No sooner does he finish this entreaty than four or five reporters again commence bleating out their questions in unison. The one with the loudest voice and the most tenacity triumphs.

Brown replies to his question: "I know I'm coming to this race late. But I'm going to bring all my energy and all my heart to it. And we'll just have to let the people of Maryland take the first step. This thing is just beginning, and I don't think there has been a fair and full scrutiny of all the candidates and alternatives. I've brought a very different kind of leadership to Sacramento. I run a tight ship. I've avoided new taxes and I've tried to promote social and economic justice. I've tried not to kid people, and I've told them that we face very serious ecological and human limits to what we can do."

"What do you think of Jimmy Carter?" asks a woman reporter, trying to bring things down to specifics.

"I don't think much about him," says Brown with a veiled smile, as if he might have said, "I don't think much *of* him."

"Governor, you keep talking about a 'new generation of leadership.' Doesn't Jimmy Carter fall in there, too?" asks a reporter.

"He falls somewhere on the spectrum. But we'll just have to see as we go along in the primaries in other states."

"Governor, are you concerned at all with the way people may feel about your starting this campaign after such a short time in office?" another reporter asks.

"Well, I feel pretty good about the fact that since I've been Governor I've had only one day off, and many times worked a fifteen- or sixteen-hour day. So I have a little accumulated vacation time that I'll use up the first week in Maryland, and I'll campaign on weekends," says Brown. And then, as though he found it irresistible to work in some boiler-plate campaign rhetoric, he says, "Hopefully I can bring the message to the people who don't want new taxes. They want someone who is able to say 'no' as well as 'yes,' and at the same time be compassionate and open and try to look at the future, not the past." By now the reporter who had asked the question that provoked this answer has not only stopped writing in his pad, but has started to talk to a colleague standing next to him, oblivious of what is being said.

"Governor," asks another reporter with the voice of a TV anchorman, "You have been very critical of the 'Democratic bosses.' Yet your first event after you arrive in Baltimore is a breakfast with Baltimore area Democratic officials who are always identified as 'bosses' and as part of the 'boss'-operated political machine."

"Well," says Brown without even pausing, "we have a democratic structure in our society. The representatives are important, since they represent all the different shades of this country. And I want to meet with them and all the people of Maryland. Left to right. Old to young."

"Including the bosses you've been critical of," the reporter insists.

"I try to convert as well as persuade," says Brown. "I don't want to just go among those who agree with me, but to those who are skeptical and disagree as well."

"Governor Brown, you've been criticized at times for being able to point out problems but not solutions."

"Well, I think it's a time for questions. I like to ask a lot of questions—of the CIA, the social service programs, etc. I think we need a President who will not just simply recycle the perceptions of those around him and take memos from the bureaucracy."

"People have called Carter a clear favorite in Maryland. How do you think you'll do?"

"I have no idea," says Brown, throwing up his hands. "I recognize that the Carter machine is well oiled, moving, and has a certain amount of support. But I'm just going to get on that plane in an hour, get off in Maryland, talk to people in their neighborhoods, and ask them what they think of America. And I'll tell them what I think. We'll just see what happens."

"Are you going back to Maryland again next week?" a man in the back cries out over several other attempted questions.

"Hey," says Brown, laughing, "I haven't even left California yet! I'd like to get there first!"

"What do you think your attraction is for all these people across the country?" the reporter continues.

"I have no idea," replies Brown, who seems satisfied with this line of questioning. "But I'd like to find out. It's the start of something new. It's unorthodox. It hasn't been the way conventional political pundits have thought about things. Maybe this isn't the way the political bosses would write the script, but this is the way I'm going to do it."

"I think we have time for one more question before flight time," says Brown's campaign press secretary.

"As a bachelor do you feel you have an advantage or a disadvantage?" says a woman reporter who has been repeatedly trying to ask a question. "For instance, your shirt is a little wrinkled, and—"

"My shirt is a little wrinkled?" asks Brown, looking down his necktie and laughing.

"I mean, who decides what you're going to take on a trip like this?"

"Well, *I* packed this morning . . ."

"You packed *yourself?*"

"Yes."

The room is on the verge of breakaway laughter. The questions may seem irrelevant to many of the "hard" news media, but there is not one member of the press who is not paying attention.

"Are there advantageous aspects to being a bachelor?" the woman reporter persists.

"Well," says Brown, groping a little for an answer. "There are advantages and disadvantages."

"Can you be specific?"

"I think that . . . ah . . . that they're rather obvious."

"What did you put in your suitcase first?" a male reporter calls out in parody.

"I put in a few shirts," says Brown, enjoying the evolving repartee.

"I see," says the male reporter, busily feigning to write down this vital information.

"Two suits, a couple of socks . . . It was three shirts," says Brown, playing it out. "But, to tell you the truth, I haven't bought any clothes since I was Governor."

Brown has a confidence that impresses people. At the same time that he wants the Presidency, he radiates something akin to indifference to it, which—whether real or unreal—has an appeal. People still do not quite believe him when he says he is serious about running. They just wonder what unfathomable Zen tactic he is perpetrating on them.

Sometimes it seems as if Brown's immense popularity stems from the electorate's inability to feel that they can totally possess or even comprehend this man—as if his charisma and magnetism grew directly out of that part of himself which he has held aloof from the insatiable appetite of the public to engorge itself on the minutest details of the lives of its public figures. Without even leaving the state, he lately has had representatives of every major newspaper, magazine, TV network and an endless string of columnists trooping to Sacramento like the wise men searching after the star. Even the venerable Walter Cronkite has sallied forth from the New York media fortress to make the pilgrimage to Brown's doorstep.

Brown feints this way, slides that way, so his interviewers and adversaries are never quite sure if they've made contact. Reporters keep searching for the ultimate question—one that he cannot parry to his own advantage with another question, humorous remark or haiku-like retort. They love it because it makes good copy and TV footage. They hate it because he can waste their time and make them look foolish.

There has been something undeniably fascinating about this young Governor's seemingly reluctant involvement in the political scene during his first seventeen months as Governor. For this is the man who only a short time ago said, "I don't even want to think about the Presidency."

Will he commence to seek coverage like every other desperate candidate, when it has been exactly his elusive unpredictability that has been his most compelling feature? One can only wonder what effect Brown's officially entering the fray will have on his image.

The press conference ends, and we board the 707 for Maryland, taking our seats in the economy section.

Allard Lowenstein, the ex–New York Congressman and political gadfly, is on board. Despite the fact that his role is ill-defined, it is clear that he is an important personage in Brown's national debut.

Though only in his forties, Lowenstein is one of America's perennial political fixtures. He has seemed to defy the need for specialization, continually popping up from some uncharted network of connecting political tunnels to embrace a new cause. Usually referred to by the press as the "leader of the dump Johnson movement," he has also been in Congress and run unsuccessfully several other times; taught at Yale, Stanford and Chapel Hill; practiced law; written and agitated on subjects ranging from Spain and South Africa to Indochina; been an assassination buff; fought in the ban-the-bomb, civil rights and antiwar movements; been a Convention delegate since time immemorial; worked for the Kennedys, and in short seems to know more significant and insignificant people in politics than almost anyone. He is a piece of political flypaper.

Lowenstein wears ice-cube-thick glasses. His dress is utterly undistinguished. He imparts a sense of confidence and reasonableness, and seems ever ready for an intelligent discussion on almost any political issue. Right now in the plane, several reporters are besieging him for interviews, having apparently decided that he is "the man-behind-the-scenes." Lowenstein is being rather evasive, eschewing this role, trying to down-play any importance that he might have had in launching Jerry Brown into national orbit.

I sit next to him, and we talk as he rummages through his legendary address book, which is swollen to truly robust proportions.

"Well, look at it this way," he says, gesturing to Brown, who is standing in the aisle, drinking a cup of coffee and talking with an aide. "What has anyone done anywhere? The question of 'What has Jerry Brown done?' raises the question of what anyone's ultimate capacity for sacrifice is. Have we set expectations that are too high for him? One of the remarkable things is that Jerry has raised people's expectations in spite of all he's said to the contrary. That's something that can't be done all the time. Although I think that the criticism that he has not *done* that much is not off the mark, I also think that the measuring stick applied to him is askew. What has any Governor done?

"Robert Kennedy's greatest gift was that he gave people a sense that something *could* be done. When you have the whole country turned off by misadventure, how do you get it turned on again? I think that there have been some remarkable changes in atmosphere around Jerry. There has been an important breakthrough in people's minds as to what power can do and what its limits are. This is one of Jerry's real gifts.

"I admire a man when he is willing to stand and fight for something," says Lowenstein, removing his glasses and rubbing his eyes. "I think the question of whether or not Jerry really has this quality is still unanswered. Maybe I'm not yet convinced that he has martyr's blood in him. But one important feeling I have is that I'm sure that he would not do anything indecent.

"You know what I think was one of his profoundest comments, one that the press considered flippant? He said, 'We are moving both right and left at once.' His unconventionality is his strongest trait."

Brown has arrived at our seats just as a stewardess is coming down the aisle with the cocktail cart.

"Okay," she says, smiling. Like an older sister she takes Brown by the waist and moves him across the aisle to an empty seat. "Sit here. If you want some lunch, I'll get you a tray."

"No, no. That's okay," he says, giving her one of his long penetrating stares that have become famous among women. "I'm just going to talk to these guys for a while."

"I listened to the *Missa Flamenco*, some Miles Davis and then went to bed," he offers gratuitously to Lowenstein. "But I finally did get some sleep last night."

"You know, Allard," he says in a manner which is both serious and makes light of the situation at hand, "we're going to need a strategy before we're finished."

Just then a woman and two children come by on their way to the lavatory.

"We think you're doing a good job," says the woman, not quite sure about the protocol of addressing a Governor in an airplane aisle.

"Where you from?" asks Brown.

"Lanham, Maryland." Then, hesitatingly, she says, "Do you think you could sign this ticket envelope for my daughters?"

"Sure. Sure." he says, scrawling the words "Don't think autographs are important. People are. Jerry Brown."

The plane is banking now on its approach to Baltimore's Friendship Airport. Governor Marvin Mandel has radioed the plane requesting that Brown stay on the flight until he can board so that they can walk off together.

Brown cringes when presented with this communication, and makes a comical gesture as if he wished to run out the back door. Governor Marvin Mandel, having taken over from Spiro Agnew as Governor of Maryland, is under indictment on twenty-two counts of federal fraud and racketeering, and is ultimately to be convicted.

Brown leaves the plane without Mandel and heads for a waiting room which is a sheer bedlam of fans, well-wishers, press and curious onlookers. It is hard even to move.

He works his way up through the chanting and cheering crowd toward a makeshift podium where a police line-up of Maryland's finest pols stands, expressionless, hands clasped behind their backs, awaiting him. One wonders if this attraction to Brown doesn't have something to do with a Maryland politician's need to occasionally be around public figures who represent some sort of purity as a kind of absolution of sins.

Brown arrives at the podium, which is festooned with an old Brown University banner, consigned to this new cause in the absence of anything more official.

He speaks in catchword phrases: "The American people need a wider choice . . . Environmental common sense . . . New spirit . . . Spaceship earth . . . It takes everyone to make this country great."

A man standing next to an enraptured woman with a sign reading BROWN IS BEAUTIFUL mutters, "An incorrigible opportunistic bullshitter." The man wears a felt business hat and identifies himself as a New York lawyer. "He did just what he said he wouldn't do when he became Governor. He ran for President."

"Have you liked him as a Governor?" I ask over the din.

"Oh, hell. Maybe as a dogcatcher," he answers contemptuously. "We're surrounded by mediocrity. It's just bad. All bad. The last politician of substance was F.D.R. I don't know," he says, watching the crush of people now trailing Brown down the corridor. One fan has even pulled a button off his suit. "It's just all so contrived," he says, shaking his head.

It is evening now. The Hilton ballroom in downtown Baltimore is seething with people. A regulation campaign Dixieland band is playing the Democratic theme song, "Happy Days Are Here Again." The crowd stands around drinking wine out of plastic glasses and waiting in anticipation.

"I'm curious. I admire his flexibility," says a young woman.

"He doesn't seem to me to be a person who is unreachable," says a pretty girl with her date. "He's a bachelor. I love it!"

"He's a little conservative," says a black man. "I don't think he's saying anything new to us. He wants to use us, but we still don't have a piece of the pie."

"He's not afraid to be different," a young male college student says. "I read in the papers that he lives in an apartment and sleeps on a mattress. And he's doing it to the big boys! Go Jerry!" he says, yelling as Brown makes his entrance.

The crowd roars.

"These two guys on the Republican side argue that if we're number two we're in trouble," says Brown to the audience, which is immobilized in silence by his presence. "Well, in Vietnam we were number one in bullets and B-52's, and look what happened."

"Oh, far out!" says a girl right behind me.

"What can a President do?" asks Brown. "He gets up in the morning and goes to bed at night. There isn't all that much he can do except set a tone and chart a vision."

Brown has succeeded in captivating this audience in some basic and primitive way. It is not so much what he says that seems to impress people, as the sense of trust that he is capable of inspiring. His refusal to live in the new Governor's mansion built by Ronald Reagan, his refusal to buy $153,000 worth of brief cases for state bureaucrats, his insistence on being driven in a 1974 Plymouth Satellite rather than a Cadillac limousine, the revelation that he sleeps on a mattress on the floor of his modest apartment— all seem to occur to people as symbols of a larger understanding. They seem to obviate the need for further questions to this unusual contender who, like a soft drink, has dubbed himself the "Uncandidate."

His brief talk ends with a delirious accolade, the kind of

spontaneous audience enthusiasm that is beginning to get the Carter people alarmed as this state's primary nears.

"That crowd was turned on last night!" says Ben Franklin of the *New York Times* as we wait in a smoke-filled private dining room at seven-thirty the next morning. "He has a sensational effect, a shattering effect on women. The crowd lingered. I haven't seen anything like it since the Kennedys. But" —he says in a cautionary note—"I just met the guy for the first time and need to see more."

The room is filling with what is listed on our schedule as "Baltimore area Democratic elected officials." They include such men as Harry "Soft Shoes" McGuirk, who, according to a colleague, acquired his nickname because "He kind of oozes up to you, puts his arm around your shoulder and starts to whisper"; Dominic "Mimi" DiPietro, once indicted for accepting a monetary endearment from a pool-hall operator; Theodore "TV Teddy" Venetoulis, who, while untouched by scandal, has a face that looks as if he has had cosmetic surgery performed on it to induce a permanent smile; and finally, ex-mayor Tommy d'Allesandro, who upon being introduced to Andrew Wyeth is alleged to have asked, "What's your line of work?"

"I'm a painter," Wyeth is said to have replied.

"Oh yeah. That's seasonal work, isn't it?"

"I can't help but be impressed by the tremendous turnout of people in state and local politics," Tommy d'Allesandro is saying now, by way of introducing Brown from the lectern. His cohorts clap their meaty hands together, cigars firmly clenched in their mouths, as Brown takes the floor. Whereas most of the other people in the room have that early-morning, puffy-faced squint-eyed look, Brown seems fresh and alert. He gives a short talk. "Verbal cellophane . . . The quick fixes are not there." And even "A spaceship earth, hurtling through the universe with only limited amounts of soil, air and water."

Though the campaign has hardly begun, I cannot help but wonder how a candidate can stomach the amount of repetition that seems unavoidable in politicking. Each audience, of course, is hearing it for the first time. But for the press, it quickly becomes an endless and boring dirge of recycled platitudes. And doubtless it is one source of the cynicism, both latent and manifest, that permeates much of what is written about politicians on the make.

"Mr. President . . ." one man starts to ask Brown from the floor. There is laughter at his mistake.

"Well, that's a little hard to get used to," says Brown, obviously not repelled by the thought.

A state legislator, ever mindful of the TV cameras present, walks up to the podium to pose his question. He almost cuddles right next to Brown as a klieg light snaps on. He launches into a question so interminable that even his fellow pols begin to snicker.

"What's he running for?" whispers a portly city councilman to his neighbor, using a hand as a shield as if guarding against bad breath.

"Sometimes people are prisoners of past perceptions. No one had more experience than Nixon for the Presidency," Brown is saying to a question on whether or not he is qualified. "There's no school for the Presidency, no place you can go to get a Ph.D. to run for the Presidency."

One of the politicians, who has been introduced as an "ex" something-or-other (a category of politician in which Maryland seems to abound), rises and heads for the coffee urn. Twenty minutes ago when I chatted with him he had not made his mind up about Brown.

"I endorse him," he says with finality, wearing the expression of someone who has just had good news from the race track.

"I spent four years in a Jesuit seminary," says Brown, pausing like a stand-up comedian before a punch line. "Praying for you all."

The pols think he is terrific.

"*De mortuis nihil nisi bonum*—Do not speak ill of the dead," recites Brown in Latin, responding to a question I do not hear. "The government should operate as servants not kings," he continues. There is an attraction between Brown and these men, although it is hard to imagine two worlds of political discourse that are farther apart. But, as Brown tells another reporter later, "Even Our Lord went out and preached among the sinners."

"What was happening last night at the Hilton?" Richard Bergholz of the Los Angeles *Times* asks Brown in the bus after we leave the breakfast. "Were you turning the crowd on, or were they turning you on?"

"What do you think?" replies Brown.

"Why do you always answer questions with questions?"

"Do I?"

The bus stops at WFRB Radio for a live interview.

"Well, he's accessible," says another reporter as we get off. "But is he saying anything?"

"My apprehensions are over his age," says Bergholz. "I don't know whether or not someone who's only thirty-eight can put together a professional government."

"He's the only candidate I've been around who's exciting people," says CBS TV correspondent Jim McManus. "That was a hell of a crowd last night. Do I think I understand him? Well, yes. His appeal anyway. He uses all these words we associate with some spiritual aspect of the Presidency. He's in touch. He's not frozen. It's incredible . . . Almost everyone else in the race that I've seen is just frozen up. The only thing stopping Brown from winning is meeting more people—and time."

We walk through the hallways of WFRB, adorned with cartoon figures with huge caricature heads of all the station's D.J.'s. Brown strides out in front of everyone else, looking confident and ready to be challenged.

We enter the studio. The song "Ruby, Don't Take Your Love to Town" is just ending. It is followed by the voice of a black woman doing a commercial for split-pea soup with ham.

"And in just a few minutes, a live interview with California's Governor Brown," says the earphoned D.J. in a loud, speedy voice. A sign over his head reads WFRB IS: BALTIMORE —MAD ABOUT YOU—MAD RADIO 13.

Brown is ushered into the broadcast booth behind a glass window with several of the station's executives.

"We've got to inject the bureaucracy with new vibrations," he says. "I would like to project a vision of compassion . . . We spent twelve billion dollars in Thailand, and they just kicked us out . . . We're a small global village, and we're all dependent on one another . . . Government is a limited instrument."

"We'll be back after this," says the moderator, signaling the engineer, who punches in a commercial from a large merry-go-round rack of spots with titles such as "Chicken Man Promo," "The Merry Zombie," "Strip Tease Contest" and "Popo Duck."

"You've been on the air seventeen minutes," says the station manager—one interviewer who seems to remain unaffected by the "Brown magic"—"and you haven't promised anything." He rears back in his chair with satisfaction over his piercing criticism.

"Well, how many minutes do we have left?" asks Brown, laughing, and leaving the manager with a betrayed look on his face.

MUHAMMAD ALI—THE GREATEST reads a banner which hangs over the reception desk of the Lanham Beltway Sheraton Motor Inn.

We have interrupted the planned schedule and driven half an hour to this thruway motor inn so that Jerry Brown can hold an audience with Ali, who is due to fight Jimmy Young tonight. Word has it that there are still some unsold seats to the match, which may explain Ali's interest in appearing on evening TV with America's most popular Governor.

"Oh God! What's the Mad Prince Brown doing here?" asks *Rolling Stone*'s Joe Klein, surveying the lobby, which is overrun with well-turned-out black P.R. men, young boxers on the make, trainers, flaks, jive-dude hangers-on and beautiful women in hot pants. It's like a *Black Orpheus* carnival. A seven-foot-tall black giant with bulging biceps, only barely shrouded by an Ali T-shirt which says, "Float Like a Butterfly, Sting Like a Bee," dances up to a buddy in a white Ali training cap. He throws a few mock punches, feints back, proffers his outstretched palm and gets five.

"Hey, man. What's happening, man?"

Brown has just disappeared into an elevator to search out the Champ upstairs.

"Jerry Brown, who once described the Governorship as 'a pain in the ass,'" intones a *Time* magazine writer piously as he surveys the scene in the lobby, "now seeks the mortification of the Presidency."

I spot an empty place on a couch opposite the check-in desk and sit down.

"Hey, you in show business?" a fleshy coffee-colored woman sitting on my left asks, eying my tape recorder and pad.

"No. I'm with the press," I say.

"Well, sure enough," she says, a calculated smile appearing on her face. "Now, I'm trying to get my daughter Yolanda into show biz." Then, turning to her teen-age daughter who is decked out in tight white pants, gold spike heels and a flaming-red halter top which strains against her ample bosom, she says, "Yolanda, honey, I want you to meet my friend here, Mister . . ."

"Mr. Schell."

"He's with . . ."

"I'm a writer."

"Yes. Well, that's just fine," she says, primping the lush curls of her wig, still seemingly convinced that she has struck pay dirt.

"Are there any producers or anything like that here?" she asks. "My daughter's so excited about a life in show biz." Her daughter is now talking with two men who appear to be sparring partners or the like.

"Johnny, Johnny," she says, tugging at the shirt of one of

the men. "This here is Mr. Schell. Who did you say you were with?" she turns to me.

"Governor Brown."

"Isn't that the group that . . . You should definitely interview this boy," she says, pointing to Johnny. "He's a fighter."

"Ali's the greatest," says the man grabbing the dead microphone of my tape recorder, "but Johnny Holmes is coming up."

"Oh my God!" the mother is saying as a black man in an impeccable white suit, open orange shirt and dark glasses walks by. "All the big people are here. They're all here!"

The tide before us starts moving toward the back of the lobby to the ballroom. Inside, the TV cameramen are jockeying for position. Suddenly the Champ appears in a velour shirt open almost to the navel. He is surrounded by massive bodyguards as if he were a foreign potentate. Brown materializes at his side looking uncomfortable and positively meager, almost as if he were a prisoner.

"I just wanted to meet him," says Ali, looking down at Brown, "because he's young like myself and pretty. And he's the underdog like myself. And I admire that."

"Well, Champ," Brown begins almost sheepishly, not sure if there is any way to dignify the occasion. "I just wanted to come by as the Maryland campaign evolves."

There is an awkward pause. The cameras are rolling. Realizing that someone has to deliver the *coup de grâce,* Brown continues, "I hope that Muhammad Ali and I both win our fights. He's had a lot of impossible fights, and so have I."

With this comparison, which probably encompasses the full range of possible similarities between the two men before us, the event ends as suddenly as it began.

Raising Campaign Funds

There are a thousand-odd people here in the grand ball-room of the Hilton Hotel in San Francisco, eating prime ribs at $100 a plate. Brown is trying to raise funds for his campaign. The din of voices in the room is deafening.

I sit down, and am just about to unburden the world of one more piece of rare prime rib, when the whole room is ordered to rise for a prayer.

No sooner have we regained our seats than a small tow-headed boy in a scout uniform ascends to the podium, stands on a chair and recites the Pledge of Allegiance. Sometimes traditions like these crop up at Brown occasions, suggesting that he and his staff are always mindful of the need "in the real world" for an occasional offering of Americana.

The room sits down once again. And if it is possible, the noise grows even louder. Almost every Democratic political figure of consequence in the state is here tonight at this campaign homecoming for their Governor, and Jerry Brown is riding high on a wave of national fascination. He sits in the middle of the room at the head table, over an untouched plate of food. There is an endless series of handshakes, greetings and one-line exchanges. Brown seems small, almost lost in the commotion around him.

A Dixieland band starts playing.

Brown gets up from his seat—just as a man, who has been moving laboriously on crutches toward him like a cripple bound for Lourdes, reaches within striking distance. Brown squeezes past, leaving a clogged aisle of devotees and waiters in his wake. The crippled man, who is almost capsized in the crush, surrenders, and begins to retreat to the fringes of the room to wait for a more auspicious moment to make contact with the candidate. The ceaseless motion of people getting up from their tables to introduce themselves to someone else is so great that few appear to have time to do more than pick at their food. By the time the waiters begin removing the dinner plates, there is a veritable carnage of half-eaten prime ribs and appetizers.

The other attraction of the evening is clearly Warren Beatty, whose interest in the political process seems to be at least temporarily eclipsed by a stunning series of pretty women who happen his way. He sits at the head table opposite the Governor, tilting back on his chair, sipping red wine and holding court out on the middle of the floor like a stall keeper in a bazaar. A platinum blonde, who has been talking to him and at this very minute is being threatened by another woman with dislodgement from her favorable position behind Beatty, slips him a name card just below waist level, as if she were passing subversive materials. Beatty pockets it, grins and has a sip of red wine.

George Moscone, mayor of San Francisco, is at the podium, saying something about "political sensitivity."

"Do you think that politics has just come down to people craving intriguing personalities?" I ask Beatty, elbowing my way in front of a woman photographer who has been more or less waiting in line, and thrusting my tape-recorder microphone before him.

"Umm. Well . . . You mean, Why do I like Jerry Brown? Well, umm . . . It basically is just a question of whether you think he is a good man or not, isn't it? And you draw these conclusions from a lot of things. In the long run what you're looking for in a politician is someone who's . . . you know . . . someone who's in the middle of his body."

"Do you think most people know what Brown has done? Or is it just a question of vibes and trust?"

"Sure. Yes, yes," he says. "Like on the environment. And that's not to imply . . . umm. That's not to imply something based on something vague.

"Well, I just feel he is a very decent man. That's just the way I feel about him. And that's a really important thing—more important than many years of executive experience." He takes another sip of red wine.

"It's a gut-level thing. People give you a reason to trust them, and Jerry Brown is an honest man. There are other people I would not trust. I never trusted Nixon or Agnew. You know? I trust Jerry Brown because he's never given me a reason to distrust him."

"I had my arm around you earlier, didn't I?" Beatty is suddenly saying, his attention shifting to someone behind me. I turn around. It is yet another attractive woman.

"Yes, you did," she is saying enthusiastically, right into my tape recorder. "I put my glass in your face." She laughs.

"Fine. Fine," Beatty says, giving one of his celebrated smiles. "You can put your glass in my face any time."

As this mini-saga is unfolding, Brown approaches the podium. The crowd is enthusiastic. This is Brown's night.

He introduces his father, Pat, who stands up beaming, and doesn't sit down until the room has come to its feet in applause.

"And my mother," says Brown, looking downward with just a suggestion of awkwardness. There is something about the fact that he is unmarried which adds poignancy to the presence of his mother and father. I find myself wondering just what the chemistry might be between a Governor/presidential candidate and his father, former Governor of California, in attendance at such a campaign speech as this. It is touching, jarring, to realize that this man on the podium was once a small boy who looked up to his father, as all small children do, with wanton admiration.

I look over at the two parents. Jerry Brown's mother has just made a brief gracious bow. His father is half standing, shaking someone's hand, face animated with fatherly pride. Jerry Brown, the son, stands at the podium, watching without expression.

He begins to speak. His talk is without notes as usual, and

is serious. There are no jokes tonight. He seems almost ponderous as he discusses his accomplishments and his visions of the Presidency.

As Brown speaks I wander to the back of the room near the doors, where I have spotted two young American Buddhist monks, with heads shaven, and wearing the traditional saffron robes. I introduce myself. They each give me name cards inscribed on one side in English and on the other in Chinese. Their cards indicate that they come from the Gold Mountain Zen Monastery in San Francisco.

"We don't follow politics," says one of the monks, introducing himself as Heng Kuan, an adopted Chinese name. "But we think that Brown is doing our work, and that in our own way we are doing his. So we thought that since he was going to be here tonight, it would be a good chance to draw close." Heng Kuan is speaking in almost hushed, measured sentences, his hands clasped in front of him.

"The Buddhist aspect of Brown is just a bonus feature for us," continues Heng Kuan, as if he wished to remove any insinuation that they are here tonight simply as Zen groupies drawn by the Governor's tabloid reputation of being Orientally inclined.

"We respect him for what he is. It seemed sort of inevitable that we get together. He seems to be saying, 'This is the kind of person I am; you can figure out the rest yourselves.'"

Brown has just finished his talk and has stepped down off the podium. He is surrounded by a crush of well-wishers and reporters. The two monks look over at this tumultuous scene from across the room. While they seem tempted to try to "draw close," they also recognize the virtual hopelessness of any such effort right now, unless they are willing to push and compete with the rest of the throng.

"Nothing can happen here," says Heng Kuan, matter-of-factly. "It's just an exercise. The Buddhists teach that all things come to those who are patient."

"Either he is an egomaniac or he has a calling," adds the other monk reflectively as he watches the crowd around Brown.

"Probably some of each. But I do believe he has a calling."

"It's rare that we come to such an event," says Heng Kuan, perhaps wishing to dissociate himself somewhat from all that is happening around us. "The decision was a spontaneous one."

The scene on the floor now includes Brown's mother and father as well as himself. They express concern that their son is looking too tired. Their son, who is attempting to leave for several other interviews, kisses his mother perfunctorily in an attempt to conclude the farewell scene with dispatch. The whole drama is being played out in front of several TV cameras, which are jockeying around him for better angles.

The two monks and I decide to leave the Hilton. We walk outside to the Tenderloin district, renowned mostly for its pornographic movie houses and hookers. We go into a small all-night cafe and sit at the counter. I order a Coke from the beehived waitress who stands with a pad and pencil in front of a griddle full of sizzling burgers and a deep-fry basket. Heng Kuan announces that he will have a cup of hot water. The waitress looks at these two bald, robed apparitions that have just swept in out of the night, and rolls her eyes as if she has just seen two drag queens. The other monk orders tea.

"A Coke, one tea and a cup of hot water, Harry," she yells to the back of the diner.

"We looked Brown up in *American Biographies* so we could do his horoscope," says Heng Kuan as we wait for our order.

"He's an Aries. Warren Beatty, Marlon Brando, Steve McQueen, Omar Sharif and Eugene McCarthy are also all Aries. They all like lost causes.

"Brown has a Cancer moon and a Cancer rising sign. His chart shows a person who is well set up for career and work, but not so well set up for personal relationships. He is a dominating, magnetic person—able to deal with large groups of people, but probably very sensitive and easily hurt and liable to throw up a protective shield around himself."

Our waitress arrives with our order and slides the cups

partway down the counter to us like shuffleboard pucks.

"Brown has a little tension between his sun and moon," says Heng Kuan, sipping his hot water. "He has a conscious mind that is not ready to accept the unconscious mind, and needs to negotiate out a settlement. Someone like him needs to act to get relief."

Union Square

The lunchtime crowd is packed into Union Square in downtown San Francisco, listening to the bands Sons of Champlin and Stone Ground. Campaign signs sprout up like seed packets on stakes in a chaotic garden.

LET THE BROWN SHINE IN says one sign waved by a young man without a shirt and with a string of beads around his neck enjoying the sunny, warm May day.

A girl with a bunch of balloons and prominent unbrassiered breasts holds a placard reading BROWN IS BEAUTIFUL.

A black singer assumes the stage and belts out a song called "Good Sign for Jerry Brown," causing a number of people in the tight crowd to begin to dance.

Overalls, jeans, T-shirts, long hair. There is a suggestion here today of the old San Francisco of the 1960's; of the flower children, Be-Ins, Golden Gate Park free concerts. There is a feeling of irreverent optimism. People seem to have come not so much to seek a savior as to have a good time. Everyone here is ready to have Jerry Brown knock 'em dead. They're ready to go up like tinder.

Three supervisors from San Francisco are introduced, to the accompaniment of boos mixed with laughter. Their introductory rhetoric about "new faces on the national political scene" committed to something-or-other is ignored.

A man with a crucified Christ impaled on a broom handle raises it high above his head into the sea of banners and HARVEY MILK FOR ASSEMBLY placards. Harvey Milk is a local gay-movement candidate for State Assembly.

The introduction of Warren Beatty creates a temporary flurry of interest. There are a few half-hearted squeals from women who give the impression of knowing better and only shrieking as parody. But the crowd quickly grows bored with Beatty's flat delivery.

Before he finishes, Brown's head pops up backstage. People begin to applaud in a gathering swell as they notice him. A hippie in a pair of Can't Bustem overalls, who has been holding a trumpet, delivers a piercing fanfare from under a palm tree. Warren Beatty is completely drowned out. He does not so much conclude his remarks as surrender in midsentence.

Brown comes forward. He talks about the newly formed California Arts Council as if he had pigeonholed this crowd as being an "arty" one. He mentions several other accomplishments of his administration. But he is clichéd and uninspired today, almost as if he had grown so accustomed to addressing crowds and cameras that he had forgotten there are people out there. He grabs familiar paragraphs and ideas and strings them together like short prerecorded messages. This San Francisco audience is bursting to applaud for their native son, but they can't quite seem to find a moment convincing enough to allow the floodgates down.

Someone starts yelling about the antinuclear-power initiative on the ballot at the same time as the primaries. Brown has angered many by refusing to take a position on it. He ignores the challenge with a look of melancholy. He is losing the crowd.

"What about amnesty?" yells someone else.

"We ought to wipe the slate clean," replies Brown. "But they should serve a period of public service."

There are a few boos.

"Hey, Governor! Where are you on Mussolini?" a jokester calls out.

Las Vegas

"Why are you trying to write a book about this guy?" asks my seatmate, a middle-aged specialist who is flying to the American Urological Association Convention in Las Vegas, where I am meeting Brown for more campaigning, this time for the Nevada primary. "I mean, what's interesting that hasn't been said, for chrissakes? A smart, ambitious man, drops some good ideas and stays away from the heavy concrete issues. That's Jerry Brown. End of book." He looks at me as if he had just solved the riddle of the universe.

Outside the plane, the red sun is setting over the dry Nevada mountains. Off in the distance "Vegas" flickers on the desert like neon lichen. The plane lands.

"Have a pleasant and prosperous day if you are leaving us here," says the airline hostess cheerfully.

The airport itself is a multimedia preview for the entertainment on "the Strip." Tennessee Ernie Ford's voice issues forth like that of an oracle, counseling people on an escalator to "stand on the right so people can pass on the left."

Further down the corridor Shecky Green's nasal voice booms out of a wall. He tells a joke and then laughs lewdly. If one pauses as I do by the drinking fountain, the joke and laughter repeat themselves.

In the main lobby, two girls in carhop-like uniforms stand around feeding nickels and dimes to the hungry departing passengers in need of one last quick gambling fix from the several rows of one-arm bandits. Their blouses have the word CHANGE embroidered in sequined letters at breast level.

The highway into the city is crowded with massive blinking billboards sticking up out of the sand. SPICE ON ICE ALL-NUDE REVIEW announces one sign. CAESAR'S PALACE. THE MGM GRAND. There are Cadillacs everywhere.

Suddenly the desert ends, and there is a lush green golf course with rain birds spraying water into the balmy evening air. It looks as though some high-level decision had been made to change the desert into a golf course by just going out and buying twenty acres of sod to spread out on the sand like linoleum.

Is the man who reads Pierre Teilhard de Chardin and the Zen masters going to preach to the uncommitted voter in the midst of all this?

It's eight in the morning, and already it is 90 degrees in the parking lot of the Library Restaurant, the first stop on Brown's campaign schedule. It is not clear to anyone why we are here at this particular place, especially since there are almost no patrons inside.

"Where's the center of this experience?" Brown asks sarcastically as he steps into the restaurant out of the glare and heat.

"The center is wherever you are," he responds to his own question when no other answers are forthcoming. "It's internal," he continues. "Let's have a cup of coffee."

Brown wanders toward a back room past a large Olde English-style fireplace which is incongruously belching heat from a gas log out into the room just under an overhead air-conditioning duct. There are no windows in this restaurant. The walls are covered with coats of arms, simulated medieval weapons and other heraldic trifles, as though it were not enough to shut out the world of Vegas, but vital to establish an ambience of a time and place as remote from Nevada as possible.

"I'll bet they could make it snow in here in August if the big money was behind it," says a sound man with a network TV crew.

Brown is hovering over a tray of Danish pastry, mumbling something about "bean sprouts, yogurt and midwives."

The few people who are eating breakfast are staring at this disorganized processional that swirls around Brown. Since there is really no one to talk to in the restaurant, Brown begins to hold forth to the press, which by now has filled itself with pastry and coffee. He is saying something about the "momentum" of his campaign, about "the pundits and poobahs of the Potomac," a piece of alliteration which is cropping up several times a day now.

He mentions Carter by name, and the TV cameras flick on their lights. It will make an unlikely scene: the Governor of California talking about Jimmy Carter on the movie studio–like set of Merry Olde England on the Las Vegas Strip.

"I compare myself not with perfection," Brown is saying, "because perfection is not in this race, but with those others who are running."

The front door opens. A man enters, apparently one of the dignitaries meant to meet Brown here. He is a member of the State Racing Commission, a beefy out-of-breath man, wearing a Stetson hat, cowboy boots, wide tie and a large belt buckle. He homes in like a torpedo on Brown and the TV cameras.

"I've lived long enough to know we can't trust everything a politician says," he drawls, draping an arm around Brown's shoulders. "But this boy's sincere." He turns and smiles at Brown just in time for some popping flash bulbs.

"Are you a Zen Buddhist?" asks a woman who has been waiting for the right moment to approach Brown.

"A what? A Zen what?" Brown asks incredulously, smiling as if he were hard of hearing. "No, no. I'm a Catholic—and always will be."

"I don't mind all that Zen stuff," says a man at a nearby

table who is eating with his wife. "He seems genuine and a lot more practical than before. I like his independence. It's an honor to meet him."

"Do you believe small is beautiful?" an English reporter asks Brown, still buried under the arm of the racing commissioner.

"Well, I believe in big horses and big football players," replies the commissioner, laughing and assuming this most appropriate question is for him.

Whatever focus this event has had—perhaps the coffee and Danish—has long since dissipated. Slowly Brown's aides cajole him back out into the parking lot for the trip to the airport.

Below our DC-3 is Ely, Nevada, population 7000. As we touch down on the landing field in the middle of the sagebrush, a marching band in full regalia begins to play like royal musicians from some small sub-Sahara capital welcoming a head of state.

"The band comes out every time a plane lands," says a reporter smugly.

WELCOME JERRY BROWN TO ELY, HOME OF WORLD RESPECT reads a banner hung on the airport building.

As we disembark, a group of local civic leaders come forward to greet Brown. Then a bright-red 1959 Lincoln Mark IV convertible pulls up, and the mayor of Ely squires Brown into it. The press follows behind in a cavalcade of other cars, down a perfectly straight highway into town, past trailer camps advertising "Hookups and flushes" and a drive-in movie playing a John Wayne film. Tall snow-capped mountains ring the valley.

We pull up in downtown Ely in front of the White Pine County High School. A group of girls are screaming and shrieking as Brown gets out of the Lincoln and pauses on the sidewalk before going into the local hotel. Two girls rush up to him and shake his hand before he disappears.

"I did it! I did it!" one girl yells as she flees back across the street to the safety of her classmates. "I touched him!"

"Well, we'd like to thank Jerry Brown for coming to White Pine County," James Santini, Nevada's only Congressman, is saying in the basement dining room of the hotel. "The only other candidates who ever come here are the ones who have had to make emergency landings."

Laughter is heard from the assembly of ranchers, businessmen and community leaders who sit at the rows of folding tables in chairs borrowed from the Ely Volunteer Fire Department.

Brown is introduced. I notice that he has eaten nothing on his plate.

"There is a book with a great title," he says after the applause has died away, "which I think applies not only to Nevada, but this county and city as well, and that is *Small Is Beautiful.* There is a lot of truth to that title. We're living in a society where large aggregates of power, business and government are part of the reality we all face. It's good to temper that with the experience of rural areas and small cities and towns which are not a part of the largeness. I can learn something from you, and perhaps you can learn something from me."

The people from this town, where the major industry, a Kennicott Copper plant, has just shut down in a dispute with the Environmental Protection Agency, listen in rapt attention.

"You know something?" one of the reporters standing beside me whispers in my ear. "I think Brown feels comfortable here. He seems to watch what he says less and just says what he's thinking."

"If we're just going to rely on government," continues Brown, "we're just not going to make it. We need private institutions, family, the churches, individuals, business, labor unions and government. We need all the diversity we have or we have no hope at all. We want a society built not on guilt but on pride. And what I'm trying to find is that common thread that pulls together the social fabric."

Portland

The transition from Las Vegas to Portland, via Ely, Elko and Reno, Nevada, is one that might best be endured in small degrees. If Las Vegas is the land of white shoes and leisure suits, Oregon is the land of hiking boots and parkas. In one short day we have bridged the gap.

We sit in the waiting room of a Portland TV station. Brown has just done a call-in show in his write-in effort for the May 25 Oregon primary. The switchboard is still lighting up. He folds his arms across his chest, and sits on the front of the receptionist's desk watching the late news on the waiting-room TV.

Carter appears on the screen. Brown watches intently, oblivious to the other activity in the room. Then he himself suddenly appears on the screen. He hunches down slightly looking almost skeptically at himself, as if trying to feel how he must be coming across to the tens of thousands of people watching their TV sets and making their minds up whom to vote for on Tuesday. He seems intrigued with himself the way a musician might be absorbed in a recording of one of his own concerts, listening for the flaws and strengths.

The last stop of the evening is the Portland Brown for President Headquarters. It is housed in a storefront which looks like it might once have been a small supermarket. There is a congenial sense of informality about the place as we walk in.

The various campaign banners around the headquarters suggest that this effort is not being made without imagination. HOW NOW BROWN? NOW! reads one. THERE'S BLACK, THERE'S WHITE, THEN THERE'S BROWN reads another.

Brown stands up on a chair in front of a phone bank to address his volunteers.

"I don't think any civilization has ever survived in which so many people have played so small a role in their communities." He speaks over the sound of a baby crying in the back. "I would like to see this nation that has led the world in economic development and technology now lead the world in a more benign relationship to the planet, with a more appropriate technology and openness. It's an experiment, and nobody knows how it will work out. But I sense a potential for renewal, and I sense that it is possible to get behind some of these divisive symbols."

One of the phones behind him rings. He stops talking, turns around just as someone answers it, "Hello. Brown Headquarters."

"Where does the power of the farmworkers come from?" Brown continues, asking his volunteers. "It comes from ideas and visions that people can identify with. When you look at who makes history change, whether it's Gandhi, Martin Luther King, Cesar Chavez or certain other cultural heroes, you find a power there. Sometimes even in powerlessness there is a power that comes from an idea."

The phone rings again.

"I'll get that," says Brown, interrupting himself. He reaches down for the phone.

"Hello . . . Well, *this* is the Governor." Pause. "What? . . . I'll be in Portland through tomorrow. What would you like to know?"

The crowd is roaring.

"Okay. But what would you like to know, Mrs. Wu?" he says, looking right into the receiver. Another long pause. "Well, you're talking to him right now." Pause. "Your daughter's what?" Pause. "She is?"

The audience howls with laughter, and then like canned audience reaction on a TV comedy, it suddenly dies away as people strain to hear the next line in the unfolding drama.

"You want me to give your daughter a better job than the one she already has?" he asks. "Well, tell her to come to the Governor's office." He halts a moment. Then quickly he adds,

"And ask for Gray Davis, my chief-of-staff. Say that the Governor said that she should be considered for . . . ah . . . for whatever job she's looking for. But only to be considered," he adds hastily, and turns to give the volunteers a knowing look.

"Okay, Mrs. Wu, let me turn you over to someone who can . . . No? No? . . . Okay. I'll talk to you. I'll talk to you," he says, reconsidering and precipitating another wave of delirium in the room.

"Right. Right. Davis. Gray Davis," he says. "And what's your daughter's name? . . . Jean? Jean Wu. Okay." He's just about to hang up.

"Oh, by the way, Mrs. Wu," he says, lifting the receiver back up to his ear. "Are you going to write my name in for the primary on Tuesday?" Pause. "Good. Okay. Goodbye."

The crowd breaks into applause.

Brown turns to face them. "See how easy it all is," he says.

Eureka

The old Sacramento airport is cool in the dusk. A balmy breeze is blowing as we walk out to the DC-3 that will carry us around California for the next few days. It looks like a plane from a Porky Pig cartoon—antiquated but still capable of putting us down at several stops at opposite ends of the state in the same day.

Brown arrives and stands out on the apron under the wing with the wind blowing his hair.

"Everyone has good intentions," one of the pilots is saying, standing over by the ramp looking at Brown. "But how can you put a guy with good intentions in shit and have him come

up smelling like a rose? What do I know about him? Only what
they tell me on TV.

"You know how I feel?" he says as Brown starts walking
toward him, still out of earshot. "I might as well put a blindfold
on when I vote."

We take our seats. The plane shudders and heads off
down the runway. As we lift off, a TV cameraman blows a
sports whistle that he wears around his neck. Brown sits up
front drinking a cup of coffee, chewing on a thumbnail and
concentrating on some legislative bills in the dim light of the
cabin. Our plane flies out to the coast and the Pacific Ocean,
going north to Eureka, California.

"Today was madness," says Brown finally, coming over
and sitting on the arm of a seat near me. A photographer leans
out from the seats just in front of us and starts snapping
pictures in rapid-fire succession.

"How long am I going to have you breathing down my
neck?" Brown asks deadpan, but in a way that suggests humor
rather than anger.

"Only to Salinas," answers the photographer, his camera
still firing away.

"Okay," says Brown, as if he were a parent chiding an
obstreperous child. "Sit down and fasten your seat belt."

Another reporter who has been trying to pin down Brown
for a brief interview arrives with pad in hand from the rear of
the plane.

"Sure, let's do it now," says Brown, sliding off the arm
into the seat. "I'm sorry you've had to wait."

Then, with no priming from the reporter, he starts talking. The reporter manages to ask a few questions about issues
and the other presidential candidates. It is not long before
Brown's attention begins to wander.

"Well, issues are the last refuge of scoundrels," he says
finally, in a tone that strongly implies that the interview will
end here.

Then he's moving down the aisle again and chatting. He's

enjoying himself. Some of the most relaxed and informal moments between politicians and the press happen in flight, when the crush of crowds, questions and business temporarily subsides.

"What are some of the big issues here?" Brown is asking provocatively, as if he were trying to stir up some verbal sparring.

"The three-gallon flush," yells one reporter from several seats away, almost in mockery of Brown's recent interest in compost toilets and toilets with low water consumption.

"Oh yeah. I supported that," he says, lighting up. "I say I support any bill I sign." It is one of the frequent moments when, growing tired of spoofing others, he even becomes flippant about himself.

"What parts of this campaign have you found enjoyable and meaningful?" I ask him, hoping to jolt the exchange loose from a level of inconsequence.

"Oh, it's a new process," he says without really thinking about it. "We're moving forward. It's emerging," he continues, as if a few more of his stand-by lines might imbue his originally short answer with depth.

"What do you mean?" I ask.

"Oh, I don't know," he says in an offhand way.

"Do you enjoy it?" I continue, curious to see how he will resolve the encounter.

"No . . . Oh, I don't know."

"What's it feel like to have sixty people around you from every major media outlet in the country listening to you, no matter what you have to say?"

"It's a little crazy." He drums a pencil on his teeth. "It's a journey. That's the way I describe my campaign. It's a journey to the East." He smiles at his own joke. And then, as if he felt that a less coy, more serious answer was required, he adds, "Anyway, it stimulates the gray matter."

"Do you find it more stimulating than peace and quiet?"

"Well, I think you need a mixture."

"Do you get enough peace and quiet on the campaign trail?"

"We do from time to time. But I guess if you're going to be in politics you have to have a certain sense of the absurd."

He picks up a newspaper and starts reading, as I go on writing notes.

"That's what it takes," he says almost to himself, looking at a story on the front page about some grisly murder. "Inflame the passions and appeal to the baser instincts."

He puts the paper down, looks over at my notebook, cranks his whole body around so that he can read what I have written. "Okay. What is all this? What are you always writing down?"

He reads a few phrases curiously and then gives up on this charade, which he often indulges in when you least expect it. One journalist has confided to me that whenever he is close to Brown taking notes, he always writes as sloppily as he can so if Brown should move in for one of his surprise raids on the notebook, he will have a difficult time deciphering it.

The plane begins descending over Eureka Airport. As we land we can see a crowd that has been waiting several hours. We taxi in and deplane. A cheer goes up. Brown strides over to the dais. Enthusiastic supporters yell questions, compliments, jokes. Instead of a speech he begins to conduct a kind of dialogue with them.

"Save the whales," someone yells.

"We're going to save the whales," Brown thrusts his arm and outstretched index finger forward like Billy Graham preaching hellfire and damnation.

"After I'm President, I won't even talk to Brezhnev until he saves the whales," he says in his most convincing promise-them-anything campaign voice. The crowd cheers and whistles.

Brown keeps up the patter with the audience like a nightclub entertainer, playing them almost antiphonically, enjoying them. Then he plunges into the crowd, breaststroking his way through his fans, grabbing clumps of hands like bunches of bananas and shaking them. He pauses to autograph the head of one student's banjo.

"God," screams a girl struggling in the mob behind us, "he doesn't even have any bodyguards!" Indeed, the absence of security men around Brown is unique, particularly in comparison to the retinue that used to accompany the last Governor of California, Ronald Reagan.

"'Bye, Governor. We're with you," one student says, laughing. "We'll see you next time you're in Ho-hum."

Brown disappears into a car and drives off leaving a chaos of admirers, who suddenly become silent.

"Sometimes I've seen him real cynical about all this madness," says Douglas Kneeland of the *New York Times*. "And then the lightning strikes, like this crowd tonight, and he starts thinking he can really win the Presidency. But I remember when we were campaigning in Rhode Island at some parade. A woman came up to him to wish him well. He said, 'Hey, say a prayer for me to St. Jude.' Then he turned to me and said, 'You know who St. Jude is, don't you? He's the patron saint of hopeless causes.'"

Maryland Victory

It is May 19th and I am at home. This man whom I have been with for so many days is on television. He shakes hands with supporters in the same familiar way, leaning over at the waist, his doelike, serious eyes are alert, he shows no trace of a political smile. He's been doing this night and day now for several weeks. He goes on like a station that keeps broadcasting long after you have turned off your radio.

Brown is on TV because he won the Maryland Democratic primary yesterday. "A significant victory," says pollster Lou Harris, commenting on the strange bent of the body politic to "keep burying the front runners."

Brown has won 49 percent of the vote to Carter's 37 percent, and the national press is snapping to attention over this interloper from the West who seems to think that he can do anything, the more impossible and outrageous the better. As in his write-in candidacy in Oregon, he is almost encouraged by the odds against him. He thrives on the long shots, and his gambler's devil-may-care attitude appeals to people. It is not that he is uncalculated or careless, but that he moves with flare and disregard for conventions, and with an infectious confidence that Americans have missed in their politics for so many years.

Carter is on the screen now, looking tired, puffy and almost angry—as if he just cannot figure out how to get this pest Brown out of his hair before his whole presidential dream is blown up.

Victories—Defeat

Brown has racked up an impressive 100,000 votes in his Oregon primary write-in effort, beating Carter and coming in second behind Frank Church. He has won the primary in Nevada, and today, May 25th, he beats Carter in California. But, although he has won over Carter in every primary where he has been on the ballot and seriously contended, Carter has just won the crucial Ohio race, and now appears to have the delegate strength to win the nomination.

All the fence-sitting delegates that Brown has been counting on are flocking to Carter. Even George Wallace, looking pale as death, shows up on TV today to throw his support behind the man from Georgia.

"I admire Brown's pluck. But he's running against a flood tide," says one reporter who has been following the campaign.

"He's intoxicated with himself," complains a state legislator back in Sacramento. "He's been successful as far as he's gone, but now he's beginning to look like someone who really *wants* the Presidency. I think he actually fooled himself into believing he could take this country by vibrations."

"I wouldn't have thought that this was the kind of situation Jerry would have wanted to find himself in," says a staff member in the Governor's office. "He's looking like a spoiler now that Carter has the delegates and he refuses to bow out.

"Well," she says with a sigh. "Maybe he just has his heart set on going to that Democratic Convention as a candidate, getting on TV and seeing if he can't stampede the place."

A reporter asks Brown about the Vice-Presidency.

"I'm not really interested in it."

"Do you intend to go to the Convention and stir things up?" continues the reporter.

"Not much," replies Brown with a sly smile.

Convention

The Democratic National Convention in New York City has ended. Jimmy Carter is the Democratic nominee.

Brown's name was placed in nomination, almost ceremonially, by Cesar Chavez, who said to the delegates, "We need a leader who will lead by example of sacrifice."

Brown garnered 300½ delegate votes. But the balloting was never in doubt, and Carter won by a landslide. He snubbed Brown's efforts to come to the podium to surrender his delegates on TV and make Carter's victory unanimous.

"Thanks for keeping Jerry Brown at home so long," says Carter, expressing his gratitude for the California delegation's final support.

"I hate to think," he says, smiling his Carter smile, "what would have happened to my campaign if he had been unleashed before New Hampshire instead of after New Hampshire."

Denver

Brown has been on the road almost a week now, campaigning for Carter. Today he is in Denver. It is afternoon, and though still only October, snow is falling. The two of us walk alone through the airport to our flight back to California. Brown has his hang-up suitcase slung over his shoulder.

We are just about to go through the security, when a young woman wearing a small gold ring in one nostril and clad in a sari glides over to us blocking further passage. Without explanation, she attempts to pin a carnation on Brown's lapel.

"Hey, what is this?" he protests, and recoils from her.

"I would like you to have this flower and this book," she says, reaching into a bag that is hanging from a strap around her shoulders. The book is a hardback with a glossy cover depicting various Hindu scenes in lurid pinks, oranges and browns.

"Are you a Hare Krishna type?" Brown asks, squinting

skeptically at a small plastic badge, similar to the kind worn by employees at defense plants, which is clipped to our accoster's sari.

"I think you will find this book truly enlightening," the woman is saying insistently, oblivious to the question.

"Okay," says Brown, taking a book about the Tibetan monk Chogyam Trongpa Rinpoche—which a devotee had insisted he take earlier in the day—out from under his arm, "Then you take this."

"Oh, no, no, no, no," says the Hare Krishna disciple, reeling backward like a vampire confronted with a crucifix. "No, no. You take this one," she says recovering, and once again thrusting her book at Brown.

"Don't be silly. I want you to take my book. I think you'll find it interesting," he says, with the barest suggestion of a smile. "I'm traveling light, anyway."

"This book will fly you," says the young woman.

"We've got to make this even. If you won't take my book, then take this." Brown extracts a box of Red Zinger herb tea from his pocket, another trifle forced on him by an admirer at a Denver shopping arcade where he spoke for Carter.

"Tea?" says our airport evangelist incredulously.

"Yeah. Tea." Brown holds the box out to her.

"Well, how about a contribution?" she counters, at last getting down to the bottom line of her mission.

"Okay. Look here. This tea is worth a dollar sixteen." He points to the price tag.

"Don't you have any money?" she asks, annoyed at being thwarted.

"I'll give you everything in my pockets," says Brown. The woman smiles broadly at the thought. Brown begins to turn his pockets inside out. No coins are forthcoming.

"You guys are too much," says the woman, backing off and evidencing signs of both disbelief and irritation. "What kind of work did you say you were in?"

Brown does not reply.

We walk through security down toward the loading gate.

"Hey, do you have a dime?" he asks as we pass a bank of pay phones. He makes a collect call to the Governor's office in Sacramento.

"What's happening?" he asks Lucie Gikovich, his secretary, on the other end. "I'm stuck here in Denver in a snowstorm. I don't know when we'll get out."

He talks on as if no one were listening, as if he enjoyed the idea of conducting state affairs over a pay phone in an airport lobby. Several people have stopped just opposite him over by a newspaper machine. They eye him curiously, seemingly convinced that they recognize him as the Jerry Brown who ran for the Presidency, but confused by the fact that here he is talking on a pay phone in a public place.

"You're Brown, aren't you?" one woman finally asks when he hangs up.

"Hi. How're you doing?"

"I wish I could vote for you for President," she says, beaming broadly.

"Good, good," says Brown, turning to walk into a VIP lounge that has just been made available. "We're going to call a special election."

The snow is coming down heavily now. All flights are being delayed. Brown sits on a vinyl couch with a pile of newspapers.

"I don't know about all these columnists," he says, glancing up. "What's going to happen when our public officials are so undermined that there is no more leadership?

"Look at this," he says, turning the front page of a paper in my direction, and reading the headline. " 'Fear Puts Candidates on the High Road.' How about 'Ambition Puts Candidates on the High Road'? Or how about 'Love Puts Candidates on the High Road'?" He laughs. "They'd just lose their jobs," he adds, his attention already moving to another article.

" 'Eight Cops Indicted in Bar Payoffs.' " He intones another headline. " 'FBI Meets Mystery Ship,' 'Fourth-graders Who Say They Drink.' What is all this? What is it supposed to do for people?"

As is often the case, he is talking as much to himself as anyone else. I sense that one reason he indulges in this thinking-out-loud is that it helps him make up his own mind about things.

"Okay. Here's one with some redeeming social importance. 'The U.S. Has First Talks with Cubans.' And look"— he measures the column with his thumb and forefinger—"it's only two inches long.

"What's wrong with us? What do you think? Maybe it's a disease of the spirit. It permeates everything. I just try and keep my eyes open." He shakes his head.

"Maybe on Easter I'll go up to that Trappist monastery in Tehama County and reflect on it all for a few days. It doesn't disillusion me. But it is often hard to keep everyone's spirits up. We're trying. One step at a time," he says, ending up in one of his familiar codas.

Then, unable to resist the silence, he lays down the paper and launches off in another direction. "Rights," he says gesturing with outstretched hands. "Everyone wants rights these days. Rights! But with rights there are obligations, aren't there? Very few people seem to want to serve the people. People want leisure. But what's leisure for?" He laughs and gives a shrug. "Well, I'll tell you, my idea of leisure is not to take two weeks on the beach at Waikiki."

I cannot help smiling myself. The thought of Jerry Brown sprawled out in a bathing suit on a Hawaiian beach is almost unimaginable.

"I guess my idea of recreation is to get out and have a look around. See what's happening in the state. Or go up and see my poet friend Gary Snyder. I'm thinking about selling my house in L.A. and buying some land up in Nevada County, California.

"Anyway, I guess there really isn't such a big line between leisure and work for me. I've always worked hard and enjoyed it. I don't buy much. I haven't even been to the doctor or the dentist lately. Oh, well, actually I did go to the doctor. As

Governor, I can go free at U.C. Medical Center. The state provides me with cars."

He seems pleased with this catalogue of simplicity.

"But I guess if everyone consumed as little as I did, the whole economy would come to a grinding halt."

The plane is now delayed another hour. We have a cup of coffee. Brown picks up the book on Trongpa that he tried to trade with the Hare Krishna convert, and thumbs through it.

"Do you think you understand the need for the kind of total religious dedication that girl in the lobby seemed to be gripped by?" I ask him.

"I think so," he replies after thinking for a moment. "It was once part of my life. I mean, what can you say? It's more or less just a question of belief. It's not bad to believe in something if it doesn't hurt anyone else."

"How do you feel about people like the Moonies?"

"Oh, I don't feel much. They're mostly young. This custody and deprogramming thing is difficult, though. I mean, how is what they are doing any different than what I did when I ran away to the seminary, rejected the world and said the whole thing was crazy? They didn't come and take me away, although my father might have . . ." He doesn't finish the sentence. "I kind of admire people who have commitment."

He returns to the stack of newspapers.

Carter Wins the Presidency

Carter has won the Presidency, but not by much. However, he failed to carry the State of California, the nation's largest, Jerry Brown's state.

Brown was on TV earlier this evening as the returns were coming in. Carter was behind in California. A woman reporter asked him how he would feel if Carter failed to carry his state. The imputation was that Brown had either not worked hard enough for Carter as a fellow Democrat on the campaign trail, or that he simply could not deliver his own state.

The interviewer had hardly concluded her question when Brown broke in, "Well, what if he *does* carry California?" he said almost petulantly. "It's still early. I think Carter's going to carry California."

And then, as if even at this late hour he were uncontrollably programmed for some campaign rhetoric, he went on to add something about how Carter "would bring new people to Washington."

"But what *if* Carter does lose California?" the interviewer persisted. "Wouldn't people attribute the loss to Brown?"

Each time the question was posed, Brown evaded it. But it was a pertinent question. And although Brown did campaign for Carter in California as well as across the country, it was not hard for anyone accompanying him to sense that he still had reservations about the man who had beaten him for the nomination. Undoubtedly a certain part of Jerry Brown did not mind seeing Carter defeated in his home territory. And while Brown had repeatedly expressed feelings that Gerald Ford was little more than a clown, it obviously had not escaped his attention that should Ford have won, as he almost did, there was every likelihood that Brown would have ended up as President in 1980. A Carter victory made his ability to run in 1980, much less win, problematic.

Carter had in fact called Brown several days before the election, almost panicked about his chances of losing to Ford. Carter begged Brown to film a TV spot supporting him for use in California. Brown refused. The Carter people asked how he could do one for Cesar Chavez and the United Farm Workers ballot initiative and not for the presidential candidate of his own party? Brown begged off by saying that he had never done a political commercial for any other *person*. That ended that.

So, for now, Brown's blitz into national politics has ended, leaving friends and foes impressed and astounded.

"Nothing surprises me any more," says California Republican State Senator and Minority Leader George Deukmejian. "Besides asking a lot of penetrating questions about government, all he's done is a few symbolic things. And then he starts going out and getting all these votes—it's unbelievable!"

Many of the comments that one hears in the wake of Brown's presidential attempt make it sound as though his entire ego and energies have been desperately concentrated on the best scheme to get into the White House. But these interpretations seem to overlook one predominant feature of Brown's political life: often he himself does not know what he is going to do from one moment to the next.

Meanwhile it's back to Sacramento, where routine and boredom will be both Brown's greatest trial and his greatest inducement to keep his eye on a possible "pilgrimage to the East."

Conversations with Brown: Campaigning

Friday evening. The phone rings.

"I just wanted to confirm your get-together with Jerry tomorrow night up here in Sacramento," says Governor Brown's press secretary, Elisabeth Coleman.

"Fine, fine," I reply, pleased at last to have a time set when I can sit down for a period of hours with this most elusive man, without events and other people crowding in around us.

Saturday morning. The phone rings.

"Jerry's in Los Angeles," announces Coleman. "Linda Ronstadt is just back from tour. It's hard to know what will happen. But, for now, you'd better unpack your bag."

Sunday afternoon. The phone rings.

"How are we going to work this out so we can get together?" a voice asks. This time it is Brown himself calling from Los Angeles. "Why don't I fly back up to Sacramento tonight, and we can talk in my office. It ought to be quiet. I'll see you up there about seven P.M."

Fifteen minutes later. The phone rings again—as I am gathering a few things together in anticipation of my departure.

"Haven't you left yet for L.A.?" asks a surprised voice. It is Susan Botnick, one of Brown's three secretaries.

"No. I'm about to leave for Sacramento."

"Sacramento! Who told you to come here?"

"The Governor. He just called."

"Oh no, no, no!" There is a moment of silence. "Does he think he's coming back here? He's got to be in L.A. the first thing tomorrow morning for a meeting between a group of builders and some solar-heating manufacturers. You're supposed to go down there. Don't worry. I'll straighten it out."

She gives me the number of a flight to catch to L.A.

"The Governor's driver will meet you at the airport."

I arrive in L.A. after dark. Wayne Waddell, one of Brown's drivers, is there in the renowned 1974 blue Plymouth Satellite. We drive to the apartment of a Brown backer.

"Come in, come in," says Brown, opening the door in his shirt-sleeves. Then he returns to a TV room, where he sits on a couch with singer Linda Ronstadt, whom he met several years ago here in Los Angeles at the El Adobe, a small Mexican restaurant that Brown often frequents. They have been watching *60 Minutes* on television.

Halfway through the show, Brown and I retreat to the dining room to talk.

AUTHOR: *Do you feel that hotel banquets, rallies and airport press conferences provide people with genuine insights about a candidate on the campaign trail?*

BROWN: It's hard to know what the alternative might be. I've thought about this problem. But there's a certain amount of interaction with a crowd. I learn things when I give speeches. By talking to students, senior citizens, businessmen and labor leaders, one is forced to communicate in terms of their perceptions and values, and that requires an empathy with their problems.

What things disgust you when you campaign? What things are just really hard to do?

I haven't found anything too—

How about that scene in Maryland with Muhammad Ali?

I didn't really want to do that, but it was there. I don't even know how it all got started. Sometimes things are going so fast—I turned it down but they said, "He's here and you can just stop by." I said, "Well, let's go say hello to him. Why not?" I went and said hello to him. So that was that. I don't really think it was a big thing. He didn't say anything that he didn't believe, and I didn't say anything I didn't believe.

The campaign is a frenetic period because you're running around just slipping into events, trying to fill out the day. It's a unique situation, especially when you're running for President with no advance notice, no advance fund-raising. I think there has to be a certain joy to it. It can't all be serious. I don't think it has to be all boring interviews on educational television. I think that's too puritanical and not an accurate reflection of what politics really is.

Do you find the scrutiny which a candidate is given by the public forces you not to do certain things which you might otherwise do?

Well, you can't simply lie on the street and smoke a cigarette or drink a can of beer. Maybe you might do that if you had another station in life, but not if you're the Governor of California. There are certain things you can do in certain positions and others which are not appropriate. When you go to a dinner you wear different clothes than when you go to the beach. I don't see anything particularly unusual about that.

Does campaigning ever bore you?

No, it doesn't.

Does campaigning get tiring?

Yes, I began to get tired on the presidential campaign.

Can you imagine going through what Carter had to go through—a whole year of . . .

That would be difficult.

How does it feel to have to draw on the same fund of themes and phrases over and over again?

Well, I've never done it that long.

REMINISCENCES

Catholic Past

"The Jesuit ideal," Brown remembers, "is that you should prefer neither long life nor short life, neither riches nor poverty, neither health nor illness—it's all a matter of indifference. All you care about is the greater glory of God. You try and reach that state of mind. When you do, then you are ready for God to use you as his instrument. But you must take direct action. You can't just wait. You act as though everything depended on you, although you realize that everything depends on God. It is in the sense that one's self has to diminish that you try and transcend your ego. I don't think I have ever achieved this mental outlook, and I don't know if I ever will. But that's the concept. I haven't forgotten it."

"It was in high school," says one of Brown's three sisters, Kathleen, "that he started getting philosophical and religious. I remember one time when his girlfriend gave him a surprise birthday party and he didn't show up. It was the Lenten season, and he was out on a visit to all the churches in the city."

"He sets his mind on anything," says Cynthia, another of his sisters, "and by God, I've never seen anybody who focuses in on something like him."

"I hated St. Ignatius High," says one of Brown's San Francisco schoolmates, remembering his days with the Jesuits. "I loved music, and all we had was a football pep band. Jerry was interested in debating and serious about it.

"Once when we had a National Forensic League debate in Modesto, Jerry overslept and missed the bus. But he high-tailed it down there in his old jalopy, burning six quarts of oil, arriving with five minutes to spare before the start of the debate.

"At S.I. we had the jocks, the debating team and various other groups. It was really cliques of people. On the debating team, we developed a whole mystique around words. Our game was to convince people regardless of the issues. We were training to become what the Greeks called sophists.

"I must admit our lady scene was a little cramped," remembers this schoolmate, laughing. "We used to visit Mercy High or Presentation High looking for girls. They had these dreadful stiff mixers. Were they ever straight! Right out of *The Last Picture Show*.

"I used to feel that the absence of girls at S.I. was warping. I don't know how Jerry felt, because he went right off to the Sacred Heart Novitiate in Los Gatos. But now as I look back on it, I think adolescence was a miserable time for both of us."

"I don't think Jerry Brown's experience in high school was any different from any other guy that I went to school with who ended up in seminary in the fifties," says Nancy Skelton of the Sacramento *Bee*, a Catholic woman reporter of the same age, who has covered the Brown administration since the beginning.

"We all went to those mixers presided over by the nuns. We were all products of the forties and fifties, stumbling around with our hangups about Catholic education, sex, religion and the priests.

"I don't think Brown could have gone through what he did and come out any other way. Jerry was a cheerleader for S.I. Crew cut, letter sweater. The status of a cheerleader then was much greater than today. It wasn't prudish. It wasn't as good as being captain of the football team, but at least they didn't think of you as a jerk. Jerry seems to me to be just another guy who took the finest option available to him at the time. He wanted to become a priest. In its way it was revolutionary then."

After a year at the Catholic University of Santa Clara, Brown entered the Jesuit seminary.

"I think that in those days," says Frank Damrell, Jr.— now a lawyer in Modesto, who left college and entered the novitiate with Brown—"it seemed to us like the last spiritual frontier. It seemed a rather heroic thing to do."

Brown spent almost three and a half years—August 1956 to January 1960—in Jesuitical isolation.

"Not many people have experienced complete solitude," says Damrell. "But it's not strange or weird, it's completely human."

"The seminary involved terrific mental regimentation," says Peter Finnegan, a friend since St. Ignatius. "It was medieval. No radio. No television. No newspapers. The Hungarian Revolution didn't exist for us."

"If you're not a Catholic," explains Nancy Skelton, "it sounds quite far out to go to a seminary. But you have to remember that Brown didn't go and become a Benedictine or a Trappist. The Jesuits are the intellectuals, the elite—the corporate leaders and bank presidents of the Catholic Church. But I think finally Brown just found that he was on the side of change. He had all those ideas, and there he was in that strict order not able to do anything."

"We felt that the Jesuit Order was out of touch with the contemporary world," says Finnegan, describing why he and Brown finally left.

"I began to think," recalls Brown himself, "that here I sit in poverty, but it isn't real poverty. I don't buy anything. I don't own anything. But the mystical Three Degrees of Humility elude me, and chastity seems like another form of detachment and separation. I decided I wanted to get into the world."

Brown's point of reentry was a year and a half at the University of California at Berkeley, where he got a degree in classics. He went on to Yale Law School. Upon graduation he returned to California to clerk in the California Supreme Court for Associate Justice Mathew Tobriner. After a short period of private practice at the Los Angeles firm of Tuttle and

Taylor, he was elected as a trustee for the Los Angeles Community College Board. A year later, in 1972, he ran for California secretary of state and won. In 1974 he was elected Governor of the state.

"I was attracted and repelled by what I saw of politics in my father's house," Brown said several years ago about his odyssey from the sacred to the profane. "Attracted by the adventure and opportunity, and repelled by the grasping, the artificiality, the obvious manipulation, role-playing and repetition of emotions. Particularly that: the repetition of emotion."

He is reported to have told a group of students and faculty members from Loyola Marymount University in Los Angeles just after his election that "If you want to know what my administration will be like, look at St. Ignatius' eleventh and twelfth rules in the Summary of the Constitution. Rule eleven is that Jesuits abhor completely and without exception all that the world loves and embraces, and accepts and desires whatever Christ loved and embraced. Rule twelve is that each Jesuit should make his first and foremost endeavor to seek in Christ his greatest abnegation and continuous mortification."

Father and Son

"Sure. Sure . . . Fine . . . Good," Pat Brown is saying over the phone. "Be glad to get together. If you're going to write a book about Jerry, you've got to talk to the parents." He laughs. "Where'd you say you were? In-state?"

Pat talks so easily. The words just flow out. There is a corny friendliness to this unreserved man, who is so different from his son. I can almost feel the glad hand and the slap on the back even over the phone. As I listen I find myself smiling.

"Oh, Jerry could have beat Carter," he is saying, one subject just slurring into another with hardly a comma in between. "If it hadn't been for that Ohio primary . . ."

I'm in a pay phone, and the operator has just signaled nine minutes and wants more money. I finally have to interrupt.

"Okay. Great. We'll get together. Just call Judy, my secretary, and we'll set something up."

Pat Brown comes charging out into the reception room of his Los Angeles law firm, Ball, Hunt, Hart, Brown and Baerwitz, to greet me. But, not knowing what I look like, he approaches the wrong man with an effusion of affability. Upon discovering his error, he backtracks without embarrassment and then redirects his energy toward me.

One senses that Pat Brown has met so many people in his day that he has long since lost the need to pin down names and intentions; his political joviality is by now almost a reflex reaction. One can imagine him being awakened from a deep sleep and performing his greetings with equal gusto on an unintroduced passer-by.

"Well, hell. Let's talk," he says, gripping my hand warmly and leading me through the door to his office.

He wears a business suit, gold-rimmed glasses, a gold watch, and has the same fluffy gray sideburns that are slowly advancing up the temples of his son.

The entrance to his office is covered with photos of Pat with L.B.J., Harry Truman, John Kennedy, Earl Warren and even Richard Nixon. With the exception of Nixon, all are dead, suggesting that the world of Pat Brown has become history.

"Jerry was a good kid," begins Pat Brown. "But he was wild as a march hare. When I say wild, I mean he was hard to control. He was very rebellious. He used to tease his younger sister a lot and drive me nuts. She was kind of my favorite, you know. Later on she told me that she used to encourage Jerry because she loved to see me give him hell.

"There were many incidents. I recall once we told him he

couldn't drive the car unless he cleaned out the garage. Well, he got right at it. But it wasn't long before there were a couple policemen knocking on our door. Jerry had just taken all the trash and heaved it into a vacant lot. He was mischievous.

"Of course, I was frequently away politicking. But we were a close family. Jerry and I used to go on pack trips up into the High Sierras together. I went every year I was Governor. I'd go out into the real wilderness for four or five days, and he'd go with me. He enjoyed that very, very much. He was the youngest person ever to climb the Ledge Trail in Yosemite. He was three and a half, and I had to push him over it right up the side of a precipice."

"What do you think of the charge that your son was born with a silver spoon in his mouth?" I ask Pat after he takes two phone calls.

"I don't think it's true. We never had any money to speak of. When I ran for D.A. of San Francisco, I was only making $8000 a year. I had won some lawsuits, but I never had any money. We never took any trips. We had a nice home in Forest Hills, but it was very plain and crowded with four kids. Jerry had various jobs. He had a newspaper route, although he could never get up in the morning. When I was Attorney General, I succeeded in getting him a job with the phone company. I think he was collecting coins out of pay phones or something. When he got his first check, he went out and got himself seventy-five dollars' worth of pennies. That's a lot of pennies. He couldn't really carry them. I don't know why he wanted them. Then, when he got through with the phone company, I got him a job up near Spokane working in a lumber camp. But he didn't like it up there a bit, and he came home.

"We never really had any money. Maybe a little savings. And we never gave Jerry a goddamn thing. I helped him when he went to the University of Santa Clara for a year before the novitiate. Then, when he went to Yale Law School, a wealthy San Franciscan friend, Louis Lurie, paid his tuition through a family foundation. In fact, Jerry used to write me these funny letters where he would outline every nickel he spent. And at the end of one letter, he wrote, 'Now, if you think I can live on $2.75 a month and have dates and things like that, you're crazy.' "

"How did you feel when your son went into the novitiate?" I ask Pat, who is still chuckling over the memory.

"I have tremendous respect for the Jesuits. They were the ones that brought me back to Catholicism. When Jerry went in, I thought, 'Well, he's going to become a priest.' I thought he'd stick to it. We used to go down on Sundays to see him. We were allowed to visit one Sunday a month for two hours. He and I would walk the paths down there in Los Gatos. Mrs. Brown would kind of trail behind, because she was a Protestant. She and Jerry weren't really simpatico. Oh, I mean, they love each other, but they're not . . . Neither one is very demonstrative.

"Anyway. There he would be in his black sacerdotal cassock. He and I would walk and argue about things."

"What do you think motivated him to begin this life of mortifying the flesh, contemplation and austerity?"

"He apparently became religious in the last two years of high school at St. Ignatius." Pat Brown tilts back from his desk. "I think he was probably influenced by the young student teachers there. I'm really not sure." He pauses for a moment, looks out the window, and then begins speaking again with his usual affability. "He knows me a lot better than I know him. I guess I'm just more outgoing than he is. Sometimes I'm not sure I really know Jerry."

"Were you disappointed that he left secular life so early?"

"Well, no. I've never tried to interfere in the lives of my children, although I think I tried to deter all my daughters from marrying the men they ended up with." He laughs. "I think I probably wanted Jerry to go into politics. He's my only son, and I've been in politics all my life. But I bounce back from those expectations and don't worry about them."

"What periods in his life were difficult for him?"

"I think that one of the most difficult moments of his life must have been when he flunked the bar examination the first

time. He just had been taking it too easy, like he did at Yale.
They don't tell you what to do back there, and besides he's not
too disciplined anyway.

"So I think that failure hurt him. Then there was a girlfriend he had in college after he left the novitiate. She was an
awful nice girl. But she kind of gave him the back of her hand
and married someone else. I think that really bothered him for
a time."

But, as always, the thing Pat Brown most enjoys talking
about is politics.

"Then, after he left the novitiate, he came up to the
Governor's mansion in Sacramento. He used to watch the
legislators come and go over there. He told me how he used
to sit up on the stairs and listen to the arguments that went
on below.

"I suppose he's got some of my genes, too. It's a peculiar
thing about politics—how so many sons of politicians get into
it. I think they do it because maybe they instinctively want to
serve. Believe it or not, that's a great conceit in politicians. I
think it is also a conceit in clergymen. They think they can
make the world better."

"Do you think the life of a politician is a good life for your
son?"

"Yes, I think it is. And I think his mother, Bernice, feels
it's a good life, too. Of course, she worries that he doesn't eat
right. Jerry's screwy about that. He doesn't eat regularly or
watch what he eats. I know that he got amoebic dysentery
down in Chile after he passed the bar examination. That's
affected his stomach. His mother worries about that. But she
doesn't worry about much else.

"She's very proud of him, although she gets annoyed
when he doesn't pay enough attention to her. She feels that
he could call her up once in a while. But in ways Jerry's very
much like her. My wife is very persnickety. Like I'll climb in
the pool balls-naked." He gives a loud guffaw. *"She'd* never
think of going into the pool without a bathing suit, even
though it's absolutely isolated and there's nobody around. She's

very modest. Maybe to a certain extent Jerry shares that modesty with her.

"I'm proud of him, too," says Pat, lowering his voice and flecking some lint from his tie. "He amazes me, because he never showed any political sagacity as he grew up. In high school and college, I was always running for everything, but he never ran for anything except cheerleader at St. Ignatius. I think he got elected, although I'm not quite sure."

"Do you think your son finds his life a restrictive one?"

"No. I don't think so. I think he's thoroughly enjoying it. He doesn't grumble about it. But I wish he were married. Not for the sake of marriage, but I found as Governor that his mother was a very restraining influence on me. You know, I had to get home by six-thirty or seven. If you're foot-loose and fancy-free like Jerry, you have a tendency to stay up and waste time. A wife can get right in there and be important. It took a long time for Bernice, who is kind of a retiring person. But she got into it, although she claimed she didn't like it. She got very good at speeches and telling stories.

"You have somebody who can help you hate the bastards that are taking you on. Obviously Jerry doesn't have this. He is essentially a loner. I think those three and a half years in the novitiate and the contemplative life he led had a profound influence on his life." He pauses a moment, reflecting.

"But I'll tell you one thing: it would be tough on the dame if he got married."

"Do you think it is difficult for your son to draw the line between his public and his private life?"

"There's no way you can do it. In politics the two just merge. You have no private life. I think Jerry's tried to handle it by just refusing to talk about it when reporters or other people ask him personal questions. But damn few politicians have the brains and intelligence to do that. I never did."

"Do you think a man has to be ambitious to stay in politics?"

"Well, I think you have to have the conceit that you can do a better job than anyone else. Otherwise the ordeal of campaigning and the humiliation of raising money by going out and genuflecting and kissing the hand of these guys who are going to give you some dough would be too much. And then six months later you're at dinner and they say they want their son to be a judge or some goddamn thing.

"They talk about Jerry being ambitious and wanting to run for the Presidency, but I don't think he ever intended to run for the Presidency two years ago. I think Al Lowenstein convinced him he ought to take a whack at Maryland because none of the other candidates seemed to be emerging. And then he went back there and did so well and got a taste of it. He was good. I think he is one of the best I've seen on TV. He's got a good poker face. He never shows when they get him or anything like that. When you're talking to him directly he'll show annoyance, but not on TV. He must have watched all my mistakes."

"The death penalty is a subject which both you and your son have had to wrestle with. How do you think your experiences with handling men who were sentenced to death affected him?"

"There were fifty or sixty capital cases which reached the end of the road when I was Governor. And every goddamn case would drive you crazy. The backgrounds of the guys who committed those horrible crimes—and they were the kind that just revolted you—were backgrounds of neglect. There was one black kid I remember who had been in institutions since he was five years of age. He never had anybody pick him up, kiss him, love him. No warmth. Never had it. He just never gained any moral maturity.

"There was another guy who was in a mental institution, and the mother begged the authorities not to let him out. But goddamn it, they let him out and he went and raped and killed a seven-year-old girl. He was a sick person. It was such a horrible crime I couldn't commute it.

"But I felt like no human being has the right to pass on the life or death of anyone else. And I don't think capital punishment did any good as a deterrent."

"How many people actually died while you were Governor?"

"Thirty-six people died. I commuted eighteen others."

"Was Caryl Chessman the last one?"

"No. No. There were twenty more after him."

"How did your wife and Jerry react when you had to make these life-and-death decisions?"

"I don't think my wife reacted too much because she was for the death penalty. Her father was a policeman. Jerry was in the novitiate when I first became Governor. I think it bothered him terribly, particularly when Chessman died. In fact, he was responsible for me giving Chessman a sixty-day reprieve. I had no power to commute Chessman because he was a twice-convicted felon. A Governor can only commute in a case like that with the consent of the State Supreme Court.

"Jerry was going to the University of California, Berkeley, at the time. I was up in that great big old Governor's mansion in Sacramento by myself. He called me and said, 'Dad, you're not going to let Chessman die, are you?' And I said, 'Well, son, I have no power to commute his sentence. I've asked the Supreme Court, and they've turned me down.' And Jerry said, 'Well, you can give him a reprieve, can't you? And you can go to the legislature and ask for a moratorium on the death penalty.' I said, 'Jerry, there isn't a chance in a thousand the legislature would pass such a bill.' He said, 'Dad, if you had one chance in a thousand to save a man's life, shouldn't you take it?'

"Well, you have to remember, Jerry had just left three and a half years in the service of God. So finally I said, 'Okay, Jerry. I'm going to give him a reprieve, and I'm going to ask the legislature for a moratorium.' And he says, 'Are you really?' And I said, 'Yes. You've convinced me.' He didn't really believe it. He couldn't believe it until I called up the warden and said, 'Send Chessman upstairs from the death room.'"

"Was this just before the execution was to be carried out?"

"Yes. That night! They take you down from the row, put

you in a holding cell, give you your last meal, and then pull you out for the execution."

"Do you think that your son has gotten emotionally involved with the whole question of the death penalty?"

"I don't think Jerry gets tormented over very many things, just between you and me. I think he has convictions about things, but I don't think he agonizes over them. He just feels things are right or wrong."

"Do you think your son wants to be President?"

"I think he's got a taste as a result of defeating Carter in all those primaries. He certainly has no inferiority complex. If the door opens, he'll grasp it and go through it."

Jim Lorenz

"My first instinct about Jerry was that he was evasive and afraid of something," says Jim Lorenz, the ex-head of the State Employment Development Department.

"When I was working up in Sacramento I kept hearing people say things like 'Well, he's a genius.' Or 'His politics are so good we have to endure the rest. Anyway, he's not going to kill anyone.' "

Lorenz is living in San Francisco now, having been dismissed by Brown. In hopes of forcing the Governor to act on his proposed public service employment program through a state-run bank and development corporation, Lorenz is reported to have leaked to the Oakland *Tribune* a copy of a draft of his suggestions, which called for state-run corporations. His unilateral action angered Brown, who quickly dismissed him because of "lack of confidence in his judgment and administrative ability." The incident engendered much hard feeling.

"For me," continues Lorenz, walking over to the stove to put some water on for tea, "the personal level kept intervening. There wasn't a good relaxed, trusting environment. The more people worked with Jerry, with the possible exception of the inner circle, the more nervous vibes and anxiety would take over, and the more our relationships would suffer. He tends to be disruptive of any work community that wants to focus beyond himself. Jerry's always dashing around from one thing to another," he says, pouring some tea.

It's quiet in the apartment, which Lorenz shares with a woman. The morning sun shines in a window. From here in San Francisco, it is hard to evoke the atmosphere of Sacramento and the Governor's office.

"I was originally brought to the capitol as an issues person. I was a little symbol because of my role as founder of the California Rural Legal Assistance for farm workers. I think Jerry wanted to add that kind of integrity and weight and an aura of being willing to take a position on issues to his administration. A lot of us were idealists and political virgins . . .

"I saw changes occurring in all of us in the administration," he says, after a pause. "We were working for the same person, but after a while we were not working together. People began saying things to make a certain impression. If you did anything unilaterally, you were taking a chance. If it failed, you were in trouble. And that set up a kind of dependency.

"It's so much easier to like Brown from a distance," Lorenz smiles thinly.

"You know, when you speak with most people, you reveal part of yourself, and in turn they reveal part of themselves. But that's not true with Jerry. He has no yen for intimacy. I would write him a very frank memo—perhaps critical of his image. But it was a no-no even to admit that he might be crafting an image. Very soon I began to realize that we were all outsiders."

"After the first year, when people had a chance to begin to be close, Brown would do this now-you-see-me, now-you-don't act. He would wait until someone who wanted to see him was ready to freak out, and then he'd give them three hours and reel them back in. I was irritated by this on-and-off business. Some of his advisors, even his secretaries, tried to counsel me on how to put up with it. They would keep saying things like 'Don't let it get you. Just remember, he's the child and we're the parents.' "

He stops talking and pours some more tea. "You know, we never really had fights in the office. I mean, I never really got in there and yelled. That might have been different. Instead, I just took the run-around on the jobs program for months. He basically didn't want to do anything, but he just wouldn't say it. I wrote about twenty-five proposals, and he would take one position one day and another one the next day.

"I never really asked him to cut the shit out. I guess I just felt too isolated and intimidated. I went through meetings when I was the only one in a room of twenty who would take a somewhat insistent position. But finally I just played the good prep-school boy and never got down to telling him that he was jiving and should shape up.

"The closest we ever came to a confrontation was when he asked me to resign. He was piqued that he had to deal with it personally. I demanded a personal explanation. But he just wouldn't give it. He simply shrugged his shoulders." He shakes his head, reliving the events.

"If I had it to do over, I think I would press him harder. But I didn't. Basically, I think you either have to submit or get spit out.

"There are a lot of contradictions between him and some of the new ideas he plays with. He picks and chooses which ones he wants. He'll take a piece of an idea, and everyone will think it intimates the whole idea. But it doesn't. Many people are very uncritical in their acceptance of him, especially young people. His ability to escape himself as well as all the rest of us is frightening to watch. He talks about limits. But there are limits one must set for oneself, especially for a Governor, because he is beholden to no one else. But Jerry would just change these limitations all the time. We were trying to practice Small Is Beautiful. Then we started to get into some trouble and he'd pull back. That's characteristic of Jerry. If you go back with him and try to discuss assumptions, you're lost. Most people are afraid of raising a discordant note.

"He doesn't like it when the press, or even his own staff, doesn't go along with him. But he also gets bored with yes men. He has a way of letting people be direct with him for about half an hour. You feel drawn to him and think, Fantastic! This man wants me to be direct! But then the hole begins to close up and he freezes you out. And of course, up there you are totally dependent on him."

Lorenz sits quietly for a moment. He seems to be reflecting, not without some sense of loss, on his demise from the scene. He is not entirely at ease discussing these personal matters. But somehow the conversation seems to have a momentum of its own.

"You know," he continues finally, "I think that it is the satirists rather than the journalists who have come the closest to fathoming Jerry Brown. If you follow the rules of day-to-day journalism, Jerry will just dance around you. He eats journalists for breakfast. He knows the game. And in a funny way he is more *here* when he is on national TV than when he is in the room.

"He's been detached all his life. It's not like he's had any experiential work himself, like washing his own dishes and clothes. Until now, his experiences have been as an onlooker."

Then, almost as an afterthought, he adds, "While I was working up there in Sacramento, I almost got to the point of wishing for the return of the old pols, because at least their venality and lust for power was out front. People believe that Jerry's interest in power has no ulterior motives. It's just those other guys who are supposed to have ulterior motives. But . . ." He does not finish the thought.

"It's a weird thing for me to be sitting on this side of the fence," says Lorenz, walking over to the window. "Jerry is running for President, and so few people seem to have doubts about him. Not that I'm a hundred percent critical, because I like some of the things he's done. But there are a lot of questions even the closest advisors aren't asking him.

"If you want to get close to Jerry," he continues, "you can't give him easy balls at the net. You have to ring his anxiety bell a little. Don't ask him anything. Just start going around him. Then he'll get interested. He really respects people whom he can't get to—people who stick it to him."

Conversations with Brown: Religion

AUTHOR: *What is your relationship to God . . . or whatever transcendent force you think is at the helm of the universe?*

BROWN: It's very difficult to talk about God. The concept itself is by definition ineffable. So in speaking of God, we fall back on ritual, ceremony, symbolism—that's the usual way we signal awe and reverence for the totality of which we are a part. We are enmeshed in a complex series of relationships, and I don't think they are all explainable by our conscious human mind. But I'm not really prepared to expound on my theology at this point. It's an area that I don't feel is necessary to disclose for my present occupation. But it's an area in which I'm continuously seeking, evolving, listening, watching and communicating. It's an area that is beyond easy labeling and categorization.

I find in the Catholic theology, in the Zen commentaries—and in other traditions I have looked at

—some basic common points, suggestions about the nature of things and people in the universe. But in spite of it all, I don't think our spiritual understanding is increasing all that much.

What is your reaction to the cartoon perception of you as the Buddhist guru Governor?

I don't know if that is the common perception. Anyway, these things change. I try to think about the real world rather than about the images some people have of me. Obviously I have Buddhist friends, and the ideas of Zen Buddhism as well as those of Catholicism interest me. I'm always looking at what people, religious and otherwise, have to say about how to live and what are the important values. Government is constantly faced with value questions in education, about people imprisoned in mental hospitals and prisons, the way we allocate our funds, the way we deal with our forests, parks, rivers, oceans and farmlands. The ethical value questions are very important to the political process, and to the extent that religious traditions have something to say, I'm interested.

How does the life of "mortifying the flesh" in Jesuit seminary occur to you now twenty years later?

I look back on it as containing a great deal of truth. Just the effort of trying to transcend one's own ego is important. The quest in the spiritual life is to find God and to find the correct path. Egotism, self-indulgence, laziness, pride—all the other negative attributes that human beings have grappled with since the beginning of time—hinder that quest. And I see those obstacles as being as real in 1977 as in 1956.

The Jesuit founder, St. Ignatius, said, "I desire to choose poverty with Christ, rather than riches. Insults with Christ, rather than be loaded with honors. I desire to be counted as worthless and a fool for Christ rather than esteemed as wise and prudent in this world." How does that strike you now—as Governor?

I think that if one could attain that, one would achieve wisdom and happiness.

Well, how can one be involved in the world at the same time one is achieving this "wisdom and happiness"?

Ultimately politicians are thought of as fools. So if one could be prepared for that at the beginning, then the tenure of public office would be more acceptable.

What about St. Ignatius' cautioning against being "wise and prudent" in this world?

That is the Christian viewpoint, the historical statement St. Paul talked about. That's the method that St. Ignatius prescribed for someone to attain perfection in the spiritual life—to detach oneself from creature comforts, to become dead to things of this world, to become totally open and available to doing God's will. The world wants one thing, and in order to detach yourself from the world you must strive to seek the other. You have to dispose yourself for understanding what God wants of you.

In the Spiritual Exercises, *St. Ignatius talks repeatedly about self-denial, even physical self-abuse by chaining oneself up during periods of contemplation. Were such practices in use at your seminary?*

Yes. The goal is to try to overcome the self-indulgent, weak part of human nature. You try to attain
spiritual perfection. I did discover that after a few
years the ego is just as strong as ever. (He laughs.)

Does it all strike you now as a bit masochistic?

Well, the words sound more harsh than the reality.
As a rule, the novitiate and the junior grad Jesuits
give a more activist application of Jesuit principles.
The basic mortification is viewed as living the common life. I thought it was a bit masochistic at the
time. But I would say that the reverse is also true—
that the pursuit of riches, glory, health and long life
can be equally destructive and equally frustrating.
It's the problem of contradiction. Humility can become a source of pride, and pride can become a
source of humility. That's just the way life is. Each
pole of any concept can distort one's will or mind or
emotions. So it is good to realize that to every rule
there is a counterrule, and somewhere between the
contradictions there's a middle path or synthesis that
has to be continually reasserted to avoid the pitfalls
of fixation on extremes.

*What propelled you out of the seminary? Was it the
search for the middle?*

The spiritual concepts and the way I was pursuing
them seemed to lose their reality, to be too abstract
and removed from the vital existential world that I
wanted to be a part of. That's why I left the seminary
and went to Berkeley. It just seemed that at that
point I'd gone as far as I could in following the rules
and the ideas of St. Ignatius. His teachings run
counter to the American flow—there's no doubt
about that. St. Ignatius and the American flow are

not reconcilable. I couldn't absorb his teachings and identify with them any longer. I began to see a lack of contact with the struggle of normal human existence.

What was it like to contemplate damnation of hell for your sins? Was that part of religious life alive for you?

Yes.

You believed that if you ate a hot dog on Friday you'd go to hell?

Yes. No doubt about it. (He laughs.) But the Church changed. It's now permissible to eat hot dogs on Friday.

How does Zen fit into the Catholic context?

Zen, just like other philosophies, attempts to teach a person how to live and what life means. That has always interested me and still does. In Zen, there is the emphasis on the immediate, on reconciliation with the specific concrete acts of each day and finding in those acts—whether they be washing dishes, making a bed, giving a speech, driving your car, chopping wood—the totality of human existence. And obviously if one could find in each moment all that there is to have in life, that would be a good state of mind to attain.

How is that different from the whole Jesuit concept of the universe?

I don't think it is. Because each has within it a range of interpretation. In some of those interpretations there's an intersection between the Jesuits and the

Zen Buddhists. Obviously, the basic principles of St. Ignatius on self-abnegation, understood in one light, are no different from the no mind, no self—the whole Zen approach. In some ways the striving for the elimination of self-will and the pursuit of the good is similar.

Do you count yourself as a Catholic?

I don't feel altogether comfortable with these boxes. I don't belong to and actively involve myself in a given organization. Since I left the seminary, I've been more a private questor of spiritual things.

Do you still believe in such Jesuitical traditions as the power of fasting?

I think fasting can have a definite power—yes.

Have you ever fasted?

I have. I may again. I don't follow any prescribed course that sets forth a predictable regimen for each day and each month. I spent three days at the Trappist Monastery fasting recently. That was good.

Do you conceive of man and society as reformable and perfectable?

Well, there seems to be a persistent pattern throughout history of inhumanity as well as heroic activity to try and reform. I think that the whole process of rehabilitation is filled with a certain amount of paradox. Rehabilitation means to change the way people operate, and I think we have to keep striving for that. I think it's possible. That's the whole assumption on which I operate. Otherwise, there would be no point in even trying. But I would say that reforming the world is like saving your soul; it should be done with fear and trembling, because improving the world can become as oppressive as saving your soul. Pride, arrogance and insensitivity can be masked in the guise of improvement and doing good. Like most things, attempts at reform are a mixed bag.

Does the current rash of groups and cults—the so-called "human potential" movement—strike you as a fad?

It can be, but the basic thrust to understand yourself better, your own emotions, your own potential—I think that's good. It's a sign that we have taken care of some of our material needs. Now we're worrying about our psychological or spiritual needs. In the midst of technological change and affluence, there is a certain emptiness that people are attempting to fill. That takes many forms. Meditation, encounter groups, psychotherapy, drugs, activisms of various sorts—all are a quest for enlightenment.

It's true, the spiritual life can be self-indulgent. All of the spiritual teachers have said that. But that doesn't mean that trying to live wisely and live rightly is not an important objective. It is the important question. It is the only question.

THE CAPITOL

Sacramento

Heading east across California's hot Central Valley, one can see the city of Sacramento from ten miles away. The dome of the State Capitol, several modern state office buildings and the grain elevators of the Rice Growers' Association of California rise up like mirages off the flat tomato and sugar-beet fields. The dust and smog in the summer air tint the distant silhouettes of the buildings magenta. The shimmering heat creates visual distortions, as if one were seeing the landscape through a piece of imperfect glass.

Sacramento is a compromise. Like Washington, D.C., itself an imperfect reconciliation of the need for a political center which served both the North and the South of the country, Sacramento represented an attempt to avoid putting the capital of California decisively in either the northern or southern sphere of the state. Thus the two largest and most cosmopolitan cities, San Francisco and Los Angeles, were passed over.

Sacramento is indicated on the road map by a large red dot, which appears to be blocking the free flow of Interstate 80 as it unrolls from San Francisco, up into the Sierra Nevada Mountains, down into the desert to Salt Lake City and across the continent.

On the road map, Interstate 80 is represented by a thick green line aimed from both directions at Sacramento, where it suddenly splays off on either side of the city in freeway bypasses which appear to be avoiding the city much the way flowing water moves around an obstruction. Indeed, the destination of most people heading east on Interstate 80 is not Sacramento but the ski resorts and gambling casinos of Lake Tahoe and Reno. And before the by-passes, which now encircle the city, were finished, Sacramento was largely remembered as an unpleasant roadblock in the way of motorists bound for recreation.

Inside this cordon of freeways lies most of the city of Sacramento and the State Capitol, which sits in the city's midst, radiating its influence out through the surrounding neighborhoods of wood-frame houses and shaded, treelined streets. As one approaches the Capitol, although still many blocks away, the streets begin to be lined with parking meters. Soon thereafter, great gaps appear in the rows of houses and trees where the state has demolished the older residences and paved lots with asphalt to provide for the insatiable parking appetite of the growing bureaucracy. On some blocks, only one or two apartment buildings still stand, creating the effect of a bombed-out city.

The Dean Apartments at 1400 N Street is just such a state-owned building, its entryway—distinguished by a few shrubs, a green awning, and an aluminum frame door—faces the Capitol. Mailboxes in the building's foyer bear the apartments' numbers and names of the occupants. The identification windows on the mailboxes for apartments #9 and #10 are empty. A security man is on duty inside. It is here on the sixth floor that California's Governor now lives, having renounced the sixteen-room, million-and-a-half-dollar Governor's mansion for a mattress on the floor.

"He just wanted a place to live that was near the office and was all his own space," says Marc Poché, a former law professor and legislative secretary to Brown. "He had no use for a large and expensive mansion. He doesn't even take the state housing allowance he is entitled to. He pays the $250-a-month rent on his apartment out of his own pocket.

"I remember when he first came up here to Sacramento to look for a place to live," Poché continues fondly. "When he found that apartment, they wanted him to leave a deposit or something, and he had to tell the guy he didn't have his checkbook. He said it was in L.A. and would take a week to get." Poché shakes his head and laughs with a kind of fatherly wonderment.

"You know, when you think of all the hoo-ha the press has made out of that apartment and the mattress, it makes you wonder," says one journalist whose beat is Sacramento. "So, big deal! Jerry sleeps on a mattress and box spring on the floor. Well, I'm his age, and that's just what I sleep on. He's not married. What should he have? A Mediterranean bedroom set?"

"I don't know how to describe it," says Brown of his own bed, "but the mattress is on a box, and the box is on the floor. I'm not much of a furniture analyst, but it's appropriate. I get enough sleep at night."

Brown's apartment looks out across N street through a row of tall fan palms to the forty-acre park that surrounds the Capitol. Beds of azaleas, pansies, tulips and roses flower beneath the redwoods, cypress, elm and fruit trees. The smell of gardenias is in the air.

A statue of Father Junipero Serra, California's first Franciscan missionary, stands in a shady grove almost out of earshot of the automobile noise beyond. Holding a cross, the good father looks down over a bronze map of California that shows the twenty-two early Spanish missions, from San Diego de Alcala in the south to San Francisco de Solano in the north. The monument has been placed in the park by the Native Daughters and Native Sons of the Golden West. It is quiet and cool here, evocative of a California of a different age.

I notice a small blue plastic plaque on a wooden post almost overgrown in a bank of flowering camellia bushes. It bears the inscription "Pat Nixon—This beautiful Camella [sic] is dedicated to Pat Nixon, a perfect example of charm, beauty and grace, in deep appreciation of service for her country. Dedicated March 4, 1972, by the Foothill Farms Junior High at the Sacramento Camellia Festival."

Just a few feet away an elderly man wearing earphones

paces back and forth across the lawn with a metal detector, searching the grass for bounty. On a distant bench another man, with several days' growth of beard and an ill-fitting suit with large shoulder pads, sits quietly in the warm sun. His eyes are closed, and he talks to himself as he takes long pulls from a bagged bottle. Another young man in soiled trousers and a cowboy hat sits opposite him, slowly spooning strawberry jam out of a large jar onto a slice of white bread.

Four tour buses pull up to the curb alongside the Capitol and disgorge a group of families.

"Hey, Dad," a boy calls to his father from a water fountain. "Do you think we'll see him?"

Actually it is just here that one might encounter the Governor as he walks to his office from his apartment early in the morning on a small footpath through the park.

The presence of the Governor hangs suggestively about the Capitol and surrounding grounds. It is hard to be here without having the expectation that at any moment he might appear, as indeed he often does. It is this sense of unseen eminence that adds drama for those visiting.

The Reception Room

"Yes. I've been here twenty-five years through three Governors," says Jackie Habecker, one of the receptionists who sit in the large outer waiting room which serves the Governor's office in the Capitol. "I really like it with the doors open. Governor Reagan always kept them closed. People can come in now and look around at the displays we have on children's art, outer space, photography and art from prisons and mental hospitals." She gestures to a display of children's paintings of whales. "Sometimes people are a little timid about coming in. They're not sure if it's okay. So I just urge them to walk right in."

Jackie's desk stands to the rear of the reception room. It is the eye of the needle through which all visitors to the inner offices of the Governor and his staff must pass.

The supplicants arrive in this room full of expectations, more often than not hoping to actually see the Governor himself in the quest for a swift and final solution to their problems. Sitting here on one of the couches watching them come and go, I can see how seductive it is for the powerless to look on the world of government as a kind of magical realm—where political celebrities can be invoked like gods in times of need.

It is the job of the receptionist at the front desk to announce those with appointments, and to deal with the others without frustrating them: to ease them into the reality that their problems may not be solvable by the Governor's office, and that they will probably never get to see the Governor himself.

"Is Governor Brown here?" a middle-aged woman who has just appeared asks Jackie. She is heavyset, wears white pants, a loose blouse, sandals. Her strangely disordered hair is restrained by a floppy hat affixed to her head with a long gold hatpin that looks like an arrow shot clear through her head and out the other side.

"Yes. The Governor is in his office today," replies Jackie.

"Well, I'd like to see him," announces the woman, as if the only possible stumbling block to their meeting would be his absence from Sacramento.

"You'll have to make an appointment," says Jackie with civility, perhaps beginning to sense that this woman may be "one of those."

"I already wrote him a letter asking him for an appointment," retorts the woman. "But no one answered. My name is Mrs. Brown."

Without further wrangling, Jackie picks up the phone. "A Mrs. Brown is here and wants to see the Governor," she says to an unidentified voice at the other end of the line.

"If you'll take a seat, Mrs. Brown," says Jackie, "I'll see if I can get someone to come out."

Mrs. Brown retreats to a couch, where she becomes engrossed in a *Motorland Magazine,* part of the bizarre laundromat-type selection of periodicals which is usually available here in the reception room.

An old man with a bald head and a gentle smile walks in the door toward Jackie's desk, holding a brief case in both hands. He places his hat on the desk top, bows slightly and hands Jackie a name card.

"I would like to get copies of this," he says in a heavy European accent, extracting a two-inch-thick sheaf of dog-eared papers from his brief case and handing them to Jackie, "and I would like to give them to the Governor."

"Is it a book?" asks Jackie, familiar with the numerous people who wish to present the Governor with their unpublished manuscripts.

"No. Not really," he replies vaguely.

"Well, it's a little too large to Xerox," says Jackie. Then she adds hopefully, "Maybe it's something the Governor already has."

"It's really a petition," says the man shyly. He advances closer to the desk and pulls out some more papers from his brief case. "Here is an amendment. It was refused." He mutters something about the Public Utilities Commission.

"You might wish to write the Governor," suggests Jackie.

"I told them I was coming to Sacramento," says the old man, registering disappointment on his face. "I told this man ..." He begins to rummage once again in his brief case without completing the sentence. He can't seem to find what he is looking for.

"The cost of gas is so high," he says, looking at Jackie, as if this statement were the best substitute for the unfound document in the brief case. "We're just going to keep paying and paying if we can't do anything," he says.

"I think it would make it clearer if you could write a letter," repeats Jackie apologetically.

"Yes. All right," he says, laboriously repacking his brief case.

"Goodbye, then," he says, puts his hat on, makes another slight bow, then turns and walks slowly out of the reception room.

Mrs. Brown is still waiting. She has said nothing until now and seems contented with the progress of her mission, whatever it·may be.

"Well, some people don't agree with me," she is suddenly saying to a well-dressed, mustachioed young man in patent-leather pumps and a perfectly pressed suit, who has inadvertently sat down beside her to await an appointment. "I mean, I think that the police are just not using Mace correctly."

He casts a sidelong glance at her, evidencing grave doubts about responding, in case he might in some way be identified with this lady.

"Don't you agree?" she is asking him, turning directly toward him on the couch, trying to establish some eye contact.

He looks furtively around the room to see if anyone has noticed his entrapment by this obviously unprofessional visitation upon the Governor's office. He says nothing. Just as he seems to be contemplating a move to another couch, the door from the inner offices opens and a secretary comes out.

"Mr. Regalia?" she says, looking around the room to see who will respond.

"Oh yes," says Mrs. Brown's couch mate, rising, clearly relieved.

Mrs. Brown returns to *Motorland Magazine* as two male politicians stride through the double doors of the reception room. When they hit the bald spot on the green rug just inside the threshold, they reach for wallets full of name cards. Foot contact with the bald spot seems to induce a John Wayne-like draw for the pocket, a motion which culminates in an out-stretched hand proffering a card to Jackie. The name cards are talismans against any insinuation that they, like the still-waiting Mrs. Brown, may be without a clear mission, or worse, without an appointment.

Next, an assemblyman in a blue pinstriped suit walks into the reception room, stops, smiles, raises his right hand as if blessing Jackie at her desk, and announces in a basso profundo, "I'm here to see the king."

Jackie laughs.

"I'd like to test the Governor's open-door policy and see the Governor for five minutes," he says, walking over to the door which leads to the inner quadrangle.

Jackie buzzes him in.

An elderly man comes into the reception room. "You know what I want? I want to make everyone into a complainer. You know what we owe complainers, don't you? Everything."

Mr. Simpson leans over a supermarket shopping cart which he has just parked in front of the Capitol elevators. He slowly extracts one of the many picket signs that are carefully stacked inside. The sign shows a picture of a reclining nude figure covered at the crotch with a fig leaf. A photograph of Brown's head has been pasted on the shoulders. The caption reads BROWN: NAKED, SLIMY, BULLSHIT.

Born near Belfast in 1880, Robert H. Simpson, known commonly around the Governor's office simply as "Mr. Simpson," cocks his head to one side with a sly grin on his face, and waits to see what reaction his outspoken political message will elicit. He turns slowly and walks around to the other side of the shopping basket. He takes tiny arthritic steps that hardly involve lifting his feet off the floor.

A family with three young children stops out of curiosity to watch this odd man holding an obscene placard aloft in the halls of the State Capitol. Mr. Simpson turns and sees the stunned children, then in halting motions takes off his suit jacket and wraps it around the picket sign to obscure the message from their sight.

"He always covers his cruder signs when he comes in to

see me," says Jackie as Mr. Simpson totters in. He stops just inside the door, replaces the Brown sign and raises a new one aloft. REAGAN STINKS it reads. The placard shows a photo of Reagan in a cowboy suit with two drawn guns.

"I've come here muckraking at the Capitol every day for forty-four years," says this rumpled old man, a mixture of lucidity and eccentricity. He reaches into his pocket for some papers and hands me one. It is marked PRESS RELEASE and reads "Robert H. Simpson, Assembly credited Muckraker-in-Chief-at-the-Capitol, Specializing in Bastard Governors Brown, Reagan and Brown."

"In 1969 they even passed the Simpson Act," he says, wagging a pale, bony index finger at me. "It was in the legislature, and they tried to get rid of me." He laughs. "They arrested me three hundred and fifty times, and they didn't stop me. But it's hell to be an idealist."

He adjusts his hearing aids, which are turned up so loud that they snap and crackle with static.

"Oh, I've not been feeling well lately," he says almost faintly. "I hope I have time to recover before I die."

Then bending over, and looking right at me with one eye half closed, he says, "Jerry's the new spirit. I just want him to hear me. If Jerry would just say, 'We will hear Mr. Simpson's complaint,' it would make him a big man." His words trail off.

"After Jerry was elected they repealed the Simpson Act. But I loved the law," he says with a gleam in his eye. "It showed just how far those bastard legislators would go against one old man."

He takes a new picket sign from his cart which reads CLEAN THE CAPITOL OR WE'LL BURN IT. Then he turns and pushes his cart back into the hallway.

Margaret Murphy, a young black woman, comes out to spell Jackie. She is no sooner settled in her seat than a tall wiry man with long dirty-blond hair, a beard, a soiled windbreaker and muddy high black sneakers is escorted into the reception room by Al Bridges, one of the security guards.

"He says he's been waiting three days at the phone booth at the end of the corridor for a call from the Governor's office," says Al.

"I hitched up from San Bernardino," says the young man, his eyes darting around ceaselessly, unable to rest on anything. "I called about an appointment with the Governor from the pay phone in the hall. They said they'd call me back, but they didn't."

"What is it you wish to see the Governor about?" asks Margaret.

"I want an interview with him about the situation in the mental hospitals. I know he's interested. I saw all the mental patients on TV who had the sit-in here."

"Could you write a letter explaining everything?" asks Margaret. "Then someone from this office can contact you."

"I don't have an address. And I have no phone," says the young man, fidgeting with his windbreaker zipper.

"I think it would be best to write a letter," repeats Margaret, growing slightly impatient with a situation that seems to have no solution.

She receives no reply. The young man is looking at his feet.

"Here. I'll go out with you," says Al, taking him by the arm. They walk out the door together.

"This sure has been some few days," says Margaret, shaking her head after they leave. "You missed the dancer yesterday who flitted in here and started dancing all over the place. It must be the full moon."

Once this processional has ended, Mrs. Brown suddenly comes to life once again. She looks up suddenly, asks Margaret what time it is, and then says in a loud voice, "Oh Jeez! I forgot to put money in my parking meter!"

She leaves and does not return.

The Custodian

It is seven o'clock in the evening. Appointments have ceased. Most members of the staff have left the Governor's office. The reception room has been locked. The doors of the various offices around the quadrangle of the Governor's inner offices have been left ajar. The remaining staff members roam the halls in their shirt-sleeves, chatting with one another.

Jim MacDonald is in the reception room, dusting and vacuuming around the desk and couches. He looks to be in his fifties, wears a blue short-sleeved shirt with the state emblem on the breast pocket, khaki pants with white socks and black shoes. There is a tattoo of an eagle over an anchor on his arm. A large bunch of keys is clipped to a belt loop, the side arm of his custodial profession.

"I wouldn't be able to keep up with it," he says, gesturing to the hallway, from where we can hear the distant voice of the Governor. "I'd just go down the tubes. There's a young man, that Brown, that drives me crazy," says Jim, stressing the word "there's." "But I got to respect him. He's a work-aholic. He's trying to accomplish something. And he's got a lot of folks trying to fight him. But he's a bulldog." Jim dumps a wastebasket full of paper into the bin on his pushcart, bristling with brooms and mops.

"I know he hasn't done everything. But, you know something, the thing of it is I think he's going to change this state. He's got a job I wouldn't have. It would drive most people crazy. Just crazy.

"More often than not he's here at one A.M. when I leave. Yes sir, that man's a dedicated working fool," he says, unplugging his vacuum and moving his cart down the hall with his keys clanking at his side.

Scheduling

"It's very difficult to explain my job," says Peggy Jellison, whose official title is "scheduling assistant" and who has been working in the Governor's office since the Reagan administration. The phone rings in her small cluttered office.

"No. No. I'm sorry. I just won't have time to do that today. But if you leave your request with the receptionist, I'll look at it this weekend." She hangs up. Sighs. Sits motionless for a moment in front of a desk which is piled so deep with correspondence that it looks like terminal confusion.

The phone rings again.

"Everyone wants to see him," says Peggy, trying not to show just how harassed she is. "Everyone has a deadline. People just can't wait. They're setting up a large convention or a meeting or something, and they want to know if the Governor can come and address their group. When we delay a clear answer they often think that we're playing games with them and get angry. It's hard for me to get a clear decision from the Governor. I try, but I begin to feel like a nagging wife.

"Brown is just not the kind of guy you can pin down. There's no way we will ever be able to say, like we always did with Reagan, 'Departs residence at six P.M.' Brown has never kept a strict schedule and never will." With a suggestion of irritation, she takes a deep drag on a cigarette.

"So, what can I do? I just have to be very candid with people and tell them that they have to be 'flexible' . . . But I will say this. When he commits himself to doing something, he usually goes through with it."

The phone rings again.

I glance at a letter on her desk. It is an invitation:

Dear Governor Edmund G. Brown:
    The Annual Calaveras County Fair and Jumping Frog Jubilee will take place May 19th . . ."

"No. We just can't. We can't tell him that," Peggy is saying into the receiver. She hangs up.

She hands me two Xeroxed sheets of paper divided into calendar squares for each day of the month. One is titled "Set Calendar"; the other is titled "Information Calendar," and bears the notation at the top of the page "These are not actually scheduled events at this point."

"Well, that's it. Two calendars," says Peggy, taking an exasperated breath. "We have to type them both over almost every day. Even then he changes it at the last moment."

The phone rings. Before she finishes the first call it rings again on another number.

"Oh God! It's someone from the Arts Council all panicked because they've just heard a rumor that Brown isn't going to make it to some event of theirs in Oakland tonight. See? That's it. His presence seems to mean so much to people.

"Often I feel like I'm getting pulled down in a quicksand of paper. I mean, for instance, almost every high school in the state invites him to their mock presidential nominating convention. When he can't come, they don't understand that seventy-five other high schools also invited him. We don't want to disappoint them or make them feel we don't care. But no matter what we do, we still get letters back that say things like 'Well, we should have known all along that we were just little fish and that the Governor wouldn't care.'

"I don't know how Brown survives this scheduling of his life. I mean, actually, he does resist being pinned down, which is my problem. But I can understand how he would want to keep some time open. I don't think I could handle it. He doesn't even have a wife like Reagan to act as his functionary and sit in for him. For Reagan, everything was set out and planned weeks in advance, but I remember seeing Reagan so overburdened by his schedule that one day he just hurled his glasses on the table, saying, 'I can't take any more!'

"Well, Jerry has a lot of energy. If I could take what he has for energy and bottle it, I could buy this Capitol."

"What the hell are we going to do about this guy?" asks another staff member, striding into Peggy's office and thrusting a sheaf of papers on her desk. "He's mayor of a large city, and it looks like he wants to back Jerry into some sort of corner. I don't think we should do a thing for him."

Peggy nods. "We'll say no."

Mail Room

Just past the elevators in the Capitol's main corridor is a doorway which leads to the Governor's mail room. A sticker pasted outside for levity's sake reads TWENTY-FOUR-HOUR PSY-CHIATRY EMERGENCY SERVICE.

Inside this tiny cubicle, the walls are almost completely covered with hanging graffiti and other mementos that have arrived in the mail.

A bumper sticker reads IF YOU LIKE OUR POST OFFICE, YOU'LL LOVE NATIONALIZED OIL. A small sign written in block letters reads IF ELECTED, I WILL GO TO WASHINGTON WHERE THE ENEMY IS.

Until the other day, a collection of photographs showing several women in various states of dress and undress with accompanying propositions for dates, dalliance and matrimony also hung on the wall. When their presence was mentioned in a large California paper, Brown became unusually angry and ordered them removed.

There are, however, still a number of eccentric and humorous messages from the Governor's constituents taped to the wall. One brief missive on a post card reads:

Dear Governor Brown:
    Today I put my television in the closet.
                                        Sincerely . . .

Another letter which arrived recently at the Governor's office reads:

Dear Governor Brown:
    I am becoming increasingly concerned about the possibility that someone will make a concerted effort to find and kill "Bigfoot" . . . for personal glory, profit, or perhaps under the guise of scientific inquiry . . . I'm afraid that pretty soon some macho individual will bring a Bigfoot in draped over the hood of his pickup . . .
                                        Sincerely . . .

Directly behind the mail room, where all the letters to the Governor's office are sorted, is the correspondence unit.

Being in the correspondence unit is like being underground, since there are no windows. But staff members have made it a relatively cheerful place to work, decorating it with posters, mobiles and even a tank of tropical fish. Hanging on the wall as you enter are scores of glossy portraits of Governors from other states in the Union. Doubtless motivated by Brown's early refusal to send out autographed photographs to his fans, some ambitious staff member took on the task of seeing how other Governors cope with similar requests. Beside accompanying form letters, the results hang on the wall, like a collection of movie or rock star photos in a teenager's room.

It is here in the correspondence unit that most letters to the Governor's office are answered. The two rows of desks in the main room are each equipped with a typewriter, a phone console and a stack of mail. The atmosphere of the room is something akin to one's fantasy of that place where childhood letters to Santa Claus are received. Although the primary task of the correspondence unit is to handle the Governor's mail, staff members also field many of the phone calls that come into the office from people with problems and requests.

Cheryl Ann Goble is the supervisor of the correspondence unit. She seems pleased, even a little surprised, that her job should have turned out to be as interesting as it is.

"We open all of the mail, except if it's obviously from some friend of the Governor that we know," says Cheryl. "Some people try and sneak letters through. We get letters that say things like 'Confidential' or 'Eyes Only.' Of course, everyone who writes the Governor wants him to read it personally. And he does sometimes come over from across the hall and browse. But usually if there is important legislation coming up, we will send a sample collection of letters over for him to read."

Behind her several women are operating IBM cassette typewriters which type form-letter responses.

"We would prefer to answer every letter ourselves," says Cheryl, gesturing toward the machines. "But we just can't do it. So we use the machines to do things like acknowledge that someone has written on a certain subject. We have about three hundred letters already on tape. Then we have two people who do nothing but compose original letters. We are very careful not to speak for the Governor, but we can quote him.

"Even that gets sticky," she adds, somewhat hesitatingly.

"We're running about three thousand letters a week. That's down from around five thousand during the first year. We had over six hundred thousand letters pour in within twelve months. It outdid anything any other Governor had received any time in history.

"We get letters on every subject imaginable, from property taxes and malpractice insurance to stuff on sex bills and the death penalty. People send pamphlets, books, personal articles, diaries, crackers, fruit, photos and even some clothing." Cheryl laughs, intimating that the items of clothing received were not all mittens and scarves.

"People bake him cookies and send them in, although this doesn't happen now as much as it used to. Some people even send money. They make gifts for the Governor. Last year, around Christmastime, someone sent him a bathrobe.

"Oh yes, we've had some funny stuff through here." Cheryl tries to hold back a smile that is leaking out all over her face.

"We got one telegram on the right-to-die bill. Someone wrote and asked the Governor to veto the 'youth-in-Asia' bill. Or we get telegrams which just say, 'Please veto *the* bill'—they don't even mention what bill they're talking about.

"Of course, we get some incoherent and obscene mail. We don't reply to these. If anything threatening comes in, we turn it over to the security unit. The special hardship cases we either work on here or send over to Janis and Mary."

Janis Shobar and Mary Sheehan have recently been transferred over from the correspondence unit to the office of programs and policy, run by Leroy Chatfield—who will later head the California Conservation Corps. They share a small office. Each has a desk equipped with a phone console. This is their major working implement. They sit over their telephones in much the same way a factory worker sits over a lathe in a workshop. Each woman has several piles of letters and a state phonebook on her desk. Their workday is an almost-unbroken string of phone calls.

"This is something I have been interested in ever since the beginning when I was in charge of administration in the Governor's office," says Chatfield. A tall blond man who was once a Christian Brother and then went on to work for Cesar Chavez, Chatfield is a man who is close to the Governor, but seemingly just as content to sit off on the margins and run whatever special projects need his attention.

"So many of the letters we get are really heartrending," he says. "I felt really angry the way Reagan would just answer all his mail with letter-writing machines. I thought we ought to try and organize some . . . Oh, I don't know . . . a way to try and help some of these people get through the bureaucracy.

I mean, most people aren't even sure who they are talking to when they call up Sacramento about a lost Social Security check."

He hands me a thick loose-leaf notebook. A label on the front identifies it as "Disposition of Miscellaneous Correspondence." It is filled with case studies of people who have written in because they have lost medical benefits or unemployment checks, people who are in jail, who are ill, who have no food or shelter, who are elderly and being evicted but cannot afford nursing homes. It is an endless list of human disappointment.

"So often people just need someone to talk to." Chatfield tilts back in his chair. "They just need someone to help them give the sluggish bureaucracy a prod. And there seems to be no greater miracle than a call from someone who says, This is so-and-so from the Governor's office."

"We got about forty letters today from the correspondence unit," says Janis, slapping her open hand down on a pile of mail on her desk. Janis is twenty-three, a recent graduate from college, who worked in a restaurant before finding this job. "We're just trying to do something for the small helpless person by calling them up and trying to get them in touch with an official or some agency which can get their problem straightened out."

"Do you think dental services would be included in that?" Mary Sheehan is asking someone on the phone. She is twenty-seven and has worked in the Governor's office for two years. "Mr. X wants a full new upper plate which has been authorized by your department," she continues.

"This is Miss Shobar calling from the Governor's office," says Janis. "Mr. Y's son is a chronic schizophrenic. The father says he is caught in what he calls 'a bureaucratic revolving door.' He wants to know how he can get some help for his son from the state."

As I sit and listen to this continuo of phone conversations, I thumb through the case book.

Mr. A is a vet on a kidney dialysis machine. He receives

$89 a month. But he too says he is lost in "the bog of bureaucracy." He notes that he has borrowed from everyone he knows and is desperate and wants to die.

The case is resolved through the Governor's office's obtaining a year's retroactive Social Security. "The wife was shedding tears of gratitude when she was called and informed," says the case book. "She wants to write a special letter of thanks to the Governor."

An epileptic woman who has been helped to get welfare and food stamps writes that it was "super-duper to get a call from the Governor's Office. I want to thank you, and give him a big kiss for me."

I sit on the edge of Mary's desk and thumb through the letters that she will try to handle today. They are addressed in every imaginable way: Dear Edward B., Dear Ed, Dear Hon. Gerald Brown, Dear Edmund J. Brown, Dear Edwin M. Brown.

The top letter is written in wavy longhand, replete with misspellings and cross-outs. It is addressed simply to: The Governor, State Capitol. It is from an elderly woman who is threatened with the loss of her house.

The letter is signed "Your Loyal Supporter. Thank you." Below she has scrawled a P.S. "This will end in February, and in that month they will put me out in the cold!!! Please, please, please, help me!"

The next letter is typed in the laborious, error-ridden style of someone who has never graduated beyond the hunt-and-peck system.

"Governor Brown. Please Read," it says at the top of the page.

"My problems all started when pressure in my drive-in restaurant, which we built in 1952, settled in on me," writes a man who has just had a heart attack and open-heart surgery. "These pressures were caused by the fact that I was unable to find meat supplies, and when I did, I had to pay high prices. Potatoes, onions and lettuce were also exorbitantly priced." He pours his life out with touching detail in this long letter, a prelude to his request for help in getting a higher workmen's compensation settlement.

The letters just keep pouring in, almost all of them from people who want to meet with the Governor. There are crazy letters, sad letters, intelligent letters, illiterate letters, obscene letters. Bales of letters that the Governor will never see, left to people like Janis and Mary to handle as best they can.

"My God," I hear a man exclaim on the other end of Mary's phone. "Is this really the Governor's office? I never expected to hear from *you*."

The Press

"No, he's not sending Christmas cards at public expense . . . What? . . . No . . . It would not be fair to say that," Elisabeth Coleman, Brown's press secretary, is saying into the phone with a mixture of amusement and irritation. "No! Whether or not he's sending Christmas cards at his own expense is a personal matter. That's as far as I can go. You'll just have to make up your own mind about whether or not it's a 'valid inquiry.'

"Hey, what is this? . . . Well, why don't you ask him yourself? . . . Okay, okay. Goodbye.

"God," she says, hanging up. "I spend more time on things like that than on transportation, mental health and the environment."

Instead of eating the sandwich that sits in front of her amidst the papers on her cluttered desk, she lights up a cigarette. "People in public life become sort of fantasies. They're like stars. So every little glimmer and glimpse of their private lives gets zeroed in on.

"Was it any different with the Kennedys? Whenever Jackie got a new hairdo or dress, everyone wanted to know. By picking up little bits and pieces of a politician's life, perhaps . . . Oh, I just don't know. I can't complete that thought, I guess we're all just interested in gossip. Why? I don't know."

At last she takes a bite of her sandwich. It is three in the afternoon and the phone has been ringing almost steadily since she arrived this morning.

"The Governor has a real sense of his private life"—she says, chewing—"that is, to the degree that he has any private life. Any public figure of course has to deal with the problems of being recognized all the time. It's hard when you need solitude."

Just at that moment, as though he had been waiting in the wings for Elisabeth to finish her thought, Brown comes bursting through the door. He is humming with energy.

"We just got another call on your Christmas cards," says Elisabeth, smiling.

"Well, what do they want? Why aren't they interested in the issues? Instead they like to concentrate on trivia, like my dead front tooth. If I send cards at government expense, that's their business," he says, already beginning to be distracted by a pile of magazines on Elisabeth's coffee table. "If it's at my expense, that's my business."

He puts down the magazines, heads back into his office. "Okay, okay. Let's get going. Elisabeth, I want to see you for a minute.

"No. No," he says, laughing. "Schell, you stay there."

The offices of most members of the Sacramento press corps are gathered on the third floor of a large new building just across the street from the Capitol. AP, UPI, the San Francisco *Chronicle* and the San Francisco *Examiner* are honeycombed together in one small suite, which allows for some symbiosis between all these reporters who normally are competing for stories.

The walls are covered with wire-press copy and photos showing the entire rogues' gallery of the last decade of California's political leaders. There are numerous shots showing a considerably younger, almost boyish-looking Brown, mixed with those of his father and Ronald Reagan. A poster hangs in the *Chronicle/Examiner* room, showing a black silhouette of the Capitol with the words LOWER YOUR OWN printed across it from corner to corner. It has allegedly been distributed by the Committee for Lower Expectations.

"It's almost a historic item now," says an AP reporter looking through the door. "We haven't heard much about that lately."

"I think Brown's running scared," says San Francisco *Chronicle* reporter Larry Liebert. "He's getting stale, and I think he knows it. People are not turned on by all that 'era of limits' stuff any more. I don't know how he can stay out there in the forefront."

"I used to find covering Sacramento a lot more interesting," says Susan Sward, a young UPI Capitol reporter who goes out with a Brown aide. She is a thoughtful, independent person who prides herself on being at once close to her subject and critical.

"In the beginning it was just all so different. Some of the excitement has ebbed, perhaps because they are concentrating more on issues. Which is fine. I've always had a healthy amount of distrust for Jerry because I sense he is so interested in moving up and on. But I've had more than one reporter tell me, 'Just when you start to hate him, he does something that makes you like him.' And then, of course, part of the affinity he has with the press is that he is close in age to a lot of the reporters.

"He does say some things which ring true, even if he tends to recycle them too much. And I think he is right when he talks about how a Governor should be a philosophical and moral leader, and how we need to lower consumption. Those are good messages. And I think he likes honest opposition. He even seems to like a certain amount of disdain. But you have to watch him because he can also use disdain, wit and sardonic comments to fend people off.

"The place where I get skeptical is where he gets into the all-things-to-all-men approach. Although I have a hunch his heart is in some pretty good places, I wonder where his soul *really* is."

"Have you found him sensitive to criticism by the press?" I ask.

"I think he holds a lot of secret grievances against us. I don't think he really understands the role of the press in a free society. I just don't think he gets it."

"What's it like being a woman around Brown?"

"There is a split in Jerry about women. On the one hand, I think he knows what's right, and has appointed a lot of women judges. He's really serious about things like that. On the other hand, his real female model in life is probably his mother. I like her a lot. But she's chiefly into being a grandmother, golfing and gardening. I mean, just look at the people close to him. Besides Rose Bird, who he appointed to the Supreme Court, and Elizabeth Coleman, it's really an all-male operation."

"Do you like Jerry Brown?"

"He feeds on attention. He has good ideas, but flits in so many directions. He doesn't delegate responsibility well, and usually won't move until there is a crisis.

"I think he is sometimes at a total loss over what to do with himself. He's like an observer in life. Perhaps too much of an observer. But if someone asked me what the bottom line was on a personal level, I would have to say, 'Yes, I like him,' although I pride myself in being just as tough on him as if I didn't like him."

Out of the open door of the NBC office, the sound of a stentorian self-assured media voice issues forth into the hallway.

"And today, here in the Capitol, Governor Edmund G. Brown . . ." It stops.

"That sounds okay, Steve," says another voice. "Let's go with it."

"Sacramento is a nice place to live," says Steve Mallory, after I introduce myself. "It's a nice place between. It's between town and city, Lake Tahoe and San Francisco, and somewheres between the living and the dead." He laughs. He is sitting just in front of a bulletin board which has a post card of Gerald Ford with a Band-Aid on his head, side by side with a card bearing Brown's oft-quoted remark THERE IS NO SUCH THING AS A FREE LUNCH.

"Governor Brown is an asshole to cover," says Steve, a man with a neat mustache, button-down shirt and hair just over the tops of his ears. "I'm not putting him down," he adds hastily. "But there is no plan or organization. He just pulls stuff. And often you're called just a few minutes before it's going to happen. It's like an air raid." He pauses. "Let's just say he's unorthodox. As a person, he's egocentric and conceited. No different than I am. But he's honest, sincere and incorruptible. Sometimes he's just like smoke, though. You just can't pin him down. Sometimes you can't get a straight answer out of him even when he knows what he is doing. He'll save his announcements for the best political moment. He's a political schemer.

"He'll talk about anything but his personal life, which I'm curious about. I think people have the right to know a little more about him. For instance, how much does this man really rely on meditation? How does he cope with the challenges of his office? How does he enjoy himself? But I'd be infringing on my rights as a reporter if I started asking him those things."

Nancy Skelton of the Sacramento *Bee* is in her late thirties, a mother, and has been covering the Sacramento scene for over ten years. She is a controversial but skilled reporter.

"I think the Brown administration is beginning to be very vulnerable," she says. "Because . . . How should I put this?

Because a lot of façades have been lifted by people probing deeper into what Brown really stands for and is willing to support."

We sit in the Baker Boy Luncheonette near the Capitol, an inexpensive and unpretentious lunch counter.

"This is a Brownie type of place," she says, as a Brown aide walks in. "It's poverty chic. Lowered expectations. Anyway, I think Brown knows more about how the press works than we know ourselves. He understands the egos of reporters and all the pressure that we're under. I mean, the Capitol beat is the big gig for these people from papers all over the state. They've worked up to it. Brown knows this, and he knows we need stories to survive. He knows how and when to feed things to people. He knows what leads and deadlines are, and he drops buzz words all the time. He gets really pushed out of shape when you don't use them.

"Brown's chief-of-staff, Gray Davis, is really the one who handles the press. He is a master and a good manipulator. He thinks in symbols and knows how an idea like, say, compassion, openness or fairness can be represented by a trip to an old-age home or a mental hospital. It's a symbol machine. I'd like to think that some of those ideas come from Jerry's heart, but I don't think so. There are very few politicians over there at the Capitol who see the press as anything more than a large megaphone. When it becomes a telescope looking at them, they don't like it." She sits for a moment drinking a cup of coffee and inhaling deeply on a cigarette. I sense that her years working her way up to her respected position as a Capitol reporter have not always been easy—that they have been both illuminating and toughening.

"No one with an ounce of intelligence or integrity could survive over there," she says, almost severely, gesturing across the street to the Capitol. "In the end, I don't think Brown is any more than a product of all those things we hold dear: some vanity, a bleeding heart, some ideals and compassion and a little bit of bullshit."

"He's just like any other politician, but he's got faster footwork," says Leah Cartabruno from Sacramento's educational TV station. She holds a pile of papers and notebooks up against her chest as she waits back in the Governor's office with her camera crew to tape an interview.

"Do you think he differs in any ways from other politicians?" I ask.

"He's just better," she replies with a laugh.

Cartabruno is in her mid-thirties. She is dressed in modern career-girl clothing: white trousers, blouse, scarf. She seems somewhat nervous about the upcoming live interview.

"What questions are there that you would like to ask him but know you cannot put to him on TV?"

"Well, frankly," she says, blushing slightly under her make-up, "I don't care what Jerry does with women."

"Does he sleep in the nude?" chimes in a cameraman to general laughter.

The crew is now moving into the small library back of Brown's office to set up, when B. T. Collins, one of Brown's legislative assistants, arrives with two teen-age girls to whom he is giving a tour.

"Okay," he says. "That's the Governor's library. His office itself is just up front, and that's the elevator to the garage."

"When you get right down to it," Leah Cartabruno is saying, "Brown really is an old-time politician who just borrows the rhetoric of our generation. He's never really had to compete like the rest of us. He's an intellectual who feels that thinking about something is the same as doing it. Like, he won't take a position on the antinuclear-power initiative, something a lot of people assumed he would support.

"He gets away with saying the most outrageous things," she continues, just as the elevator doors part, delivering Brown on the scene like some supernatural character. He is smiling, enjoying his sudden and unannounced materialization before the surprised assemblage. His jacket is off. His face appears slightly sunburned.

"Hi. Who are you?" he asks, looking past Cartabruno and

addressing himself to the two high school girls.

They reply timidly. Collins is smiling paternalistically.

"Sure. Great. Give them a tour of my office," says Brown to Collins, and then walks into his library now crowded with cables, lights, cameras and sound equipment. I move across to the press office to watch the interview on the TV set there with Jacques Barzaghi and Stewart Brand, two of Brown's special assistants.

Barzaghi smokes. Brand eats cheese and crackers. Suddenly Brown's visage flashes on the screen from the next room, so close that we can almost hear their voices across the hall.

"They have become us. We have become them," intones Brand, looking at the screen, shaking his head and laughing. "There is no more *they*," he pronounces with biblical finality. "Given the choice of becoming an outlaw or a citizen, I'd take the role of citizen every time. When Jerry called and asked me to come up here, and he asked how we were going 'to slow *it* down,' I knew *we* had become *them*."

"Governor, what have you done over the past year that will last?" Cartabruno asks Brown on the screen.

"Well, I don't know if I'll ever leave permanent monuments, massive skyscrapers that someone will put my name on," he replies.

"Well, then, how about a couple of examples of your fallibility?" she asks.

"I'm not sure I'm prepared to give you a catalogue of my failures," he says. "I'm not sure I know what a failure is yet."

She follows with several other questions, trying to find one so perfectly phrased that it allows for no verbal escape.

But Brown practically ignores the question. He's ready with a reply even before her sentence is finished. The questions are little more than starting guns to get him off the blocks to run in any direction he chooses.

Cartabruno probes him on legislative successes.

"People think that when you pass a law, that's it," he

replies impatiently. "All you get when you pass a law is more paper."

Legislation

Saying that he hopes "those with the least income are treated fairly," Brown today signs into law a piece of legislation that he proposed earlier this year, giving almost all state employees a flat monthly pay raise. Both janitors and heads of agencies will have their wages raised equally by $70 a month.

"This is a bill which no one thought would pass," says Brown proudly. "It is extremely controversial and took a great deal of work in the legislature.

"It's my feeling," continues Brown—who upon assuming office required his staff to take salary cuts and threatened to veto legislation raising his own salary—"that wage differentials in society are going to diminish. I think it's right and proper that they do. I think that this effort by California provides an example that I hope will be picked up by both other governments and the private sector. As inflation eats away at our incomes, it makes no sense to give those with the most discretionary income the highest raise."

He also signs another bill that he has lobbied hard for. The bill establishes the California Conservation Corps, or CCC. Modeled on the old CCC—the Civilian Conservation Corps—of the Depression days, this will be a kind of outdoor work camp with pay for young people interested in conservation.

"I want something more than the old make-work type of job program," he tells me. "I want something that will really affect the lives of kids who've had no purpose until now. I think both the CCC and the flat pay raise express a part of my philosophy of government to help people who are trying to help themselves and who are looking for some kind of creative solution from government."

The State of the State

"New wine in old bottles," grumbles a workman in painter's overalls as he wrestles a large mahogany desk out the doorway of one of the legislative offices in the Capitol. It is time for the post-election changing of the guard. Forty old legislators are on their way out to pasture. Forty new ones are having their furniture moved into the vacated offices. Today the new political year of the Capitol begins, and at eleven o'clock the Governor is scheduled to deliver his annual State of the State message to the senate and assembly.

Yesterday there was much coming and going around the inner hallways of the Governor's office as Brown huddled with his senior staff members. Although Brown almost never formally prepares a speech in advance of delivery, he seems to take special pains with the State of the State. Today there is a sense around the office that something significant is about to happen.

"I'm not even sure what he's going to say this time," says Brown's legal affairs secretary, Tony Kline. *He* is of course the appellation used by Brown's staff to make reference to *him* in absentia. It is a neutral designation lying somewhere between the familiar "Jerry" and the rather distant "Governor."

"He may write it down," adds Kline, "or he may just immerse himself in certain ideas and deliver the address from notes. It's hard to tell. Anyway, he has been asking us all for the ideas that we feel are important to express."

"He wings most of his speeches," says another staff member. "He just gets out there and starts talking. But I don't think he'll do that this time."

As it nears ten-thirty, people begin to move down the hallway to the assembly Chambers. Legislators and aides stand chatting outside. Although the Chambers of both houses of the legislature share the same building as the Governor's office, they are an entirely different universe of power, residing, as they do, on opposite sides of the system of checks and balances. The legislature is another political world which, although in contention with the Governor's Executive branch, is also welded together with it in a common enterprise like a Siamese twin. Today is the yearly ritual where both officially meet in full force face to face.

Inside the Chambers, the legislators sit at their desks, lined up like children in a large classroom. Each desk has an electronic voting button and a gooseneck mike connected to a central P.A. system. The votes are tabulated on three large electronic boards behind the Speaker's desk, which give the whole room a suggestion of a Nevada keno parlor.

Many of the legislators are at their desks waiting. They too seem to feel a sense of anticipation, but one which is mixed with a chafing sense of the possible indignity of being kept waiting, like nobles summoned for an audience before the king.

"I don't think there is any feeling of affection for Brown here," says Assemblyman Charles Warren of Los Angeles. "But there is a lot of respect for him and his ability to conduct himself so as to attain such unparalleled voter approval."

"The legislators trust him to be honest," says Republican Senator and Republican Minority Leader George Deukmejian. "But I doubt that they trust his political motivations. He's so inconsistent, and many people feel that he does it deliberately and shrewdly. You never really know where he's coming from."

Assemblyman William Thomas of Kern County is bounding around the assembly Chambers with a pen and a sheet of paper. He is taking bets like a bookie on how long Brown's speech will be. Last year he astounded the legislators and citizenry with a brief nine-minute discourse. The longest bet so far for this year is thirty minutes. The shortest is five minutes.

Thomas' lottery activities are abruptly curtailed by the assembly speaker, Leo T. McCarthy of San Francisco, who suddenly rises and announces, "Ladies and gentlemen—the Governor of California."

Brown sweeps in, bathed with TV lights; everyone in the room rises. He shakes a few hands as he moves swiftly toward the podium.

His delivery is direct and businesslike, although extemporaneous. There is neither cosmic philosophy nor flippancy. He works through the problems confronting the State in grocery-list fashion: property taxes, school funding, conservation, drought, quality of life, crime, mental health.

Some legislators listen attentively. A few take notes. Others stare off into space. A few doodle. One is reading.

As he reaches the five-minute mark, Assemblyman Thomas, who has arranged the names of his bettors according to the times they have chosen, begins to scratch entries off with a smile on his face.

"That leaves us one other question," Brown is saying somberly. He has been talking almost nine minutes.

"The Supreme Court recently struck down the death penalty in this state. This is something I have thought about for a long time. My position is very clear on the subject. I respect each one of you." Almost everyone is looking up at the podium now. Brown's voice seems to gain conviction as he speaks.

"I respect the judgment of the people," he continues. "But as you begin your deliberations, I feel it incumbent on me to share with you what I believe. For me, this is a matter of conscience . . . I feel that way. And if a bill should come to my desk, I will return it without my signature. Thank you very much."

The whole speech begins and ends so fast it leaves people electrified, as if they had just heard some short virtuoso recital that was over before the audience had even settled into their seats.

There is a moment of silence, then applause.

"He's up against a strong tide," says one legislator as Brown moves through the crush to the rear door. "Two thirds of the people out there want that death penalty."

"He didn't talk about the business climate or the environment," says another legislator. "Does that mean that's all down the tubes?"

"I thought it was one of his best speeches," says a UPI reporter. "No mush. Nothing phony."

"Why didn't he just come right out and say he'd veto the death penalty instead of all this confusing junk about 'returning it without his signature'?" asks a senator.

Assemblyman Thomas is standing at his desk toward the rear of the Chambers with his left hand full of bills like a cocktail waitress. He is surrounded by a throng. He gives Brown a sheepish grin as he passes, and then returns to squaring his accounts.

Willie Brown

Willie Brown is a black assemblyman from San Francisco who represents large numbers of minority constituents. His relations with the Governor have been on-and-off. When he finally endorsed Brown for the Presidency, it was only after a long wait-and-see period, finally doing so with as much political realism as fervor.

"It hurts! It hurts!" he comically told one reporter who spotted him wearing a BROWN FOR PRESIDENT button in the

Capitol hallway. Willie Brown has never been at a loss for frankness.

Willie drives a Porsche. He is an expensive and flashy dresser and a man of seemingly boundless confidence and good humor. He is acknowledged as the foremost crowd warm-up act in California.

"Hello, man," he's saying on the phone as I walk into his office. "Sheeeee-it! You just call my San Francisco office and we'll find you one . . . No, she's black," he says, laughing and mimicking someone who is procuring women. "But we got white ones too. Vassar girls! They still have white gloves on." He winks at me and explodes into uproarious laughter. It is a special Willie Brown parody laugh that starts off like any other laugh but ends up in the sinuses.

Resting on some shelves full of lawbooks behind Willie's desk is an antique soap-powder box. Its logo shows two darkies with arms around each other's shoulders, big minstrel-show grins, fat lips and white eyes. Other office trivia include a photo of a chimpanzee wearing a banana peel on its head and a scroll that reads THERE IS NO DIFFERENCE THAT LOVE WILL NOT CONQUER.

"What parts of Jerry Brown ring true to you?" I ask.

"In the professional sense of the word," says Willie, removing his perfectly pressed sports coat, "Brown is close to being the best politician in this country. But I don't think he speaks from the heart at all. Like most politicians he desires to exercise power. He is probably one of the outstanding examples of a man who thinks that his exercise of power can best benefit the world. But I'd also be the first to admit that most of us have a hard time standing back and self-evaluating—distinguishing between what drives us to pursue power for our own benefit and the public good. If you can really combine what you want with what the world wants, you're really it. Brown does that better than any of us. And nobody advertises himself as well as he does."

"Do you think Brown has a nonpolitical side to him?"

"No. That's why I'm not as good a politician as he is. I'm certain that Brown is a full-time politician, as distinguished, say, from one of us who have other jobs and kind of play at being politician. There are few people who are totally consumed by the political process, and Brown, in my opinion is one of those few people."

"What reins in a politician besides defeat?"

"Another politician of equal ambition and power."

"Is there anyone who is Brown's equal in California?"

"There's nobody."

"Do you think he has staff within his administration who feel themselves his equal and can dress him down?"

"Well, it's absolutely necessary to have people around whose survival is not tied to whether you're pleased with them or not. Otherwise they become court jesters. The worst example was Nixon. He had talented men who submerged their talent in order to ingratiate themselves with him.

"I think Brown has one or two people who stand up to him. They're the sort who have offered considerable strength to his administration."

"How do you explain Brown's popularity?"

"I think that Brown has read the public as somehow being turned off with the beautiful things of life, because in so many cases people are not personally experiencing these things. They just don't go for excesses. Anyone who engages in excesses is doomed to be unacceptable. But Brown is careful not to overstep the bounds of being too deprived. He gets close, and then he goes and shows up with a starlet or somebody else who is a visible symbol of success. Then the next day he'll appear very spartan in his conduct and attitude. I think it's totally conscious."

"Do you trust him?"

"Yes, as a professional politician. Whereas I would tend to do what is necessary, he will tend to do what is politically possible and acceptable."

"Where do you think the compassion he talks about enters into all this?"

"Compassion doesn't figure very high in the arena of the professional practicing politician, because it can cause you to do things which are not politically acceptable. I haven't seen Jerry Brown do anything out of compassion that was not politically beneficial. That may be a bit harsh, but I'm waiting to see the act which doesn't have any political pluses for him."

"How do you account for the fact that bachelorhood has suddenly become politically acceptable?"

"People are slowly becoming aware that family affairs interfere with the actual functions of a political office. It's difficult to make twenty-five speeches a week, eat thirty-six meals out and still have time to go to church, teach your fifteen-year-old how to drive, and be part of a Boy Scout troop. In addition, public life just doesn't pay enough to allow you not to hold two jobs, which is hard if you're married."

"Do you think Brown will ever get married?"

"I would not think it in keeping with his being the all-consuming politician."

"Do you think he will be President?"

"It's a possibility. Yes."

Prayer Breakfast

It is 8 A.M. as the faithful, thousands of them, move into the Sacramento Convention Center Hall. Generals, businessmen, clergy, politicians, blacks, Mexicans, members of the Salvation Army sit down to a breakfast of orange juice, melon, quiche and coffee cake. Already the surface of the melons is dehydrating and turning brown. The coffee cake, which has been on the table several hours, is growing stale.

The hall is a cavernous room with epoxied floors and

steel-beam construction that suggest storage more than spirituality. Five or six TV cameras are setting up at the back of the hall as the sixty waitresses, who have been here since 4 A.M., move swiftly in and out of the kitchen at the far end. They wear yellow and black uniforms, which creates an effect at the jammed doorway of yellow jackets buzzing around the entrance to their hive. Somewhere in the vast hall, a waitress drops a tray, creating a distant sound of shattering china over the din of the guests.

"You know, when Pat Brown first started these prayer breakfasts," says Brown advisor Tony Kline, "Jerry got real indignant. He wrote his dad this outraged letter from seminary protesting the fact that his father was praying with Protestants. Well, times have changed," he says, wandering off into the crowd.

Jacques Barzaghi, another Brown advisor, moves about the hall smiling, greeting people like a general reviewing his bivouacked troops.

"Who organized the prayer breakfast?" I ask him.

"The Prayer Breakfast Committee, of course," he replies with an inscrutable smile. But everyone remembers how, last year, he and Brown astounded everyone by inviting the Sufi Choir to perform; the Prayer Breakfasts are one of Barzaghi's favorite events.

Brown walks in through the back door, almost unnoticed at first. "All right. What do we have here?" he asks, scrubbing his hands together and surveying the crowd.

Then, as he moves down the aisle to the head table to sit beside the guest speaker, Martin Luther King, Sr., the TV cameras spot him. They surge after him as if sucked along by some large unseen vacuum, their lights ablaze. Brown sits down.

Two young boys in suits and ties come up to his table rather cautiously. One holds an Instamatic, the other a portable tape recorder. They move right up behind Brown's chair. But, seemingly paralyzed by their easy access to celebrityhood, they are unable to utter their request and consummate their mission. The Governor is not aware of their presence. No one seems to notice them. The juggernaut of the press advances. The boys are finally forced to withdraw with disappointed looks on their faces.

"Lord, we have come here together this morning to renew our awareness of your presence in our worldly acts and decisions," Justice Leonard Friedman of the third district court of appeals intones from the podium. "In the pressures of our secular concerns we tend to encase ourselves in the arrogant armor of our intellectual pride."

Brown's head is half bowed in a compromise somewhere between the position of those whose hands are clasped beneath their bowed foreheads, and of those who sit upright in secular defiance throughout the prayer.

"Grant us, oh Lord, awareness that economical and political inoculations will not cure America's epidemic of spiritual malaise," continues Justice Friedman.

The Coro Hispánica of San Francisco begins to sing some seventeenth-century sacred music, "Ya Viene El Alba," a song of the California Spaniards.

The sounds are haunting yet incongruous as they carry up under the asbestos-coated steel beams of this modern California cathedral.

"Beautiful. Rich. How lovely," says Martin Luther King, Sr., so loudly that his voice is audible at the surrounding tables.

Dr. King ascends slowly to the dais to thunderous applause and launches into a brief encomium of Brown: "God knows how far your Governor is going."

Brown is looking a little uncomfortable.

King talks about the "ungodly" things that have been done to black people, and about the assassinations of his son and his wife, about how he is afraid that America has taken the wrong path.

The room is absolutely silent, save for the sound of the forced-air heaters overhead.

Then his voice begins to sweep up into a gospel crescendo. "Man will never be God! He isn't good enough, righteous enough, holy enough. . . . I'm preachin' now!" he adds at fever pitch. "If there is a man who knows right and doesn't stand up, that man is blocking traffic!"

There is deafening applause.

Brown strides to the podium. He stands there silently for an instant, looking out across the hall.

"Freedom is knowing what you live for, as well as knowing what you are prepared to die for," he says. "In this business we must be practical and get things done, but the real strength of this country is in the ideas, the faith, in the human energy that is willing to commit itself to dreams that haven't been dreamed."

The audience is listening attentively. But with King they were bound by their hearts. With Brown, they seem bound by a kind of curiosity.

"Moments come and moments go," he continues. "Languages come and languages go. Countries rise and countries fall. But the human spirit keeps moving. Let us move with it."

"Real good, real good," says Dr. King, grabbing Brown by the arm as he returns to the table.

Soon Brown rises and moves toward the door; a crowd follows.

"The prayer breakfast is okay," I hear one man say, "but what I want to know is when he's going to release that $240 million in highway funds."

Another man squeezes up to Brown to ask him about the bill—which Brown did not support—banning disposable bottles. People are shaking his hand. A bald man in a powder-blue double-knit suit manages to edge forward and introduce a colleague with his arm in a sling. The colleague seems as impressed with his friend for knowing the Governor as he is with actually meeting the Governor himself.

"Stop by. Drop in," Brown is saying to someone else.

We walk out of the Convention Center, and across the park to the Capitol. He talks all the way with several people who are concerned about a strike in San Francisco.

"You've got to understand," Brown is saying. "I can't go

getting involved in every strike in the state. I'd use up all my credibility."

"Yeah, yeah. I see," says one beseecher agreeably.

We are about to enter the Governor's office through the side door when a group of property-tax protesters waiting outside of the reception room see him. They come running down the hall.

One carries a sign that says YOU CAN'T GET BLOOD FROM A TURNIP. Another runs waving a placard that reads GIVE US SOME TIME, GOVERNOR BROWN. WE'RE AT THE END OF OUR ROPE.

"Why don't you support a good property-tax relief bill?" one of the men asks with a mixture of nervousness and anger.

"Well, that's a loaded question," replies Brown with a smile. "How do you know I don't?"

"Pretty soon no one is going to be able to afford a house except the rich," a woman chimes in. By now a small throng has gathered in the hallway, watching the encounter. Although Brown is showing no evidence of wishing to retreat, a staff member is holding the door ajar, ready to squire him into the safety of the inner office.

"What's this all about?" Brown asks. "You don't want to pay any more taxes?"

There is a chorus of no's. Then they all start talking at once, attaching themselves to him like barnacles.

He listens, quips with them. They start smiling, then laughing. It is hard for them to maintain their anger when Brown is not resisting them in any way.

"Okay," he says finally. "Thanks. We're working on it. I'll see ya."

He disappears through the door to his offices, leaving the protesters outside to discuss their victory, such as it is.

Conversations with Brown: the Media

AUTHOR: *Do the reflections of your life and politics that appear in the media ring true to you?*

BROWN: There's usually an element of truth. But as in everything, there are nuances and contradictory aspects of any given act. How people want to play these nuances depends on the reporter's perceptions and on the rules that govern political reporting in this latter half of the twentieth century. And those rules require a generous amount of negative reductionism in any analysis.

People can only see what the culture will allow to be communicated. Media people usually don't say that the President is trying to do X. They say that the President is trying to improve his image by doing X.

Do you try to manage your image at all?

Well, I certainly don't try to put my worst foot forward. But I don't try to be something that I'm not. I try to become what I'd like to be. The word "image" connotes unreality. The presentation of a man and the reality should be fairly close. Some people think there are only appearances.

I don't have any packagers around me, but I think that in some senses the press itself is into a packaging game. There's a two-way relationship between the press and the candidate or the public official. The press believes that there's got to be something wrong, and the candidate tries to communicate what is best in what he's doing. So that creates a certain amount of tension. Here's what I'm curious to know: How would a media person recommend a Governor or a President conduct himself to avoid all consideration of what they call "image"?

What do you think people want from the media?

The media seems to have decided that people want personalities and not issues. So they take the issues and make them appear to be a mere aspect of a politician's personality, and say he's trying to bolster his position, his political life. The media doesn't like to be used, yet it is exactly this medium by which the politician and the people interact, communicate— and that's all there is to it.

You often speak of "representing all the people," while the press often criticizes you for being two-faced and being all-things-to-all-men. How do you view this dichotomy?

Yes. Often trying to serve the majority of people is viewed as something less than honorable.

You mean, because it involves certain compromises?

No. Because people are saying you should just do what you believe, irrespective of what the impact is on the people you serve. Yet the whole idea of democracy is to pay attention to the impact of what you do on the majority of people. Otherwise there'd be no point in having an election every four years. There is a strong amount of cynicism in the media about politicians attempting to please the electorate—and yet democracy requires that in a very fundamental way.

Do you feel that the media grows easily bored with incumbents, and has a tendency to eat up politicians in office in a search for new excitement?

I don't know. Given the reductionism of the media, it strikes me that no matter how wise a person in public office, the popularity curve has to be downward in a very short time period . . .

Why do you think the media is so interested in squaring you off against Carter in the next presidential election, which is still so far away?

It's part of obsolescence. Cars are built on an obsolescent principle. Fashion is designed to grow obsolete. The culture requires obsolescence to sustain its basic momentum. Obsolescence pervades everything from politics to relationships. In one sense that generates a great deal of innovation, but also a great deal of frustration. There obviously are people in the media who try to perceive trends, give voice to them and help make them happen. The media needs conflict, needs contradiction, in order for there to be anything to talk about. Popular taste must be appealed to. The media cannot survive without it.

The media has a relentless commercial obligation underlying much of its objectivity. Advertising space must be sold. Circulation must be maintained and expanded, ratings must be attained.

So, as Governor, you feel you get sold in the media like cereal?

The fact of the matter is that a newscaster on a show that loses ratings will very quickly be changed. A newspaper that loses circulation loses advertising space. That is the ever-present underlying reality of the entire media process. Drama creates interest. In order to have drama, you must have a protagonist and you must have conflict. You must have the challenger; you must have the incumbent. And if you're writing for a national publication, you can't write just in terms of California. You have to find a national angle. And that creates this relationship of antagonism with the President.

Why do you think they're so interested in you?

I don't know if they are.

Let's assume they are.

Well, that gets too easy. They may not be. And in a few more months they may lose their interest.

What do you make of publications like Penthouse *and* Playboy, *in which you yourself were interviewed, which mix serious literature and politics in with photos of women's genitals?*

It's just part of the media. It's a media product, part of one mélange: politicians, sex, comedy, murder, soaps, commercials—it's all stuff that is put through the media machine. There's no difference between being layered in between the centerfold and being layered in between deodorant commercials or soap operas.

THE
INNER CIRCLE

Brown's Office

"Sometimes he doesn't even go back to his apartment at night," says one of Brown's women staff members. "He just uses his office as if it were his home. "He's not used to taking care of certain aspects of his life, like cleaning up," she continues. "And because of this trait, he evokes a maternal instinct from many women.

"You'll see him pacing around his office thinking about something. Then he'll come out into his secretaries' room almost like a little boy and say that he's hungry. So one of his secretaries has to go out and get him something to eat. They usually get him dull, plain, healthy things like avocado and alfalfa sprout sandwiches. But his late-night eating habits are kind of a joke. Maybe a Shakey's pizza or some Kentucky Fried Chicken. When he began to get a paunch, he started carrying Sego diet drinks around in his brief case.

"Often when he is in the office all alone at night, he just wanders around the offices looking for candy or other snacks on people's desks as if he were a mouse or something. Sometimes staff members play games with him—they'll put candy and cheese out on the desks to see how many nights it will survive.

"But anyway," she goes on, "he has collected this bevy of loyal and efficient women assistants around him. These secretaries see themselves as kind of behind-the-lines queens of the roost. They are called the 'Big Mamas' because they are so close to power. And in fact they are very powerful, because not only do they take care of Brown but in important ways they control who gets through to him on the phone, what mail he reads, what gets brought to his attention. When he is in the office they are like a giant filter screening his points of contact. I think that's why he likes to get out and visit projects and ride on public transportation. But the trouble is—and I've seen this happen many times—after people talk with him casually and he's told them to 'Stop by' or 'Drop me a line,' they can't understand later why they can't get through the Big Mamas when they try.

"And while we're on the subject of women," she adds with a forbidden smile, "there's this whole other group in the office who have secret crushes on Jerry. It is very important to them that they have succeeded in getting a job in the Governor's office, and they are almost possessed with making themselves evident and available to him. A few even confess that their foremost passion is to sleep with him, and they purposely work late at night when they know he is here. They'll go out and pace around the halls, hoping to just run into him and get a conversation going. I mean, Jerry loves to talk, particularly after members of the inner circle—like Gray Davis, Tony Kline, Jacques Barzaghi and Stewart Brand—have left for home."

Gray Davis

"Come in," says Gray Davis with a slight smile, closing the door to his office. Then, almost in the same motion, he takes an inflatable plastic beach toy out from behind the door, places it in the middle of the floor, pulls out two foam Boffer swords and lunges at the figure, in his very proper way, knocking it over.

"Great therapy after a long hard day," he says grinning and sitting down on the couch. He folds his hands in his lap, crosses his pinstripe-suited legs and begins to talk.

"It's always difficult even for me to understand, much less explain, what I do here," he says with a smirk that suggests that the ambiguity is not entirely unpleasant for him. "My title is chief-of-staff. I suppose you could liken it to a managing editor of a newspaper. Actually, the Governor has let me define the role. I guess the most important aspect is to help him do his job, to help bring his attention to the array of activities that are begging for consideration. I try to select out those which I think most warrant his personal involvement, and then to attend to the others myself. The other thing I do is just guide people in this office and the Cabinet and try to give some direction to the activities of the principal staff members.

"Sometimes it's like being a ringmaster, with all the ideas that pop up from everyone," says Davis, laughing the way a father might laugh over the naughty deeds of his bright young children. "I mean, nine out of ten are clearly felonious or crazy!"

The ambience in Gray's office is late-fifties. Large, faded, travel-poster-like colored photos of outdoor scenes hang on the walls, perhaps left over from past administrations. There are potted plants on the floor, bookcases full of lawbooks and veneer paneling. The office, like Gray, is neat. Papers are piled in an orderly fashion on the desk next to the speaker phone. In one dark corner there is a photo of Davis with the Governor, although one wonders why such a reminder is needed for a man whose office is directly across from Brown's, and who spends most of his waking hours in his company.

"I'm thirty-five," says Davis, reflectively pulling at his dark sock as if to coax it a few inches further up his calf. "I was born in New York. I lived in Bronxville and Greenwich, and moved to Los Angeles in 1954. My life was a new twist on the American dream: riches to rags. I was in high school when my parents lost it all. My father worked in advertising with *Time* and *Sports Illustrated*. There's no question, it drove me to the wall. I had this sense that what he was doing was so ill-defined and uncertain. As I look back on it, I think my decision to study law had a lot to do with his rise and fall. I figured that as a lawyer I would at least have a profession and trade. So, after I graduated from Stanford, I went to Columbia Law School. Then I worked in L.A. for Mayor Thomas Bradley, ran unsuccessfully for state treasurer and finally hooked up with Jerry."

"Do you find that friendship plays an important role in an office such as this one?"

"I don't think that it is necessary to be personal friends with the people you are working with, but I think you have to be attracted by the energy and interested in the flow of ideas they generate. There is a kind of bond that I think has developed here—not so much out of social experience outside the office as from the satisfaction and sense of mutual achievement shared within the office. What makes this job exciting for me is that the Governor is a serious thinker. His ideas are a cutting edge and quite aggressive. We've had . . . I can't tell you how many discussions we have had, many of which go on until early morning. We tend to move from the specific to the general conceptual level. This is one of the Governor's strong suits. He can see relationships between problems, people, nations and societies that are not as apparent to me or some of the others. I find it exciting to contribute to this thought process and then to see something happen because of it."

He reaches up to scratch his scalp by carefully inserting one outstretched stiffened finger in between the hairs and wiggling it in the manner of a woman who does not wish to disturb her hairdo. Gray is coiffed in the "dry look," hair neatly trimmed and held in place as if by some unseen force. His shoes are always immaculately shined. His stylish double-vented suits rarely show any signs of being rumpled. There is a crispness and exactness about him that seems to remain uneroded by the ceaseless assaults and demands made on his office each day.

"I don't reserve too much time for myself," he says. "When I got into this, I realized that I wasn't going to do it for thirty years. It was not going to be a lifestyle that I wanted to perpetuate over the rest of my life. I have to keep reminding myself of that. Frequently I get up in the morning and I don't relish the prospect of another fourteen- or fifteen-hour day."

His secretary comes in with an urgent message. He goes to his desk and makes a phone call.

"I'm not like Jerry," he says, setting down the receiver and returning to the couch. "I mean, he can literally relax just by focusing on a problem which isn't an immediate one. And he can do it with the same energy that he focuses on a crisis. There are some times when I know I am reaching the point where I'll have to throw the switch off. One of the quickest ways for me to do that is to get into the car and drive immediately to the nearest movie house. It doesn't matter what's playing or when it started, if I can get a couple of hours uninterrupted.

"When I get back, my desk is piled high with pink slips. But that's all right, because I start with the premise that I enjoy what I'm doing. The only thing that changes this judgment is extreme fatigue."

Davis talks easily and earnestly. When an answer is not immediately forthcoming, he has a habit of throwing his head back and looking at the ceiling. Then, if the precise response still does not formulate itself in his mind, he may ramble as a kind of warm-up. But even this vamping has an orderliness to it and frequently takes the form of several enumerated points. Then, when he finally catches on to what he means to say, he takes off clearly and concisely.

"A by-product of the rather spontaneous existential approach we seem to have to government is that people realize that we will not commit our time in advance. This style obviously creates problems as well as flexibility. But I sincerely believe that something like the Farm Labor Law—which was the result of intensive concentration and negotiation here in this office between Chavez's farm workers and the growers— would not be law today if Jerry had been a prisoner of traditional executive scheduling. There's no question in my mind that the free-flow approach to things has its advantages, although sometimes it can frustrate people."

Taking a deep breath in and letting it out slowly, Davis talks about the difficulty of remaining accessible. "Sure, there are times when you just want to shut everything else out and focus on one problem and try to bring some creative energy to bear on it. But often that's impossible."

"What is your policy around the office regarding security?"

"Jerry's only complaints are that it is too heavy," says Davis, not overly eager to broach the subject. "He just doesn't like it. Our attitude is to deal with it as much by keeping spontaneous scheduling as anything else. And I think it is also true that if a political personality shows some vulnerability, it tends to diffuse hostility. People feel so shut out when a person is all cordoned off by bodyguards. I think it creates a very hostile situation."

When Davis converses, he frequently says something like "As I think I mentioned to you the other day" or "Well, I think we may have talked about this before." These caveats before a statement suggest that he is not always quite sure if he has told you what he is about to say, or even worse, whether or not he has already used a certain metaphor or joke. These asides attest to an ongoing effort to make each encounter personal and avoid falling into the boorish trap of repetition.

"What do you find difficult about working here in the Governor's office?"

"What I find personally difficult about the job, as I think I've mentioned to you, is to deliver less than the best news to people. All day long there are people calling because they want something: grant an appointment, push a bill, get some funding, give an interview with the Governor. And obviously I can't say yes as often as I have to say no. So that's kind of sapping."

"Does marriage fit in anyplace for you in all this?"

"You know, it's really amazing. But what was considered a liability in terms of getting into office has proven an asset now that we're here. I mean, being unmarried really allows you to focus. This is obviously not an easy context in which to have an enduring relationship. Any relationship with a woman which would amount to anything . . . Well, let me put it this way. A lot of people, and perhaps validly so, judge a relationship by the amount of time two people spend together. I remember one friend wanted to see me during the primaries, giving me a choice of any one of ten nights. And I had to tell my friend that I just couldn't make it. I know it sounded preposterous. But that was it."

"Do you have any fantasies about your life that remain unfulfilled?"

"Well, to a large degree I'm doing what I always wanted to do. Maybe that only happens once or twice in your life. So, I'm in my fantasy now."

Jacques Barzaghi

Barzaghi looks as if he might play oboe for some Continental symphony orchestra. He is short and wiry with small feet. His hair is beginning to gray. He smokes Camels, wears wire-rimmed glasses and speaks English with a noticeable French accent. He listens well when he is interested, and becomes elusive, vague and distracted when he is bored. He wears shirts with the letters J.B. stitched on the left side at kidney level, an affectation also in evidence on Brown's shirts, since they share the same initials. This common embellishment has been noted ad nauseam in the press, as if it signified a cryptic connection between the two men. If not cryptic, the bond between them is indeed strong. For Barzaghi is probably Brown's most trusted advisor, as well as a close friend with whom the Governor can relax.

"It is clear that Jacques and Jerry have a very honest relationship," says one woman who has worked with both of them. "They trust each other and don't have to play games. Jerry uses Jacques as a sounding board for almost everything. Jacques is in and out of his office all day long. He's not really accountable to any job description, but he is close to Brown, and a very loyal and powerful man. He can be stern and very abrupt with you, but he is one of the realer people in the office."

Barzaghi was born in the small southern French town of Beausoleil near Monte Carlo in 1938. He worked as a merchant seaman before being drafted for service with the French Army in Algeria in the late 1950's. He came to the United States in 1968, and worked in film for a while before going to work for Brown after he was elected secretary of state in 1970.

Although Barzaghi sits in an office next to Brown's, marked on a small placard outside as Secretary of the Cabinet, this is a misnomer. His actual title is Special Assistant to the Governor, one which does not do justice to the depth of connection between the two men.

Barzaghi's office consists of an antechamber for his secretary, Dotty, and a small back office of his own. He often has classical music playing from a portable radio. Other than a few books on the shelves and a scroll on the wall that reads LIFE IS A MYSTERY TO BE LIVED, NOT A PROBLEM TO BE SOLVED, the office bears no particularly distinctive imprint of his presence.

"Did you see this?" he asks, smiling and holding out a length of paper off the wire-press ticker. The story recounts the birth, assisted by Barzaghi himself, of his child. He and his wife Connie have named their new son Vajra Kai Khan Barzaghi.

"Vajra means 'thunderbolt' in Sanskrit," says Barzaghi proudly. "Kai means 'open' in Japanese. Khan means 'the great ruler' in Mongolian." He describes this smorgasbord of names with playfulness rather than the cosmic sanctimoniousness which is fashionable in some California circles.

Barzaghi's involvement with Zen Buddhism, martial arts and other bits and pieces of Orientalia have given him the public reputation of being somewhat mysterious—even kooky. Journalists writing about the Brown administration have not infrequently portrayed Barzaghi as the unfathomable spiritual mentor of the Boy Governor. Barzaghi has been referred to as "The strange Mr. Barzaghi," a "freaky chauffeur" and a "Rasputin-like" power behind the throne. The media has seemed to love the notion that there is some shrouded spiritual force at work behind the scenes.

"I don't believe Jacques is a Rasputin or an evil malevolent force around here at all," says Tony Kline, Brown's legal affairs advisor. "Jacques is a very whimsical and direct man," says another member of Brown's inner circle, laughing. "He just happens to be occupying the body of a bureaucrat at this moment."

While Barzaghi may be a searcher, he is also a down-to-earth and practical man.

"I'm intrigued by the way the press likes to make me and Jerry sound so bizarre," he says over lunch in the public cafeteria upstairs in the Capitol. "Like this Zen thing. I mean, it's really nothing. We know Baker Roshi [Richard Baker, head of the San Francisco Zen Center]. He's just a fine man. He cannot be in the wrong place. Do you understand what I mean? Wherever he is, is right. It feels good to be around him. Jerry likes to go there, meet with some interesting people and take it easy. No one hassles him. It's very pleasant and nothing profound.

"I still feel funny about reporters who keep calling me up and asking me why Jerry gave me this job as an advisor, as though there were something sinister about it. It makes me feel dirty. It's upsetting."

He pauses. We eat in silence for a moment.

"I only think in the present," says Barzaghi. "The future doesn't belong to me. The past is already dead. My hope is that everyone can rely on themselves rather than on government. But even though they don't want to pay for it, people want to be taken care of. I don't think that we should be using the government as parents."

"As one of the few married men in an office of bachelors, do you think families have an important role to play in politics?"

"It's tough for me to answer that question. Personally, I've been married three times and have four kids. I'm a great believer in sharing. I think that there is more sharing in Europe than in this country, even if it's not on a material level. An image in my mind is of evening time in a small French town. All the elderly people bring chairs outside their houses and sit together and talk. Here that doesn't exist. At six o'clock people turn on the TV. That's it. There's very little communication between people and households. So, if we're talking about that kind of family life, I don't like it. It means isolation. I don't think people can survive it."

"Why do you think that people feel the Governor is unique?"

"Probably because Jerry is the first politician who is not a politician in the traditional American way. Just for comparison, try and compare Jerry with the Chinese Communists." He waits for a minute, takes a long drag on a cigarette, as if to allow time for the image to sink in.

"You see," he says, as if the object of the lesson were now self-evident. "It's *almost* a possibility . . . a plausibility. Now take another politician and try." He pauses again.

"See? It doesn't fit, does it? The key link between Brown and the Chinese style is commitment—to self, to party, to nation, to a redwood tree, to pollution consciousness, caring, sharing.

"The thing I think I appreciate most about Jerry is that he takes words seriously. In his gubernatorial campaign when he said that he would not raise taxes, I remember how he looked for the story in the papers the next day. But it didn't even make it in, because every hack in history had said the same thing. But Jerry meant it."

"Is there any grand design for California here at the Governor's office or are things just going to 'emerge,' as the Governor always says?"

"Both. Both at the same time," says Barzaghi, finishing his sandwich. "I believe that the most important end product is just to have vision."

"But is there any cohesive vision of the future among people in the Governor's office?"

"No, no," says Barzaghi, almost as if he were waving away a bad smell. "We don't have a model, because we don't want one. Do we need to know where we are going? If we know where we are going, it means creating restrictions. Do we want to have more restrictions in our lives? I think restrictions stop the imagination. Do we want to limit ourselves?

"Jerry's said again and again that government is a big mess, and that the only way to begin to understand it is to slow it down. I mean, that's a very simple notion. I'm very naïve in politics, but to me that's a revolutionary notion. You can stop a few things. Stop a freeway. But it's so small. To slow things down you probably have to use more energy than just to let them go faster and faster. It takes more courage to stop and do nothing than just to approve things as they move by.

"In most governments you can only survive by spending more and more money. You get pressured into spending money by people who need it. If you don't do it, they say, 'Okay, you're out!' So in government, to survive, you make many compromises. And at some point politicians turn into cream cheese."

"People always talk about the Brown administration's being so spartan. Do concepts like hedonism, escapism, leisure have much of a place in this office?"

"If you're into what you are doing, time does not exist. There is no need for leisure time. Jerry gets completely balanced by what he is doing. He mixes hours in the office with time outside the office. But it's not a question of needing pleasure. Needing such escapes is being out of your center. Instead of reaching for your center, you seek pleasure outside of yourself, which is dangerous, because there is no end to it and you become attached to it.

"If you really want to work on yourself, there is no better

place than California, because everything is all here all the time. All the goodies are surrounding you."

Suddenly he puts down his coffee cup, and without comment begins to roll up one of his sleeves, revealing a tattoo. The three Japanese characters for *bushido,* or the cult of the warrior, are inscribed on his arm. Then, still without speaking, he rolls up the sleeve on his other arm, revealing a red and blue tattooed mandala.

"I have four of these," he says with no expression on his face. "I'm not sure why I have them."

Even though he is French, Barzaghi enjoys living in California. "Compared to all the other countries I have visited, there is nothing better than this place. California is really the . . ." He gestures grandly with his hands, trying to complete the thought. "If something starts, it starts in California. California moves all the time. There is a great sense of insecurity here. But when you get a lot of movement, there is also a possibility for new ideas. You can buy a pair of shoes in a store. Six months later when you want another pair of shoes, you go back to that store and they don't exist any more. It's fabulous! Absolutely fabulous!

"Something is happening in California. It's like when you pull a carrot out of the ground to eat it, all those little teeny pieces of earth are going to get crumbled around the carrot. Well, that's California. I mean, I can feel it. There's something coming out of California. At the same time we're pulling out the carrot, there's all this mess. If it were possible to film very close to the earth, it would look like an explosion as the carrot comes out."

"How does the Governor feel about campaigning?"

"Well, he's just not the sort to go out and put on a lot of hard hats and hold snakes at the zoo. He couldn't campaign on that level and still keep his balance. You know, after he got back from campaigning in Maryland, I asked him how he could have done that event with Muhammad Ali. He just gave me a kind of pained look. I know he was uncomfortable. He said that there was just a kind of momentum which swept him along. I don't know if it was a mistake or not. But let's just say it certainly wasn't his style."

Barzaghi closes his eyes as if in deep thought.

"You know, when we were shooting the commercials for the gubernatorial campaign, we didn't use a script. About five of us wrote out questions. We didn't show them to Jerry. Then we got him on camera, asked the questions and just let him ad-lib the answers. Howard Berman, an assemblyman from L.A., asked some technical question on oil depletion or something, and Jerry just looked straight into the camera and said, 'Hey. I just don't know the answer to that.' It was fantastic!"

"Did you use it as a spot?"

"Well, no," Barzaghi sighs. "It would have been powerful. But do you think America is ready for it? But it would be such a relief to see a politician stand up on a commercial and say, 'I just don't know.' " He is grinning from ear to ear as he so often does when an appropriate but outrageous idea is suggested.

"I don't know if you saw the commercial that Carter made. It showed him walking through a field plucking pieces of grass and chewing on it or something. He says something about the environment, and then they cut to a shot of trees and sky.

"Well, Jesus!" says Barzaghi, coming forward on his chair. "It was just like a commercial for air freshener."

Tony Kline

"One thing about Jerry which is a real relief," says J. Anthony Kline, Brown's legal affairs secretary, in between phone calls in his office, "is that he doesn't have any machismo.

He doesn't go for cowboy solutions because he isn't the kind of person who always feels personally threatened and challenged."

Tony is a voluble, often blunt man, whose dedication to his work in Brown's inner circle is apparent. He works behind the scenes without great fanfare, and is the man most directly responsible for Brown's judicial appointments. Kline, a classmate of Brown's at Yale Law School, is co-founder of the West's largest public-interest law firm, Public Advocates, Inc.

Kline has allegedly told the Governor in no uncertain terms that he would resign should anyone be executed during his term. He is the kind of brash, confident person who can stand up to Brown.

"When he's full of shit," says Kline, "I just tell him, 'Jerry, you're full of shit.' I think he appreciates it. He doesn't respect yes men.

"I know that I can really get intimidating," says Kline with a self-effacing smile, stroking his bushy black beard, which contrasts interestingly with his bald head. "I mean, you've never seen me in court. I can give the third degree. I can even get insulting. And sometimes with Jerry I'll get totally carried away. But Jerry doesn't go overboard. He just tells me to cool off, and invites a dialogue. I've never seen him personally affronted by someone's aggression—where he felt he had to retaliate to protect his reputation or something."

He stands up to give Cindy, his secretary, a large pile of correspondence to file. "I don't think the public perceives Jerry as a very threatening or pugnacious individual either. Even if you disagree with him, it's hard to get all steamed up and feel that what he really needs is a punch in the nose."

Stewart Brand

Stewart Brand sits with his feet up on his cluttered desk. The walls of his office are fashioned from cardboard boxes filled with back issues of *The Coevolution Quarterly*, a magazine which spun off from the *Whole Earth Catalogues*. Stewart is editor of these publications.

The offices of *The Coevolution Quarterly* are located in a small tilting building on the Sausalito waterfront near some decrepit houseboats. The signs from the building's former incarnation as Harvey's Lunch still hang outside. To say that this office is "unpretentious" would overstate its majesty.

Brand also serves as a part-time special consultant to Governor Brown. As such, he has had an often-unseen but nonetheless profound impact on California politics. Not only has he been responsible for arranging the steady flow of notables (such as Buckminster Fuller, Herman Kahn, Ray Bradbury, Ken Kesey, Carl Sagan, Jacques Cousteau, E. F. Schumacher, Ivan Illich) that have visited the Governor's office to speak with the staff and Brown himself, but an impressive number of his contacts and friends have surfaced as Brown appointees.

Brand is a lanky blond man, who looks a little like an Ingmar Bergman character and was once one of Ken Kesey's Merry Pranksters in the heyday of the acid generation. He has been at the established center of the counterculture ever since.

"How does it feel to be enmeshed in politics and working for someone else?"

"Well, there's an advantage to being an appointee rather than an elected official," says Brand, who is attired in his usual ensemble—so bland that I cannot even recall it, except to say that his clothes usually look as if they had been bought and put right on at the nearest branch of St. Vincent de Paul Thrift Shop. When Brand first began working at the Governor's office, he felt somehow compelled to wear a three-piece pin-stripe suit. The concept was good, but this particular piece of haberdashery hung on him like a shroud over an unveiled statue.

"I don't see myself as representing anyone," says Brand, clasping his hands behind his head. "I've got two customers. One is my boss, Jerry. The other is my client, the state of California. In terms of actually being the house hippie and representing some sort of group of people, forget it.

"Politics is so much more a process than I realized. I do very little reading, no writing, and an enormous quantity of meeting, being available, talking on the phone. That sea of pink slips of unreturned phone calls just keeps piling up on the desks. There is a lot of process and very little product."

Just at this moment the phone rings. It is Carl Sagan, the noted astronomer. A conversation on an article about space colonies ensues.

"Is it easy to get out of touch?" I ask Brand when he hangs up.

"Everyone is aware of the problem, feels it, warns each other about it. The same pressures that destroy marriages distort the lives of politicians. You get a very fish-eye lens view of things. What is immediate looms enormously large, and what is three or four inches away seems way off on the horizon. There is so much going on up close that you're endlessly immersed in emergencies. Some are real and urgent, and others only seem urgent. You don't always have time to make the separation.

"One thing I think the office is remarkable for is that anyone who works for Brown feels heard and heeded. He actually consults and responds to people. I've noticed that the press sometimes gets a little boggled when he does it to them. They think he is being patronizing when he asks them what they think. The unusual thing is that Brown accepts a very wide range of people around him. It's not just types like me. But some of those old hard-nosed financial types go back several administrations. In many ways he gets along better with the old pros than us 'groovy guys.'

"But the system is automatically reductionist. It's continually just . . . just drawing conclusions from insufficient data. And I think part of Brown's popularity is that he acknowledges this.

"One of the things that I think I have come to realize is that the office actually doesn't have much power. I think that everyone that finally gets into politics finds this out, whether it's being around a Governor or a President. The only moves that are left are fairly small subtle ones that have to be done adroitly.

"Brown is now able to say things like 'You should get credit for things you don't do as well as for those things you do do.' A lot of Brown's flashiness and good moves tend to be fairly symbolic things, like the Arts Council, the Office of Appropriate Technology and the California Conservation Corps. I think they have the possibility of going a long way, but they're not things that are difficult to get out of.

"You don't have to do much to encourage appropriate technology. If a fair wind blows from high office, these things will come into their own. A lot of times it's just a question of reducing obstructions. You sort of fly the symbol out there, and it either gets picked up or it doesn't.

"Okay. Time for volleyball," says Brand enthusiastically, taking his feet off his desk top, and stepping out the door into a small mud yard with a volleyball net strung across the center.

After the game with other office members, we return sweating to his office and continue to talk.

"The perceptions non-Californians have of Brown seem surreal. You read about some event which you attended, and the account in the papers has so little to do with what you saw that . . . Well, you wonder where the reporter was.

"But there's an even trickier problem I'm still trying to figure out. The common belief is that the Brown administration talks good but hasn't done anything. My perception is that no administration in this century has done much. Maybe because people got so used to him talking about lowered expectations they think nothing has happened. They think Eisenhower is back.

"Every criticism people make is true. And every criticism in isolation is a goddamn lie. It's the same feeling I had when I was a doper back in the old days. My mother was always telling me all those terrible things that dope was going to do to me. She was correct. And I had to acknowledge that she was correct. But what pissed me off enormously was that she didn't know all the other stuff that was also true, which the hippies were always calling 'psychedelic heaven.' "

"Are you down on the press?"

"Well, take the death penalty. Even Brown's personal clarity on that issue is seen by them as some sort of political adroitness. They don't distinguish the bone of political honesty which flashes white there. The press will take one point and keep examining it in terms of what it means for Brown's reelection, even if it's insignificant. Here's Brown, who's bright, articulate and deliciously dialectical. Given anything like a good straight line he will fly around the room with it. But I have this terrible sense that the press is just wasting its time with a man who could really entertain and inspire readers if the press would just use a little personal contact and draw him out."

"How do you mean?"

"I'll give you an example. Right after the Carter election, Leslie Stahl from CBS called up and said, 'Governor, remember me?' And he said, 'Yeah, of course.' And she said, 'Well, I'm just calling to see if you have any particular remarks to make about the election.'

"Well, then they really got into it together. She drew him out. And that's when he made his remark about the 'fundamental mystery' which has to be respected in elections. He said that he thought if you got too quantitative about elections, it led to the fallacy of 'misplaced concreteness.'

"Leslie Stahl went 'Gosh!' because she had clearly gotten her best item of the day."

"If most of the press is just pecking, why doesn't Brown try and provoke them into a more meaningful exchange?"

"Well, you can't turn off the pecking. Also, as far as I can tell, the job requires that you be good at standing there and getting pecked.

"The position of Governor is already sufficiently insane. You have to have someone who really understands the illusion of power. What we need is a man who can handle insanity. Maybe part of the testing procedure for high office should be 'How much madness can you handle before vulnerability shows?' It's like some Iroquois Indians torturing a Jesuit explorer to see how strongly he believes in God."

View from Below

Every year there are a number of low-paying positions available in the Governor's office for young people to work for short periods of time and gain some familiarity with government and politics. Some of these "intern" jobs are interesting, while others are make-work jobs. Occasionally an intern will be retained after his or her period of internship ends, and be integrated into the Governor's staff on a more permanent basis. But more often than not they simply leave when their time is up.

"My job is the pits," says one woman intern who is still in law school. "Before I came here to the Governor's office I already had a general sense that politics was bad. Now I have some concrete reasons," she says, sitting at her temporary desk in the back of the windowless research room. There is a forgotten quality to this back office that lies across the hall from the main quadrangle.

"Politicians are almost all so self-concerned," she continues dyspeptically. "Since I've been here, I keep seeing parallels between the office and fraternities, or even first grade. If you are in the inner circle here, it's probably okay. Who you are is determined by who you get to hang out with. I keep thinking about religious orders. Like if you call Brown 'God,' the inner circle are the prophets. Everyone else is just the multitude trying to get as close as they can to the seat of power.

"I'm not even sure what I'm doing here," she says, pushing a yellow legal-size pad to the side of her desk. "One of the problems is that everyone expects so much when they get a chance to work here. This office has a hard time living up to people's fantasies."

"You know, before I started working here," says another intern, smiling and shaking his head, "I'd never even heard of those guys in the inner circle. From the outside it was all Brown, Brown, Brown. Anyway, all these guys are sort of middle-aged quasi-counterculture people. But I don't see how you really can mix counterculture, Zen and capitalism. They're okay people, but I don't see how they make all their values compatible with each other. I mean, how does Herman Kahn fit in with E. F. Schumacher?"

"It's true that people here are fascinated with power," says another young staff member, who has just returned from lunch to join the conversation. "They resent it at the same time that they are drawn to it. But some people really do stand in awe of Jerry, even quite sophisticated people who are quite powerful themselves. I see it every day. They feel uncertain about whether they will be received well by him. You know—whether to shake hands, whether he will ask them into his office. They get uncharacteristically confused.

"I just don't think Jerry realizes what a profound effect he has on people," she says after a moment's reflection. "I mean, I know he knows he's Governor. But I don't think he is always aware of the impact it is having around him, even when he is just sitting quietly in a corner talking to someone at a party or something. Everyone at the party would like to be the one talking to him. They all feel a little slighted if he doesn't give them some attention. Then, if they get some attention, they think they have the inside line and want a little follow-up. It's impossible. I mean, we're talking about millions of people.

"In any event, he just is not the kind of person who will dutifully make the rounds of a whole room, signing menus and giving everyone a little piece of the action like his dad. He'd rather just wander around. If he's at a friend's house, he usually ends up at the refrigerator pawing around to see what is available. He just wants to pretend that he is no different from anyone else."

As the months go by, and as my vigil of watching, listening, waiting and getting to know the people in this office plays itself out, the story begins to emerge as much a human drama as a political epic.

The cool, efficient tone of the reception room, which I first encountered months ago, suggests nothing awry behind the doors in the unseen offices. To a visitor sitting on one of the couches, the Governor's office might seem somehow above the normal gravitational pull of human affairs.

But there are scenes here, too, where a secretary, tired of the grind, doing her boss's laundry, late hours, and frustrated by all the irritations which punctuate a day of intense work, will just get fed up and give notice. There are people in adjoining offices who hardly speak with one another. There are affairs which begin and end, leaving two people who must work together as colleagues, if not as lovers. There are feuds, hurt feelings, firings, slights, promotions that are not forthcoming, as well as moments of great friendship and kindness. There are incidents which are unrecorded in this book, not because they are uninteresting, but because they seem so unalterably on the private side of the great public-private continental divide.

I have often watched one or another of the men or women in the Governor's office after some painful inner-office conflict or after some particularly scurrilous innuendo has surfaced against them in the press. There is a sense of hurt which follows the public exposure of a person's most vulnerable side—a hurt which very often has no defense, because the charge, rather than being political, had something to do with family, friends, the past, lovers or sexual prowess. These intrusions are endured as part of the wager of becoming public men and women of high office.

Office Photo

It is just after 11 A.M., and the Governor's office has more or less ground to a halt. Even Jackie and Margaret from the reception desk have gotten substitutes. The couches are filled with people waiting for appointments. The phones continue to ring. Callers are told to call back shortly. Today is the day for the official photo of the Governor's staff.

Staff members slowly assemble in the outdoor courtyard that lies at the center of the Governor's quadrangle. The chatter and laughter of the eighty-odd people echoes through the court. The photographer is trying to prod and cajole the staff members up onto risers into an orderly group. The feeling in the courtyard is akin to that of a class reunion picture, as the photographer squeezes people together, turning a shoulder here and moving a person there. Some wear suits and ties and dresses. Others wear blue jeans and janitorial uniforms.

Two chairs remain empty in the middle of the front row, awaiting like ceremonial thrones for some as yet unseen eminence. Suddenly Gray is sitting in one. Then, just as the photographer has gotten everyone else into place, Brown appears. There is a ripple of applause and a few cheers, evocative not so much of the spirited greeting accorded to arriving royalty as of the kind of acknowledgment a large family might give the arrival of a member who is chronically late to collective events.

Brown pauses with his hands thrust into his trouser pockets and surveys the assemblage. "Hey. How can there be only men in the front row?" he asks, laughing, and then sits down. No one provides an answer to his question.

The photographer barks some orders.

"Stop standing in front of me, B. T.," someone yells.

Brown cracks a joke in the front row, causing the people within earshot to chuckle. Then he turns, sits bolt upright, and looks at the camera without expression, not being the kind to give the camera a big cheese smile. Gray Davis wears a smile no broader than that made famous by the Mona Lisa. Tony Kline is looking stern—like a Smith Brother from the cough-drop box.

The flash pops once, twice. Suddenly everyone's facial expressions reappear. The staff swarms down off the risers in a festive mood like kids on a recess break.

Dinner

Lucie Gikovich and Susan Botnick, Brown's secretaries, sit in the antechamber of his inner office. There is a coffee maker at the rear of the room behind them, which causes a good deal of traffic in and out as various staff members drop by for periodic caffeine pick-me-ups. A sign just above the coffee maker reads "Jerry Brown was once a Jesuit novice. While in the seminary, the master rebuked his charges for being too dependent on their morning coffee. He announced that in order that the practice of austerity might be encouraged, coffee would no longer be served. Young Brown piped up with a counterargument: 'Let the coffee continue to be served so that the novices might be free to exercise their power to refuse to drink.' "

Opposite the coffee maker is the doorway to Brown's own office, from which he has not infrequently appeared with a wooden paddle and rubber ball attached to an elastic band, slapping the ball to see how many times he can hit it without missing.

The floor of the inner office is covered with a regal red carpet, which, like many of his shirts, is at once stylish and somewhat frayed. There are numerous large potted green plants arrayed around this spacious room. A photo of the earth as seen from outer space hangs on the wall. Against the window a long baronial table is heaped with books, pamphlets, studies, tracts, leaflets and government documents on a great variety of subjects that interest Brown.

His desk is also a tablelike piece of furniture without drawers. There is a speaker phone on top, which enables him to speak on the telephone without actually having to put a receiver to his ear.

At the far end of the room, next to a door leading into a seldom-used study, is a group of couches and chairs placed around a glass coffee table. On the tabletop is a small polished rock that bears the inscription "Bloom Where You Are," next to a wooden percussion instrument which was given to Brown by a young man who has done experiments playing music to whales and dolphins.

Underneath the table lies a heap of books ranging from *The Whole Earth Epilogue* and a Webster's dictionary to a book by Ivan Illich, some NASA studies, several volumes on Buddhism, and a paperback about the hazards of sugar called *Sweet and Dangerous.*

There is a suggestion of unkemptness lingering about the room. Although it is here that Brown spends countless hours talking with the seemingly endless string of dignitaries, scholars, counterculturalists and politicians who float through his office, it is also the place where he meets with his staff, and where serious matters of state are decided.

It is almost 8 P.M. Only Lucie, one of Brown's secretaries, is still in his anteroom. He is in his inner office now, door ajar, sitting at the table which serves as his desk, doodling on a pad with a felt-tip pen and talking on the speaker phone. His voice can be heard all the way out into the hallway where Gray Davis is waiting by the water fountain with a sheaf of legal-size yellow pads under his arm. Jacques Barzaghi steps out of his office, jacket off, tie pulled down. For the past fifteen minutes the coming and going has allegedly been focused around getting together to go out for dinner.

"Let's go," says Davis, leaning into Brown's office.

"Okay, okay," says Brown. "We'll talk to you soon." He punches the off button on his speaker phone.

The daily-early-evening-Governor's-office-mill-in is in full swing. Tony Kline has arrived. Brown is in his anteroom, pawing through some papers on Lucie's desk. It is not clear whether he is looking for anything in particular or just rooting around on the odd chance that he will find something interesting.

"What are we going to do with these bureaucrats?" he says, glancing at a document.

Finally, everyone gets mobilized and partitioned into groups to go in various cars.

As we settle into the blue Plymouth in the basement parking lot with Gray Davis at the wheel, Brown turns toward the back seat with a half smile, and says, " 'Each time I left my cell and returned, I felt a lesser man.' Thomas à Kempis said that. I don't know why I remember it, but I always do."

We cruise through the already-deserted streets of Sacramento to the Peking Restaurant on the outskirts of town.

About eight of us sit at a round table, drink beer, eat and talk. The conversation is a strange disjointed one, and we seem unable to decide whether to hold a common discussion embracing everyone at the table, or a collection of individual chats.

Brown's voice rises above the others, as if he were a teacher trying to draw a class together.

"What if they stopped all the wine presses for two weeks?"

"Is too much compassion a vice?"

No matter how searchingly these questions are asked, responses to them are usually derailed by a new question before they are completed. Brown's wit and intelligence are sharp and fascinating as well as distracting.

"Why don't we send everyone down to work in the mail room awhile," he asks, attracting the attention of the people several tables over. "How about that, Gray? Or maybe send them out of their offices to work in the country."

There is a pause for eating.

" 'Do ut des,' " Brown suddenly says. "I think that's Virgil. 'Get by giving.' You receive what you give," he adds, reaching out and spinning the Lazy Susan until the *mu shu* pork swings around in front of him.

"What do people really want from leaders?" he asks, in a way which does not beg a response. In fact, the rest of his staff are busy eating, and seem moved to make no reply.

"Hey, Gray. What's this trip to that military base scheduled for tomorrow?" Brown holds his chopsticks aloft.

"It's disaster mobilization maneuvers for the National Guard," says Davis.

"Who's going?"

"I'll probably go to represent civilian authority."

"Why?"

"Because you're not going. You're the one that got invited."

"Are you going in fatigues?" someone asks Davis.

"I've arranged to rent a pair of blue jeans for the occasion." The table bursts into laughter. More beer is ordered.

It is almost eleven by the time we have finished the beer. We have long since disposed of all the food. The platters sit on the Lazy Susan, the sauces cold and congealing. None of the fortunes in the cookies have been provocative.

The bill arrives. Tony Kline picks it up and starts collecting cash from each person like a card shark at a big game. There are no credit cards. Each person pays for his own share, except Brown, for whom Davis pays.

"Oh, hell," he says later. "He never has any cash. I usually get back about twenty cents on the dollar."

Brown sits through the collection like some intelligent member of an aristocratic family for whom the necessity, and thus the inclination, to cope with the minor details of life has become vestigial. It is not that he seems repelled by details such as buying food, doing laundry, paying bills, keeping the car repaired, or that he feels above them, but just that in the life he now leads they seem magically to have become the province of others.

Conversations with Brown: the Job

AUTHOR: *Why would anybody want to do your job?*

BROWN: Well, obviously my father was a Governor, and I grew up seeing the job close in. I studied law, I've been interested in politics, I understand what the job is. I feel I have the talent and the skills and the ideas that I believe are relevant to our society. Being Governor is like any other profession. In one sense, it is no big deal. Politics is like any other job.

Some people have called you a dabbler—fishing a little here, then fishing a little there. Lacking in long-term focus . . . How would you respond to that?

There's the hedgehog . . . and what's the other one?
The fox. The hedgehog digs his hole and the fox runs
all around. Those are the two different approaches.

Which are you?

I'd say a little of both. The nature of the job of
Governor requires that I be interested in many
things at once.

*How do you shut certain problems out? Obviously you
can't deal with everything at once.*

I've also been criticized for only doing one thing at
a time. I do think I do a number of things at once,
but you have to have a sense of priorities. That's what
a leader does—he sets priorities. I just assess what is
the most difficult and pressing problem of the moment and try to deal with it. I looked at the farm
labor problem and said, Well, I'm going to have to
deal with this—so I dealt with it. I looked at nuclear
energy and said, Well, I've got to do something
about this.

   People find it interesting how I go from Whale
Day to Space Day, from one issue to another. Life
is a mosaic. Life is many themes. Life is many sea-
sons. So is a governorship. So is a culture. So is
history.

*Do you often feel the weight of the electorate pushing
you in some direction?*

The electorate is the ocean in which you swim, and
to feel alienated from it is to be separated from the
entire process. There are two extremes. There's the
person who has a single-minded view of what should
be done, irrespective of what anyone else wants.

They just forge ahead, even if 99 percent of the people don't want it. That's one extreme.

The opposite extreme is the person who will just try to figure out what the people want at any given moment and will then just float, trying to read the electorate as perfectly as possible to survive in office as long as possible.

Where do you see yourself?

I see myself as attempting to confront the problems of society and communicating them in a persuasive way so as to win over a sufficient base of support in order to realize certain goals. I try to learn what has to be done and faced up to by society and communicate that back to the people.

Do you think the role of "teacher" is an important one for a Governor or President?

That's the most important part of the political process—placing ideas in the public domain. I see my role as identifying ideas that are on the margin and bringing them into the mainstream in a way that people can grapple with, digest and assimilate. The one thing that I've made a very determined effort to avoid is becoming a prisoner of a limited number of perceptions provided through the bureaucratic channels. I noticed during the Vietnam war that ideas I would read about in publications that went counter to the official doctrine were not really taken seriously in Washington, or even by my father when he was Governor. The only way ideas could achieve currency and credibility was if they were uttered by significant players in the established decision-making apparatus: the Governor, the executive secretary, the director of finance, the Speaker of the legislature, a publisher of a major newspaper, a significant campaign contributor, a campaign manager. There may be only ten, fifteen, twenty people, but they are the keepers of the approved perceptions—of what is thinkable. And I have been struck by the narrowness of that process. So I've tried to surround myself with divergent perceptions and alternate channels of information. And that is a time-consuming and sometimes painful process. How did we get into Vietnam? I think because the perceptions that surrounded the President just made any other solution unthinkable. Someone who's not from a prominent Washington law firm, from Congress or from the President's own entourage finds it very difficult to gain a hearing for a new idea.

I see the government as having a persuasive power that is often ignored in the concentration on coercive power. And the coercive power is the ability and the capacity to pass regulatory and tax legislation and give out rules that then can be enforced with lawyers and auditors and policemen. But the persuasive power of government is the power of ideas to influence the culture, influence the thinking, which then will shape the response that society makes to external and internal challenge. The White House or the Governor's office tends to be like the end of a funnel. Ideas are funneled before they get to the Chief Executive. What I've done that is different is to get out from behind the funnel and take the time to learn for myself alternative interpretations and recommendations for possible policy choices. I try to meet with all kinds of different people, allowing both sides to talk, taking time—hours, days—getting the various thinkers together.

You are renowned for getting state officials and contending forces together in your office for long sessions to work out various problems. Is that an effective technique?

I kept a group until midnight last week. After these marathons I go back and have more meetings. Yesterday I spent from twelve-thirty P.M. until six going through nursing homes and board-and-care homes. The Health and Welfare Agency head came along with me. I had the directors of licensing for the state and L.A. County, a black psychiatrist who works in the ghetto, and various other local officials, including a deputy public guardian who puts mentally ill people under conservatorship. I'm trying to reexamine the whole system of mental health and community care. But I'm discovering something very curious. In a mental hospital we reward the people who do well by letting them out and sending them to a nursing home where the care is not as good. If they do well in the nursing home, we reward them further by putting them in a board-and-care home, which is even more miserable. So that there is progressive punishment for improving and becoming more sane, which is in itself an insane situation. I have just discovered that. But I don't know yet what we're going to do about it.

Do you think a President can operate on this kind of micro-level?

I think he has to do it. It's the only way you'll change anything. Otherwise the President doesn't exist. He is a puppet. One has to go back to places again and again. I don't just want to get advice from my own advisors, but from their staffs. You have to get down to primary material, until you get the contradictory perceptions of people involved. Then you put them all in a room and keep them there talking day after day. Then I come to my own conclusions.

It's a very valuable process, one which might work on the international level too.

Without this sort of probing, a governorship is just ceremonial—like a puppet presiding over the conventional wisdom that has percolated up through the bureaucracy and been safely put on a memorandum to the executive.

Have you ever woken up in the morning and wished you didn't have to go to work?

I'm sure that I have, but no such time comes to mind. I'm sure there are days when I've not wanted to deal with the world. I certainly had days like that when I was secretary of state, when I was often bringing actions and having press conferences in regard to campaign contributions. I never felt I could really get at the problem of money and politics in an intensive, fundamental way.

Do you think people want to know your doubts and weaknesses?

I think the information revolution does not allow for the artificial propping up of particular leaders. So whether people want it or not, the demand to know, the need to disclose is so great that it's not really viable to create a false presentation over any long period of time. I don't think it's possible.

Do you think the Nixon administration was the last of the false presentations?

That might well be. Nixon tried to manage the government and his own image.

Do you think your governorship is instructive to write about, as so many seem to be doing?

(He laughs.) If I say no, it sounds silly. If I say yes, it sounds arrogant. I'm just trying to apply myself to the problems at hand.

FAVORITE
PROJECTS

The California Arts Council

If you ask Brown or one of the members of his inner circle what has been accomplished by way of legislation during their administration, they will refer to the farm worker legislation, to the California Coastal Act (set up to protect the Pacific coastline from excess development) or to the three bills that limit and regulate the building of nuclear power plants. Some of these pieces of legislation happened without much, and in some cases without any, help from the Governor's office. But three new bills that the Governor and his staff consider to be thoroughly their own are those which set up the California Conservation Corps, the Office of Appropriate Technology and the California Arts Council. Rather than being restrictive or regulatory, these bills established ongoing projects in which Brown has taken a personal interest.

"I'll tell you what it feels like to be working for the state," muses Peter Coyote, né Peter Cohan, who took over the chairmanship of the California Arts Council from Brown's friend Pulitzer Prize-winning poet Gary Snyder. "It feels wretched. But I love it."

Peter is tall. He wears moccasins, blue jeans and a leather knife scabbard on his belt. His hair is long and clipped behind his head. He wears a fishbone necklace, two gold earrings and a turquoise belt buckle. He has mainline California counterculture credentials, being a refugee from the East Coast twelve years ago—just in time to catch the first shock waves of the antiwar movement and acid/flower generation. He was a mover and shaker in the San Francisco Mime Troupe and the Diggers, who distributed free food in the Haight-Ashbury in 1967.

Before moving to its present headquarters in Sacramento, the Arts Council was housed in an old mortuary. Its offices are now located in a restored gold rush–vintage brick building with wooden boardwalks, gas lights and rough-sawn fir interior. This museum-piece building stands incongruously beside a roaring maze of intertwined freeway off-ramps. It is as if astronauts were delivered to their Apollo launching pad in a stagecoach.

Julia O'Connor, the deputy director of the Arts Council, is an intense, cheerful and energetic woman, not unmindful of the power of some good press for her organization, which is this year seeking to expand its budget from $1.4 million to $4.7 million. Such an increase, as many legislators have pointed out, is most un-Brown-like in this "era of lowered expectations."

On her office wall Julia has hung a framed copy of the assembly bill first establishing the Arts Council. Brown has scrawled across it in pencil "C.A.C. Go!—Jerry," as if he might have been composing a cultural football cheer.

"Art is the form of the liberating recognition of what is, through an act of fusing and harmonizing opposites," says the Council's lofty if grammatically confusing Statement of Objectives.

The long-range goals of the Council call for "encouraging expression that draws from and clarifies the actual places we live, to the end of a better life for both people and redwoods" so that we might "ultimately have a society so deeply dyed with art, craft and style, as to render an arts council unnecessary."

A secretary looks over my shoulder and winks. "I think all that was written by poets. But I'll say one thing. This is a bureaucracy which is pretty much run *by* poets and other artists."

The main concrete function of the Arts Council is to sponsor projects and provide small grants to individuals and community groups.

"I thought of all poets as far off, distant, dead people," writes a twelve-year-old after participating in one such Arts Council poetry project. "But I found that people who write poetry are normal."

"What did I think about the poetry teachers?" asks another child. "I liked both of them, even though one had a broken nose."

And a fifth-grader: "Did I learn something about poetry that I didn't already know? No. Nothing. No way. No. Dig it?"

"Maybe our main contribution is that the Governor and the state have given us license to see problems—political problems—with a new insight," says Peter Coyote, removing a toothpick from his mouth. "We have been given permission to bring a more intuitive understanding to politics."

Peter is matter-of-fact about his notion of the function of art. It is easy to forget that one is talking to a man of the bureaucracy, whose function is to dispense grant money like food stamps.

"You know," he says, smiling, "we've angered a lot of traditional arts organizations, the so-called 'empire arts' by taking money from their projects and tipping it toward grassroots arts organizations. California is split now between two different visions of art: art-for-art's sake, stressing refinement and excellence, like a large city symphony on the one hand, and maybe a small Chicano theater group on the other, where the process rather than the final product is important.

"We are under attack here at the Arts Council for eroding standards of quality; for emphasizing amateurs over professionals. But actually"—Peter pauses to reemploy his toothpick—"actually, there is nothing in either form that is exclusive of the other. Schools, prisons, housing projects, traveling theaters, racial minorities need to assume their rightful place among the arts. A symphony which employs ninety people shouldn't take up to ninety percent of the funding. Those who have made their whole living at art are often those who have made so many compromises that their art shocks, titillates and offends no one."

When the new Arts Council budget was announced, the San Francisco *Chronicle* called its members "unpredictable free spirits." The conservative Statewide Conference of the California Confederation of the Arts called the Council "ass-kissing liberals, muddy Marxists and Sufi intangibles."

"We're all in the garbage can together, and someone is sitting on the lid," was Peter Coyote's response. "Instead of putting our shoulders together to get out, we're jostling for position."

"Why in the world should that aid come out of our minuscule arts budget, and not out of the school or prison budget?" counters an "empire artist." "Call that social work, not aid to the arts."

As I leave the Council offices, sun is streaming in the upstairs window of the room where the budget and policy committee are regrouping for their afternoon session on grant guidelines. Feet on the meeting table. Chairs tilting backward. Myriad empty coffee cups piling up before them.

The meeting goes for the rest of the day.

The Office of Appropriate Technology

"We're sort of like the bastard prodigy of the Governor," says Jonathan Katz, Project Director of the Office of Appropriate Technology, an idea Brown hatched up with several "small is beautiful" technologists and Sym Van der Ryn, the State Architect who has just designed and put to bid a new four-story block-size state office building. Called "Site One," this building will employ cooling systems which use cool night air to flush heat from the thermal mass of the building—itself designed to absorb heat during the hot daylight hours. During the cold winter months a reverse system of passive solar heating will be used.

OAT—as the Office of Appropriate Technology is known around Sacramento—sponsors a variety of projects in alternative energy sources, aqua-culture, waste disposal and small-scale agriculture. They have initiated a Solar Technician Training Project (which installed a solar hot-water heater on the roof of Brown's apartment building), the New Possibilities Show, which is a circus-wagon exhibit of appropriate technologies that travels all over the state to county fairs and public events, and the Capitol Bicycle Program, which provides bikes to state agencies and employees for errands and transportation, much the same way a motor pool provides cars.

"It's pretty well understood that government favors and subsidizes large-scale activity at the expense of small local enterprise," says Van der Ryn. "Our interest is to remove some of the barriers to smallness. It's nothing more conspiratorial. More and more regulations are just making it harder for the small guy."

"Great expectations are held for us," says Katz. "We are officially part of the Governor's office, but as you can see, we are removed physically."

Indeed, OAT's office is located several blocks from the Capitol in a building that looks like an old motel. There is a temporary feeling to the place, which is just upstairs from Planned Parenthood. Some ecology posters are taped to the concrete-block walls. Makeshift bookcases have been put up, dormitory style, with bricks and boards. The furniture is all gray steel governmental issue.

"A world of limited resources demands a conserving technology," reads the OAT brochure. "We must carry out governmental responsibilities in less wasteful, less costly, less bureaucratic ways, and in ways that are less harmful to people, and our environment. We need to encourage tools, techniques and processes that are simple, direct, small-scale and inexpensive; a balanced technology that is appropriate to maintaining the health of California's people, economy and environment."

OAT is empowered to deal with developing jobs, resource conservation, environmental protection and commercial development. The OAT logo is a rainbow rising out of some clouds.

"It's easy to get into new buzz words," says Gigi Coe, an OAT staff member in charge of information publication. "The info junkies are really into appropriate technology. We are paying the price for all the talk and no delivery."

"You can't make policy from the top around here and have it stick," says Katz. "It's hard for younger people like us to understand this, but you don't just turn the whole state bureaucracy around on a dime with a lot of good far-out ideas. It's like L.B.J. said about the bureaucrats, 'They're hunkered down like a jackass in the snow.' "

"Last year," says Gigi Coe, "our budget was only $90,000. This year we've requested $260,000—no more than is spent for landscaping a short stretch of freeway.

"I'm still not exactly sure I know what 'appropriate technology' means to everyone out there," says Katz, with a smile. "I know that they really ate up the whole 'era of limits' business when Brown was out on the presidential campaign trail, although I'm not really sure why. But I know that it's very important to be able to say that we are part of the Governor's office, especially in trying to inject some of those 'small is beautiful' ideas into the veins of the state."

The CCC

The road into the rugged San Bernardino Mountains north of Los Angeles winds up the steep rocky slopes on hairpin turns and switchbacks. The Governor's car moves slowly. As we gain altitude, it starts to snow.

By the time we arrive at Camp Radford, a training center for the California Conservation Corps, there are several inches of snow on the ground. We pull up to the central building, a large wood and stone structure, built in the 1930's. Giant sequoia trees arch out over the snow-covered dirt road.

A gang of teen-age corpsmen, wearing bulky army overcoats and hard hats, greets us with a cheer as we step out of the warmth of the cars. Brown is attired in a dark business suit, tie and black wing-tip shoes. He looks rather incongruous standing out in the middle of the snow.

"Hey, all I've got is a sweater," he says, walking over to the trunk of the Plymouth and rooting around in his suitcase. "And I borrowed that from a friend," he adds, as if he were addressing the suitcase itself.

"Governor, let me see if we can't dig up an overcoat," says Wayne Waddell, the driver, who heads over to the main office. Moments later he reappears with a coat like those worn by the corpsmen, a pair of galoshes and a hard hat. Brown dons everything but the hard hat, which he twice refuses. Then we are swept off by the crowd of enthusiastic corpsmen up the road to a freshly dug hole on the road bank, where Brown is to plant a ceremonial tree.

"So you can leave a footprint on the earth," says a black kid, handing the small tree to him.

Two other corpsmen immediately close in to help extract the tree from the planter can. Finally, they take it from

Brown's hands, leaving him an accessory, standing in the quiet falling snow, watching.

They have the tree out now and in the hole. Brown squats down and starts pushing the earth around it with his bare hands. But there is an awkwardness to his posture. He is crouched tentatively in his oversized coat with his suit pants flopping out over his newly acquired galoshes, a half an inch of snow on his head. It is the first time I have ever seen him do anything even remotely physical.

"Hey, where's a shovel?" yells one of the corpsmen. But it is too late. The job is done.

"Instead of just providing for this $22 billion bureaucracy," says Brown, standing, holding his dirt- and snow-covered hands outstretched before him, "I hope I can plant a few seeds that will germinate in future generations."

"Hey, Governor," yells a reporter. "When was the last time you got your hands dirty?"

"I'm not telling," says Brown, smiling.

"Hey, get him a towel," says one of the girl corpsmen. A bath towel is found. As Brown is cleaning off his hands, two girls present him with a banner they have made.

"It's . . . That hits the spot," says Brown sounding almost like a commercial. And then, as if he realizes that some more heartfelt words were in order, he appreciatively says, "It's beautiful. It's really beautiful. I'd like to hang it in my office."

The group troops off through the snow, with Brown surrounded by the corpsmen, to visit some of the small wood-stove-heated cabins that serve as home during the four-week CCC training period.

"How is it living with these wood stoves?" Brown asks, inside one of the sparsely furnished cabins.

"It's okay," says a Chicano boy with hesitation. Then, a smile creeping across his face, he says, "Actually, we're freezing our asses off."

"Is that right?" says Brown deadpan.

Back in the main building, fires are lit in the huge stone

fireplaces. There is a festive ski lodge–like atmosphere. A coffee urn has been set out on a tabletop. A small sign on the table beside it reads "Friends, Cups Are Made from Trees. Put Your Name on One and Use It Again."

Brown, who has been milling around the room, cheeks reddened, necktie still on, takes a paper cup and heads to the sink for some water. He has a drink, and then surreptitiously returns the cup to the top of the pile of clean ones. I catch his eye.

"I'll just put it back here," he says, smiling faintly and almost whispering. "There's nothing wrong with my germs."

"The purpose of the CCC," reads a placard on the wall, "is to provide young people from eighteen to twenty with an opportunity for personal development and employment through performing public service in conservation of the natural resources for the people of California."

"If you have questions about the way your life is developing," says one of the brochures for the CCC lying on the table next to the coffee urn, "and if you are ready to work, earn and learn together with others for a year or more, the CCC may just be the chance you've been waiting for."

A corpsman in this pet project of Brown's earns from $325 to $450 a month working at such tasks as building trails, clearing streams, developing public parks, helping plant community gardens and farms, water conservation, forest-fire fighting and assisting in emergency and disaster work. Although the project has been beset with many problems and leadership struggles, it is one in which Brown still takes a personal interest.

"I see it as an experiment," he says as we wait in line for dinner at the cafeteria. "It's an idea. Part work, part public service. It's a concept I wanted to make into a reality because I think the environmental movement is a very important part of the political process."

There are kids running around everywhere as he talks.

Some are setting places, carrying food. Others are just standing around him watching, listening and asking an occasional question.

"You know what I think our society lacks?" he says. "It lacks good passage between adolescence and adulthood. I envision what's going on here as an opportunity not only for kids to learn about themselves but to learn about the countryside."

He pauses for a moment. And then, by way of adding a personal testimonial of his own passage from adolescence to adulthood, he says, "I went to scout camp. I learned a lot." He smiles ironically. "I learned how to tie knots."

"In order for this thing to work," he continues, now in a more serious vein, "it's going to have to start small and grow slowly, or it will go the way of all the other job programs. I think that the boredom we are seeing in schools these days is because there is not enough mixing of mind and body. There is so little physical labor. The tradition of kids growing up and doing chores is perishing. William James talks about the "moral equivalent of war." We need an alternative to the military, where one can serve one's country not only in a time of war but in a time of peace. The notion of public service is one that I like."

The line is moving now, down toward the kitchen, where a special meal has been prepared in honor of the graduation of this first batch of CCC corpsmen from training camp.

"I want to get this thing about public and private service out in the open," he says, putting some chicken on his plate. "You know, we were trying to find a chancellor for the community college system. Everyone wanted to raise the salary to fifty thousand dollars. They said we couldn't get anyone good unless we did it. I said, 'No. I don't want that kind of person. I don't want a fifty-grand-a-year type of chancellor.'

"I hope these kids will learn something about working together and service here," he says, stopping in front of the fruit salad to inspect it. "If policemen, teachers, sanitation people had a little respect, they might enjoy their jobs more. That's what I call 'psychic currency.' All the professors went

wild when I suggested that just the enjoyment of their work
... a good job ... was worth something! Perhaps even a higher
salary."

It is after dinner now. The main hall is filling with kids
and counselors for the "graduation" ceremony. The hall has
been decorated in a hybrid Christmas/birthday/high-school
prom motif with balloons, crepe paper, tin-foil stars and a large
banner painted on shelf paper which reads A WARM WELCOME
TO OUR GOVERNOR BROWN.

Brown walks in, still be-galoshed, and sits down near the
front of the room. One of the corpsmen goes over to him and
hands him his walking stick. "Will you carve your initials in
this?" he asks.

"Sure," says Brown, taking the stick and pocket knife, and
hunching over to go to work.

There is a ripple of applause.

"Quiet," he says, holding up a hand in mock sternness, as
if to imply that the master could not possibly perform without
silence in the room.

He fumbles around a minute or so. There is some laughter. "I'm going to carve my name on this stick, or I'm not going
to leave," he announces defiantly. Brown busies himself with
the task at hand. The crowd cheers.

The camp director walks to the front of the room carrying
a boxful of framed certificates for the matriculating corpsmen.
He introduces Brown, who steps forward to a chorus of screaming and stamping from the kids. He stands facing the audience,
looking a trifle ill-at-ease in the face of such unabashed adora-
tion. The kids, sensing that they have him at their mercy,
refuse to stop their laughing, clapping and stamping.

Brown mumbles something about "liking to stay low,"
which is only audible in the front row.

"I'm very proud and impressed," he says, when the furor
finally dies down. "You've come a long way. You have a lot to
learn, but then we all have a lot to learn.

"We live on the whole earth. That's what we're on," he

says, now breaking into a mini-address. "It's our earth. The obsolescent-throwaway culture is coming to an end. And I see many of the possibilities I envision for the future unfolding against this potential humans have developed for destroying themselves."

The room is absolutely quiet. The kids are now sitting in rapt attention, as if listening to a prophet.

"I believe that time for the human species is running out," continues Brown. "One of the most important outgrowths of technology and progress is concern for the environment. You're the generation that has the possibility of binding up all the divisions which have divided our society."

As he finishes speaking, a girl in blue jeans and a hard hat bounces up and presents him with a scroll, thanking him for attending the ceremony.

"Why do I get this?" he asks, as if he had momentarily forgotten that he was Governor. "I didn't do anything," he says. Then, as if to terminate this particular moment, he reaches for one of the certificates he is to bestow upon the corpsmen.

The first corpsman called forward is a young woman. She accepts the certificate from Brown, pauses in front of him. Then, having sized up the situation and made a split-second decision, she turns and kisses the tall black camp director standing next to Brown.

Her choice brings cheers, boos and laughter from her fellow corpsmen. She stands awkwardly for a moment, flushing with embarrassment, then wheels around and throws her arms wantonly about Brown, giving him a big hug.

The crowd is beside itself with enthusiasm for this move, as Brown half endures and half reciprocates the gesture, blushing a little himself.

The next few recipients are men. But the room is supercharged with anticipation of the next young woman to go up.

Finally one is called. There is much hooting and cheering. She works her way forward, head down, trying to control a nervous smile. She reaches Brown. As if she had decided to find a way out of the extremism of a hug or the cop-out of a handshake, she accepts her certificate, and then kind of grabs him for a moment by the elbow. The crowd explodes in disapprobation, like Romans at the Colosseum demanding fresh Christians for the lions.

"I guess she's embarrassed," says Brown, an embellishment which sends the audience to a fever-pitch.

Three young blacks stride forward for their certificates, and give Brown black-power handshakes with great bravura. A Chicano boy leaps up and runs forward, almost knocking the Governor over when his name is called. The kids are irrepressible, hamming it up, kissing, hugging, spoofing.

Another girl moves up and gives Brown a long embrace. By now he seems not only resigned to his role but enjoying it.

The ceremony ends. It's been snowing ever since we arrived. There is concern that we will not be able to get out of the mountains tomorrow morning. It is remote and quiet here. The darkness, the snow and the impassability of the roads all lend to the sense of solitude and isolation. But still the calls for the Governor come in. Short whispered conferences go on throughout the evening. Staff members are summoned to the phone to manage some affair of state. Even though it is by one thin wire, we are still connected irrevocably to the outside world.

The kids have cleared the room, turned off the lights and started to dance. The "blacks" and "rednecks" have worked out a music treaty. They alternate, one black rock tune for one country and western song.

Outside, a large bonfire has been lit in a fire pit underneath the falling snow. In-between phone calls Brown wanders around by the fire, then back into the dance hall and to the downstairs office used as gubernatorial headquarters. He has a strange way of at once helping to create confusion and blending into it. He seems to appreciate these scenes of quasi-confusion almost as a means of leveling, of upsetting protocol and loosening stiff situations in which people may be tempted to defer to him as a ranking foreign dignitary.

It is one o'clock in the morning. The dance has petered out, and groups of young couples have positioned themselves on cushions around the massive stone fireplace. Brown emerges from a back room where he has been talking with several corpsmen. Many people have already gone to bed.

"Hey, is the dining room still open?" Brown asks, perhaps sensing that if he doesn't get something going, the evening may terminate.

"He's a night owl," says Jacques Barzaghi, shaking his head and looking weary.

Several corpsmen rise to the challenge of raiding the kitchen with their Governor, and our small band walks out into the snow to make the trek across a footbridge to the dining room.

It is cold and silent. The towering sequoias are covered with snow. Suddenly Brown pulls a ridiculous red and white wool ski cap out of his pocket and puts it on.

"Hey, watch out!" says one of the corpsmen. "Maybe there's a photographer behind one of those trees."

Brown says nothing. He has an abhorrence of looking foolish in hats pressed on him by well-wishers. But there is safety here in this dark snowy night. There are really no photographers behind the trees. The Governor's appearance in this comical pointed wool cap will go unrecorded.

Once in the kitchen, our band fans out like an army of cockroaches. All the leftovers from the evening meal are out on the counters, covered with wax paper. Brown is all hands. Eating pieces of fried chicken, a glass of milk, some pineapple, some chocolate cake, buttered buns. He doesn't bother with a plate. He just moves from platter to platter with no apparent regard for the proper sequence of a normal meal. He stands up throughout this entire gastronomical smorgasbord, his wool hat riding down over his eyes so that he looks about eight years old.

He is laughing, talking, asking questions with his mouth full, joking. The accompanying corpsmen are eating with equal abandon, and appear to be greatly enjoying Brown's company.

"Maybe we all ought to have a moment of silence here," says Brown Jesuitically while gnawing on a chicken leg. "After the meal or something," he adds, smiling.

"No way," says one of the corpsmen. "We have exercises before breakfast. That's enough." The corpsman breaks himself loose from the chocolate cake, and begins doing push-ups on the floor by way of illustration.

"What's the longest period of time you've ever gone silent?" someone asks Brown.

"Oh, about eight days," he replies. "Then I think there was one period where I only talked about four out of thirty days. In seminary we had these periods of meditation—twenty minutes kneeling, twenty standing and then twenty sitting. We had to meditate on our sins. Then we had to . . . Oh, what was it? Oh boy. I can't even remember," he says, slicing off a piece of pineapple upside-down cake.

"In seminary we always had to get permission. You even had to have permission to drink water. It was automatically renewable for a month." He smiles at this notion. "Then, we had to have permission for a siesta. After we got it, we would hang a little sign up which said SIESTA 1:00–1:30. It was like getting a permit. We even had to get permission to do nothing."

The kids listen, not sure how to respond to all this. They seem more fascinated by this man than by what he is actually saying.

"The Jesuits have this phrase," he continues, *"Agere contra,* which means 'Do what you are doing.' It's just like Chairman Mao. They also have a phrase *Age quod agis,* which means 'If you're going to do it, do it.' That's it. That's just what you are doing," he says, turning to one of the corpsmen who has started cleaning off the mess we have made on the stainless-steel counter.

Conversations with Brown: Nuclear Power, Small Is Beautiful

AUTHOR: *How do you feel about nuclear power?*

BROWN: Well, it's not completely clear to me what a reasonable scientific position is on nuclear power—except to say that where there are other potentially less destructive alternatives, it doesn't make much sense to rush to increase dependency on nuclear power plants. In California there are alternatives such as conservation, cogeneration combined cycle, geothermal and solar energy. In the aggregate they make it possible to slow down the growing use of nuclear power. And I am supporting them because I believe that with enough incentives these other alternatives can become practical relatively rapidly.

But at this point, we're faced with a nuclear technology that is already proven—although the questions of storage of wastes over a long period of time, the capital costs and nuclear reprocessing are difficult to answer. So it seems to me that in California, at least for the present, it is worthwhile to encourage and stimulate the utilities to try every alternative other than nuclear. I find it difficult to weigh the competing scientific claims and arrive at a definitive conclusion.

Don't you think we are already sufficiently aware of the hazards and benefits of nuclear power for you to make a decision pro or con?

There are a number of serious questions about nuclear power. The knowledge curve is increasing. I would put myself in midpassage in the analysis right now. I see the use of oil and gas in various combinations as a way to buy time for the other alternatives. To the extent that we push those alternatives, they will become more feasible and possible. Besides that, all I can see now is the necessity of trying to make the nuclear laws on the books work well.

Handling nuclear wastes—do you find that a frightening proposition?

Well, I don't at this point. But I see it as a potentially irreversible dependency that creates serious problems for human beings. If it can be avoided it would be wise to do so. A number of people that I respect feel that it has serious consequences for society, for the environment. They are asking important questions about the ability of society to store these wastes. And giving these people the benefit of the doubt, I would like to try to find economically and environmentally sound alternatives. But whether the prospect of this frightens me . . . Well, I'd like to know how much radioactive material there is, and how much more waste power plants are going to create in the world.

Nuclear energy raises the specter of a more controlled society arming itself to protect its energy. Now, that could alter our democratic and humanistic society into a more paranoid, militaristic society. That's one of the risks that opponents raise. I think it's worth serious consideration.

I would put myself in the position of trying to

understand nuclear power, of trying to slow it down pending more information about its hazards and more information about what its alternatives are. I don't see any real necessity of going further than that now. Twelve months from now or twenty-four months from now I might see it a little differently.

So you're thinking it through to some potentially more decisive conclusion.

Right.

Does the largeness of government ever occur to you as a problem?

No. The size doesn't bother me.

Do you think there is any difference between operating as President, Governor or county supervisor?

I would say state government is a very manageable size. Though it is big, there is significant power available. While local neighborhood or city governments are perhaps more human in the sense of face-to-face communication, which is extremely important, there are other problems.

For example, to try to solve the problem of mental health in a city may be hard without state decision-making power. Every scale has its own constraints and limits. There are limits to dealing with state government. You see in person just a fraction of the people who are affected. So that is a limit, a very profound limit. On the other hand, there is more authority to change and remove obstacles in the various laws that have an impact on things like education, environment, mental health and taxation.

Many people identify you with the notion of "small is beautiful." Indeed, I believe you even went to London to speak at a memorial service for E.F. Schumacher, the author of the book Small Is Beautiful. *How does this jibe with being Governor of the largest state in the Union and running for President of the world's most powerful country?*

Strangely, many of the people talking about "small is beautiful" are involved in large international organizations, conferences, are traveling on jet planes and using satellite telephone communications—all of which are very much a product of large-scale technology. So the concept of "small" has to be a part of the overall picture. The earth is a small part of the universe. It's just a speck. Human history is just an instant. I would say that what Schumacher noticed was the deficiency of economic systems which look at aggregate terms and quantities like GNP rather than at human impact, human scale and the value of face-to-face communication. So "small" and "human scale" are important insights that had been lost sight of. Schumacher brought us back to them. It isn't enough just to worry about macroeconomics. There is the irreducible human individual—the family, the small group—which is also important. But I would like to see strong small-scale organizations as part of a network which in itself might be viewed as a larger-scale organization. From the building blocks at the bottom on up there have to be units that are internally consistent and human. The quality of "small" life at the bottom affects the quality of life at the top. As the family or the neighborhood disintegrates, then society becomes confused. "Small is beautiful" is a corrective to the big bang, the big organization, the big bank, the big house, the big car

—that overexuberance with ever-increasing quantity.

But America is a big place. Texas is a big place. We make big airplanes, big bombs, big cities that capture a lot of glory. I mean, what is the connection between communications satellites—which interest me—and "small is beautiful"? (He laughs.) I'm not sure. But I'm thinking about it. Maybe the connection is that a communications satellite allows rural people in small towns to have better access to information.

Do you feel people misinterpret you when they assume that because you are interested in the concept of "small is beautiful" you must feel it is a universal truth that applies across the board?

Nothing applies to everything. There are limits to everything. There's no idea that doesn't have a boundary, unless it's just the pure light of the visionary. All action involves limits and most ideas have their polar opposites. Obviously some things have to be done on a small scale. What I see in the idea of small scale is that things don't have to be big to be better—that organizations can be good that are small —like a small business, a small church or a small college. There's an esprit de corp, an intimacy, a face-to-face interaction that provides for a certain quickness of response and collective effort that gets lost in the mass bureaucracy of a large-scale organization. Now, on the other hand, large-scale organizations such as the United States telephone company, the Post Office, and multinational corporations can produce some powerful effects and technological innovation.

So you don't feel that smallness and largeness are necessarily contradictory?

No. But some people, who are totally concerned about the environment, for instance, can't develop an interest in technology. I don't see why the two can't be connected.

Has your understanding of how business and the environment fit together undergone some reevaluation since the environmental red tape caused the Dow Chemical Company to withdraw its application for a styrene plant in California?

What I've learned from the Dow situation is that business is a constituency that has to be communicated with, just like minority groups, labor unions and environmentalists. Given the fact that business is traditionally a Republican constituency, their feelings of estrangement are easily stimulated by a Democratic Governor. And Dow became an occasion for some alienation. There are some hard trade-offs. Environmental protection has a cost. But if there is a sound environmental position, it probably makes sense in the long term to take it. Investment has to be made. The question is at what rate. Each side in the Dow case tended to talk past the other instead of confronting the problems at hand.

What is your reaction to those people who now criticize you for abandoning some of your environmental rhetoric in favor of a more sympathetic position toward business?

I don't see life as a static picture on the wall that is frozen forever. Life is flow, life is evolution; times change and we change with them. "Things are changed and we are changed by them." That's an old Latin saying. But I would say that my understanding is broader than it was two years ago. I can also see that technological innovation is important, that growth does provide benefits to people all over the world, that many political problems can be dealt with more easily in a period of expanding economic growth than with an uncertain, stagnant, declining economic growth rate. You have to be able to accept other people's reality. You can't be too finicky about the different styles of political communication. Speaking to the Sierra Club and speaking to the Laborers' Hall in Baltimore is a very different experience. And you have to be able to communicate with both. They're all part of the system.

It's hard to communicate effectively with labor unions and spout off environmental platitudes—it just won't fly. So therefore one has to come to grips with people who are worried about growth, who are worried about jobs, who don't see the value of certain environmental programs. So if you really want to persuade people to get behind a certain environmental program, you have to be able to convince businessmen and labor leaders about it.

So for you it is not a question of speaking out of both sides of your mouth but of trying to reconcile opposing interests?

I try not to contradict myself. But how do you get one group to talk to another? That is one of the central problems of America. Assimilating differences has always been part of the melting pot. A big part of politics is getting one group to accept the other.

I see myself in a majoritarian democracy. I'm

trying to communicate new themes that strike me as being essential for the future—themes which can reconcile conflicting constituencies by finding the larger generalization that brings them together.

JAPAN

Japan

"I don't know," Brown is saying with characteristic non-chalance. "It's a holiday, so I thought I'd take a trip." He gives a cryptic smile. "It's also my birthday.

"I'm going to pay for myself," he adds hastily. "But we'll do a little business. See some Japanese auto manufacturers." He is standing in his shirt-sleeves in the hallway just outside his secretaries' office. He drinks a cup of black coffee with indifference.

"Why don't you come along?" he says to me with a sweep of his arm, as if he were ordering some kind of cavalry charge.

Elizabeth Coleman, his press secretary, stands behind him, shaking her head.

"He'll invite anyone along," she groans after he has disappeared back into his office. Elizabeth is often the one to work out the practical details of these magnanimous gubernatorial invitations extended on the spur of the moment.

Brown has decided to go to Japan over Easter weekend on a day and a half's notice. As usual, those who are doing his scheduling are tearing their hair out by the roots.

"Why are you going to Japan?" a reporter with a basso profundo voice asks Brown, who just arrived at San Francisco Airport with traveling companion Richard Silberman, his future secretary of business and transportation.

"I think that the people of California should be able to share in that very fast-growing market for Japanese cars here in America. I hope we can get a Japanese car plant to set up in California. It will create jobs and might provide some competition for Detroit and help force them to meet the clean-air standards that they are now stalking the halls of Congress to weaken."

And then, almost as an afterthought, he adds, "Besides, I may schedule a few other visits while I'm there."

"Like what kind of touristy things?" a woman reporter asks.

"Oh, I don't know. Maybe a Jesuit seminary," he says, leaving his questioner unsure whether or not she has been the butt of a sarcastic joke.

"Why are you paying for your own trip if you're going on business?" asks another reporter.

"Because I feel like it," he replies.

Brown is looking rather natty today in his double-breasted blue blazer, gray flannel trousers, blue oxford-cloth shirt and polka-dot tie—which he will wear every day for five days. He somehow can look quite sharp and well turned out, and at the same time exhibit signs of haberdasheral erosion.

"Can I give you a kiss for your birthday?" pleads the woman reporter.

"Do you have to ask?"

She gives him a noisy kiss, leaving the lipstick imprint of two large lips on his cheek.

"Oh my God!" she gasps, noticing what she has done, and then lunges at Brown to wipe off the evidence before he sweeps out of the VIP lounge into the airport lobby. He stands stiffly for this ablution like a young boy tolerating a public face wash from his mother.

Once on the plane bound for Tokyo, Brown becomes lost to the world in a pile of newspapers from San Francisco, Los Angeles, New York and Washington, D.C. He rifles through them wantonly like a financier checking his investments.

Suddenly he's up and roaming around the aisles. He shakes a few hands, checks the magazine rack, poses for a Pakistani who wants to take his photo, and then moves toward the lavatories.

A young girl approaches him. "Do you give autographs?" she asks cautiously, apparently unclear as to whether or not his one-time policy of refusing to sign things is still operational.

"No," he says. "But for you I will. What do you do?" he asks, taking her ticket envelope and reaching into his pocket for a pen.

"I'm on vacation."

"From what?"

"From school."

"School? School is a vacation from life."

The little girl is nonplused. She stands silently as Brown scrawls his name.

He returns to his seat. Restless. Trying to stir up a conversation. Rummaging through the stack of newspapers for an overlooked article of interest.

Finally he alights on a *New Yorker* article that I have written on China. For forty-five minutes he is silent.

Somewhere high above Alaska he casts the magazines aside. "Hey, Schell," he says across the aisle as if he were hailing me on a street corner. "What about this place China? Why don't we go to China?" he asks with the devilish look of one who enjoys provoking seemingly impossible challenges. "Who would we contact? Just call them up? Would we have to tell our State Department we were going?"

He is a fountainhead of questions, suddenly preoccupied with the idea. Our immediate destination, Japan, seems to have momentarily slipped from his mind.

"Hey, Dick," he says, turning to Richard Silberman. "Do you think we'd have time?"

Dick is sitting bolt upright in his seat with his stereo headset in one ear, as if someone had suddenly turned the volume up a few hundred decibels. He is electrified by the idea. A long slow smile starts to creep across his face. He grabs a fat International Air Transport Association book of air schedules and turns to the Tokyo-Peking route.

A lone middle-aged man who is sitting in a seat directly behind us, and who has been listening incredulously to our conversation, has a look of "Oh Lord! Is-this-the-way-the-government-is-really-run" on his face.

"What do the Chinese think about human rights?" Brown is asking. "I wonder if we could just go and live in a village awhile without all the banquets?"

The sheer brazen unpredictability of just deciding to up and go to China on the spur of the moment excites Brown.

"Where's the U. S. government on this one?" he asks. "Well, why not go?" he continues, without pausing for an answer. "We want to do business with the Japanese, why not the Chinese?"

There is a moment of silence, as if he were mentally digesting some new aspect of this idea.

"I met the Chinese Ping-Pong team when they were in California," he says anew, as though the Governor of California needed to establish some connection, however tenuous, with his potential hosts before offering himself up as a guest.

"What about the press?" he half asks and half ruminates. "Do you think they'd let them in, too?" He pauses. "Oh, it doesn't matter. They'll just think we schemed this thing up a long time ago like Kissinger and never told them," he says, dismissing the idea.

The notion that the Chinese, not unlike the Japanese, are rather formal proper people when it comes to visiting dignitaries is not one that would seem easy to raise at this moment of spontaneous enthusiasm. And besides, I find myself curious to see what kind of fate this idea will endure, imagining with relish how Brown, the scheduler's anathema and organizer's nemesis, might make out with the good comrades from China who have taken the world's most chaotic country and made it the most ordered.

"Let's just call up . . . what's-his-name on the phone. You know . . . Yes—Hua Kuo-feng, the Chairman, and ask if we can come," says Brown audaciously.

Just then, four Pan Am airline hostesses appear beside Brown's seat, bearing a small chocolate cake with one large white candle on the top. They are singing "Happy Birthday," with broad foolish smiles on their faces.

People in the surrounding seats crane around to see what is happening. Brown appears both embarrassed and touched by the scene.

"Thank you. Thank you very much," he says sincerely, and takes a piece of cake on a paper plate. Then, having dispatched the cake, he pulls the arms out of the vacant seats around him.

"Let's see," he says, "I got two hours of sleep last night. So I better sleep three hours tonight."

That said, he lies down, takes a red blanket down from the overhead racks and pulls it over his head like a hood. He sleeps for several hours.

"Why did you want to come on this trip anyway?" he asks, as we sit and eat lunch from our trays six hours out over the Pacific Ocean.

"I don't know," I reply. "It seemed like it might be an interesting trip, since I'm writing a book about you and your office."

"Why would you want to write a book about all this . . . about this funny farm?" he asks, smirking.

Brown has asked me questions like this several times over the months, apparently both curious about my motives and interested in the prospect of hearing in detail how he might appear to someone from the outside. He has the capacity to be vain and concerned with the kind of image that he is projecting, at the same time that he is able to dismiss and forget that he *is* in fact Governor. Indeed, when I have been around him for periods of time in a personal rather than public context, it is often difficult to maintain full consciousness of his position —to remember that the man beside you asking these unusual questions is both the Governor of California and a major contender for the Presidency of the United States. He seems to derive satisfaction from defrocking potentially ponderous and important situations of their superficial seriousness with his facile banter. This insistence on being unconventional can be a great relief in a high-ranking figure. It is also a quality which can prove disconcerting to a person who views a particular issue or problem with a sense of gravity and concern. There is something about his attempts to keep the heart of the matter at a distance, to keep talking, lest a certain problem evoke strong feelings, that can be unsettling.

We arrive in Tokyo in the evening. Brown wants to get in touch with the Chinese immediately about a possible visit. Our waiting Japanese hosts from the Bank of Tokyo have lined up last-minute weekend meetings with the presidents of Datsun, Toyota and Honda, a feat which they freely admit is almost unheard of in Japan. One of our hosts, in spit-polished black shoes and dark suit and tie with white shirt, stands ready to present Brown with several mimeographed copies of his meeting schedule. No sooner does he hand it over than he is asked if he might check the airline schedule to Peking. And although I fully believe that Brown takes his mission here to Japan with some seriousness, right now it seems rendered obsolete by this new rush of enthusiasm.

We head to our rooms in the luxurious Okura Hotel, beginning to feel the letdown from ten hours of jet lag. Dick and I take baths before our approaching banquet with the Japanese Minister of Trade. Brown sprawls out on his bed without his shirt, talking to Gray Davis in Sacramento. We are fifteen minutes late for the banquet already, when two Japanese aides enter the sitting room of Brown's suite, repeatedly inspecting their watches, as if this might hurry things along. They bring the air schedules between Tokyo and Peking. The flights leave and return at such inopportune times, and so infrequently, that even requesting a visa of the Chinese looks unworkable. But Brown remains undeterred.

The Minister of Trade

We arrive at a small banquet hall upstairs in the hotel, which is incongruously filled with Impressionist paintings and Chippendale furniture. As we enter, the Minister and his aides begin the bowing-and-presenting-name-cards ritual, a quadrille that older Japanese still indulge in.

Not having any name cards of his own, Brown stands off to the side while the Japanese accompanying us become acquainted with the Japanese from the Ministry of Trade. He seems only a trifle bemused by this display of Japanese politeness.

We are seated and served cocktails by a ramrod-straight butler in a white jacket. I am tired. It is all I can do to keep from falling out of my chair onto the expensive carpet. But Brown is wide awake and going full throttle.

"Okay. You say that the Japanese car manufacturers may want to consider building plants in the U. S. because they fear being cut off from U. S. markets by increasingly high protective tariffs?" he asks, as we move to the table for a six-course French dinner.

"I think that they will find California the perfect place," he continues, "because our state is a pacesetter. I think it is important to realize this." He is staring right at the Minister of Trade, who is eating a piece of filet mignon. He is a short man, in the usual dark business suit, who chain-smokes. He looks up from his plate, squints in preparation for the exhale, and says to Brown, "I like your aggressive, dynamic approach." He lets out a startling and abrupt laugh. "The Foreign Minister was surprised by your direct approach, too—of deciding to come here the day before your departure. Most people plan weeks in advance, and go through the American embassy." He laughs loudly again. "Nobody just comes over to Japan this way and gets some contacts at a bank to call up the Prime Minister."

Brown listens and looks both amused and pleased. I am wondering what the Chinese reaction will be to this approach.

After the banquet ends, we walk alone back to our rooms at the other end of the hotel.

"Why are we doing this?" Brown suddenly asks, as we stop to wait for the elevator.

Dick Silberman just smiles.

It is eight o'clock. Brown is out of bed, but still tousled and unshaven. He has slept in his jockey shorts and blue dress shirt. He is sort of hanging out in his suite, wandering around and discussing taxes with Dick Silberman.

He walks into the sitting room and takes a banana from a basket of fruit which has been left as a gesture of hospitality by the hotel management. He returns to Dick's room, leans in the doorway munching his banana, "All right," he asks. "So who are we going to see today?"

A Datsun "President"-model limousine arrives at the front door of the hotel to take us to our meeting with the actual Datsun president, Tadahiro Iwakoshi.

Once at the Datsun world headquarters, we take an elevator up to the top of the building, where we are ushered into a plush-carpeted meeting room by three uniformed women, all wearing plastic name tags. Their demeanor is obsequious, suggesting the near presence of high-ranking and respected personages. There is a hush about this sequestered complex of rooms. The three of us sit alone, waiting on couches that are arranged around a tea table decorated with a delicate and tasteful flower arrangement. One American flag and one Japanese flag have been stuck side by side into the midst of the flowers in jarring contrast to this otherwise-traditional Japanese arrangement.

Brown inspects his tie, and finding a small spot on it, he

commences to scratch it off. Then he looks around the room to size up the scene, his eyes finally fixing on the flower arrangement. "How does that relate to Zen?" he asks. "I think we ought to make small cars that we can fix ourselves," he continues, eliding one thought into another. "Well, it's just a thought."

The door opens, and President Iwakoshi, surrounded by a coterie of assistants and aides, enters the room. As introductions are made, a house photographer scurries around the room, flash bulbs popping. All of the men entering with the president wear dark suits and Nissan Motors corporate lapel pins. The Oriental mafia effect their collective entry has produced is partially dispelled as one of these modern black-suited samurai sits down and allows his suit pants to ride up his ankle, revealing the bottom cuffs of a pair of gray long underwear. We sit beside these wealthy and powerful Japanese businessmen, all about sixty years old, as the three uniformed girls appear again and noiselessly begin to move about the room pouring tea, bowing slightly at each stop. I glance over at Brown. He seems utterly unimpressed by the affectations of respect and hierarchy around us. There is something about his presence, his youth, his irreverence, his confidence, his California-ness which makes these men before us seem almost preposterously remote.

Although I find myself struggling to dismiss it, the one question that I cannot banish from thought is, Just what were all you guys doing around 1944 before you started making cars? Perhaps I've been watching too many late-night movies.

"Wherever you go," Brown begins, getting right down to the task of wooing one of these car plants to California, "people know California and have a pleasant association with it. I think any product that is made there cannot help but pick up that association," he says, amplifying on an idea which he tried out on the Minister of Trade last night. He is talking about California as if it were a country with its own identity and culture, like a salesman trying to peddle industrial lots to the

Japanese. But what is this man, the Environmental Prince of saved redwoods and compost privies, doing here in this den of capitalist Japanese pirates?

He is plunging forward into the whole subject of international trade: protective tariffs, unitary tax, pollution control, his concern that Japanese imports generate more jobs for California. He is feeling his way, picking up information with agility. He leads the conversation, asking questions rapid-fire until he understands the problem, any problem.

President Iwakoshi raises his head slightly and looks down his nose at Brown as he speaks. He watches Brown with unbroken concentration even while the interpreter is translating into Japanese, as if he were trying to read something from the face of this man who has, with two days' notice, succeeded in getting him to a meeting on a Saturday.

We lunch at a traditional Japanese restaurant, sitting at low lacquered tables on tatami mats. We are served numerous beautifully arranged courses which seem to lean toward sea slugs, parsnips and seaweed. We eat and discuss cars and trade.

"Are you familiar with the Zen Center in San Francisco and the Tassajara monastery several hours south of San Francisco?" Brown suddenly asks, attempting to move the conversation from an industrial to a spiritual plane.

"Oh yes," President Iwakoshi affirms, perhaps only hearing the part "south of San Francisco." "I have visited the Ford assembly plant in San Jose."

There is a cultural collision happening in this room that is not easy to describe. Brown's presence here with these polite and opaque Japanese *zaibatsu* evokes the scene of some mad scientist who wantonly mixes various potent chemicals together, uncertain whether he will end up with no reaction at all, some sizzling and smoke, or perhaps an incredible explosion.

Japanese Environmental Protection

The Tokyo Metropolitan Institute for Environmental Protection is in a shabby municipal building with a cold concrete interior. It is a far cry from the plush corporate world of Datsun. As we walk through the door, we enter a different universe: from the stronghold of the automotive polluters to their environmental antagonists.

"This is really Jerry's style," whispers Dick Silberman. "Get in both worlds, one after the other."

Indeed, this is one aspect of Brown's political personality which confounds people on each side of a particular political issue. Each side sees his willingness to meet and discourse with the other as a sellout. Brown seems to see his method of approaching contending factions as neither hypocritical nor inconsistent, but simply as logical.

"I represent all the people, not just one faction," I remember him once telling me as he read an article about some environmentalist who was mad at him for supporting the construction of a large dam.

"Well, from Tokyo in 1965," says Tokue Shibata, the institute's director, a scholarly and merry man, "we saw Mount Fuji less than thirty days. In 1970, we saw it over 70 days."

He then launches into a long historical discussion of the city's fight with the automobile industry over emission standards. But like a professor trying to cram too many details into a fifty-minute lecture, he loses us in statistics and minutiae.

"Okay, okay." With more than a hint of impatience, Brown injects himself into the discourse. "What about right now? What's happening with the car companies in Japan right now? I hear they're way out ahead of the U. S. manufacturers on pollution control."

There is a long discussion on automobile pollution and waste management in general.

"You've got free time?" asks Mr. Shibata, suddenly turning from the blackboard on which he has been scrawling figures. "I'd like to show you important point in Tokyo." He is beaming widely now. "We go to Dream Island. Big garbage dump and incinerator."

Everyone in the room bursts out in laughter. There is something absolutely hilarious about Mr. Shibata's sudden and kind invitation to visit Dream Island. Once we have stopped laughing, Brown expresses interest, but says he is not sure his schedule will allow it.

As we leave, Mr. Shibata asks us to sign the guestbook. "It is up to all men to protect the earth," writes Brown.

Champagne Gift

Brown sits in his hotel-suite living room engaged in one of his marathon phone conversations back to Sacramento.

There is a knock on the door. A room-service boy in a white jacket stands at attention outside over a tableclothed cart bearing twelve bottles of champagne. One bottle is enticingly at rest in a silver bucket full of chipped ice.

The boy hands a card through the door. The champagne is a gift for "the Governor" from a Tokyo representative of a California vineyard who has learned of his presence in Japan.

"What's this? What's this?" Brown says, cupping the phone receiver with one hand.

I hand him the card.

"No. No. Take it back! Take it back! I can't accept this. I don't take gifts." But he is virtually talking to himself, and to whomever is on the other end of the phone back in the United States: the room-service boy has already vanished leaving "the Governor" trapped with this effulgent cart of champagne.

The champagne remains untouched in his suite for the next few days. It is finally I who am elected to track down the donor and write a letter refusing the gift.

Another President

Mr. Morita is one of those rare Japanese men so deeply imbued with international coloration that it is easy to forget that he is Japanese. The president of the Sony Company, he is a small man who wears longish gray hair tucked back behind his ears in a manner suggesting the respectable flamboyance of a liberal professor. He is spry, genial and outspoken.

"So, I am telling all my friends"—this diminutive mogul is saying to Brown in English with strident charm—"my Japanese friends, my German friends—all of them! I'm telling them not to invest in California because of your unitary tax." (This taxes a foreign corporation a percentage of its U. S. profits, computed on the basis of its total world-wide profits.) "You see," he says, sitting opposite Brown in his hotel sitting room, "I don't want them to get stuck!"

Brown wears the expression of a man who has just bit into an unripe persimmon. He is peeved. "Just the man we are looking for on this trip," he says caustically.

"Yes," says Morita. "We have opened a color TV plant

in San Diego, and we are very unhappy."

"Okay. We'll have to take a look at this unitary tax," replies Brown, staring off into the room.

"Japanese people are very polite. I'm too Americanized," says Morita, as if to apologize for himself. "Anyway, I can be frank with you. Everywhere, all over the world, people are very unhappy with California."

"So you're at war with California," says Brown, looking for some way to terminate the encounter.

"Can you imagine that guy?" Brown says incredulously, down in the hotel bar later in the evening, as we conduct a late-night search operation for something to eat. "He was just rapping our ears off. He just wouldn't stop. I thought he was insulting."

He orders another glass of white wine.

"What do you think? You don't think I was too heavy with him, do you?"

A Zen Monastery

It is Sunday morning. There is nothing scheduled today. We sit around Brown's suite talking about what we're going to do and the feasibility of requesting permission to go to China. Various members of the press are calling for interviews. Two California businessmen whom Brown has run into in the lobby drop by. The hours pass.

"Let's get this China thing rolling and get out of here," Brown says finally. "This suite is costing me a hundred thirty dollars a day. It's too expensive. Why don't we go and stay at a Japanese inn or something? How about visiting a Zen monastery? That's what you're supposed to do when you come to Japan, isn't it?"

Dick gets on the phone to the manager of the hotel. A little while later he reappears. "Okay. Let's go. I've got a car and found out the name of some monastery or other. Let's get a cable off to the Chinese and get out of here."

We take the elevator down to the lobby, stand at the cable counter and send a telegram to the Honorable Huang Hua, Foreign Minister, Peking, the People's Republic of China, expressing "the Governor's" interest in visiting China. But somehow, it all seems too unofficial and ungovernmental: the Governor of the most populous state in America, standing at a counter in a hotel lobby, discussing the wording of a telegram to the Foreign Minister of the most populous nation on earth —while bellhops move suitcases and tourists wait in orderly groups for their buses?

We finally leave the hotel and arrive at the Tokyo suburb of Seijo. It is springtime, and cherry blossoms float through the air, blowing into small drifts on the narrow asphalt lanes. It is quiet. The scale of the city seems to suddenly shrink to more human proportions in these outlying neighborhoods. Though the houses are squeezed together, the Japanese have preserved every tree and every piece of greenery as if it were human life itself.

The Ko-un-ji temple is on a back street so narrow that there is hardly room for one car to pass. There are strings of bright-colored pennants hanging from its sloping roof, which make it look at first glance like a cross between a used-car lot and a yacht flying code flags.

"It must be for Buddha's birthday," says Brown. "It's the same day as mine, you know."

A young Japanese with a shaven head and wearing brown robes leads us into the garden, through some shoji screens, up a narrow flight of stairs and into a small room with tatami mats. There is a flower arrangement on a low table, a picture of Buddha under the bodhi tree, and an air conditioner. A wall

hanging done in a very cursive style of Japanese calligraphy
reads "Water Like Buddha's Teaching Flows Everywhere."

Since we have no interpreter, and since none of us speaks
Japanese, we just sit and wait, not quite sure what for. It is not
even clear to us if *they* know why *we* are here or even who we
are. For all they know, we could just be three crazy *gaijin*
(foreigners) who have wandered in off the street.

Finally, a man dressed in a T-shirt and slacks arrives,
slightly out of breath. His English is at best rudimentary.
Brown sits with a bemused smile, apparently enjoying this
unfolding event, as well as the utter anonymity he seems to
have at last attained in this small temple.

Our translator is apparently a parishioner who comes to
Ko-un-ji temple several times a week to meditate. Introductions are made. But since no one's name seems to have any
significance for anyone else, all are quickly forgotten.

"Today is Buddha birthday," says our new host, smiling.

"Buddha has many birthdays," replies Brown, falling into
a kind of modified pidgin English. "Do you pour water and
sweet tea over the Buddha today?" asks Brown, still trying to
establish some common base of discourse.

"What?" replies our host.

Brown repeats the question very slowly.

Our host smiles wordlessly.

"I'm interested in learning if there are many people here
in Tokyo who practice Zen," says Brown, trying a new tack.

"Yes. Many peoples want to practice Zen," replies our
host, like a student in a foreign language class who is given the
task of converting an interrogative sentence into a declarative
sentence.

"I come here three times a week to meditate and pray,"
he continues. "Then I return to my company and work. I sell
pharmaceuticals. I sit three days *sesshin* [a long period of Zen
meditation] each year."

The abbot of the temple, an older man in robes, with
shaven head, arrives. He bows, smiles and sits down on the
tatami mats at the end of the table. Tea is served.

"This is sweet tea," says our translator. "After Buddha was born, sweet rain fell. Please." He gestures toward the tea.

Brown picks up his cup and sips the tea. Then, shaking his head in disbelief, he says to Dick and myself, "It's kind of amazing how we arrived here, isn't it? I'm not sure I even know how it happened." He looks first at the translator, who is grinning, and then at the abbot, who is expressionless, then fixes his gaze out the window at some budding bamboo blowing in the breeze.

"Do you think Japan is getting any closer to Buddha-mind?" asks Brown.

"Farther away, to my regret." Our translator seems to puzzle over the question more as a linguistic problem than a philosophical one. "Some people want to study Zen again because they want to study human beings and human spirit. They want to be strong again. Me too. When we want a calmer mind, we will realize real meaning of Buddhism."

"What are the three truths?" asks Brown as if he were a host on a quiz show.

"Yes. This is old question," replies the translator, looking at the abbot to see if he is still tuned in.

"Do you study Buddhism?" asks the translator.

"Not really," replies Brown. "But there are some people in America who are interested. I talk to them often."

"Is it a . . . How you say? A . . ." He pauses. "A . . . a boom?" he asks triumphantly with a smile.

"A boom?" retorts Brown, laughing.

"A boom," the translator reaffirms with added surety.

"Oh, not really."

"Why did you come to Japan?" asks the abbot, breaking silence for the first time.

"Oh . . ." says Brown searching for some comprehensive answer. "For Buddha's birthday. And I'd like to give you something." He hands the abbot a copy of Shunryu Suzuki's book *Zen Mind, Beginner's Mind: Informal Talks on Zen Meditation and Practice.* Suzuki-roshi was the original master of the San Francisco Zen Center (now also encompassing Tassajara

Hot Springs and Green Gulch Ranch in Marin County, which Brown often visits on weekends).

The abbot thumbs through the pages in a desultory fashion. His face finally breaks into a smile as he stumbles on the one thing in the whole book that is in Japanese, an inscription on one of the title pages.

"Ahhhhhhhh . . ." he says, in that characteristically Japanese way of first sucking in air and then letting it out in a long nasal expletive of understanding.

"In the beginner's mind there are many possibilities, but in the expert's there are few," says Brown, as if reciting from the Scriptures.

"Do you know the difference between the Rinzai and Soto sects of Zen Buddhism?" the abbot asks. "Well, in Rinzai they sit and talk of many questions. In Soto we sit against the wall and think of nothing." The abbot lights up a cigarette.

A silence ensues.

"We thank you for your hospitality," says Brown. "I think we should be going."

The abbot bows. The translator shakes our hands, and we depart.

"I find that studying Zen makes it easier to understand Catholicism," says Brown as we leave. "It's really quite similar to Zen in a way. There are only so many philosophical principles, and they seem to permeate all philosophies. By studying one, you can understand something of the others: Zen, the Jesuits, the Communist Chinese." He is in a relaxed and reflective mood.

"Hey, are there any other Zen temples we can go to around here?" he asks the driver.

The driver thinks; nods his head.

We arrive at the Rotokuji temple, one of the oldest in Tokyo. We get out of the limousine and wander around among the graceful buildings, uncertain about what we are seeing. Brown is intrepid, willing to go anywhere whether invited or not.

A young man with a shaven head greets us as we walk into

one of the ancient tile-roofed buildings. We try to communicate. But the young man can make no sense out of us, and we can make no sense out of him. We part, giving each other smiles of futility.

As we walk back to the car under some tall gnarled pines that look to be hundreds of years old, we pass a bronze bell hanging outside under a small roof.

"There's a bell just like the one at the Green Gulch Zen Center," says Brown, pleased at last to recognize something familiar.

"I think I'll go up and ring it a few times for Buddha's birthday," he says, with a naughty look, enjoying the obvious sacrilege of the idea.

"Ah well," he says, abandoning the idea, and moving again toward the limousine, "I never made much of a tourist anyway."

"You know how I first got involved with the Zen Center in California?" Brown continues. "I was driving around one weekend with a girlfriend. We were down near Carmel, and we just decided we'd go up to Tassajara Hot Springs and have a look. I really didn't know much about it then.

"As we climbed up that narrow road in the mountains, I remember there were signs everywhere that said 'Closed— Turn Back.' I guess it was that time of year when the place is closed to the public.

"Anyway, I just wanted to keep going. When we got there, everyone was very gracious. They called their head, Dick Baker up in San Francisco, and he drove out. So, that's how it began."

"Opportunity is the great enemy of commitment," Brown says as we ride back to Tokyo. These out-loud ruminations that he shares with anyone and everyone present at once establish some form of communication and keep the listener at a strange distance. Although many of them are phrased as questions, they are posed in such a way that there is almost a tacit understanding that they need not, perhaps should not, be answered. If it were not a contradiction in terms, one might say that Brown holds dialogues with himself.

"In seminary they were always speaking to us in Latin." Brown returns, as he often does, to his novitiate experience for examples and anecdotes. "They'd tell us, *'Ad Majoram Dei Gloriam'*—'To the Greater Glory of God.' It's almost like the Chinese slogan 'Rehearse for the Revolution.' One should work for something outside of the self. In seminary we all had to sign a will which gave away everything that we had. I don't really know what the legal ramifications of it were. But anyway, we felt like we were signing away every possession that we had. We were supposed to be 'In the world but not of it,' " he says, as if it is a wager that is still not entirely resolved in his own mind.

"The Jesuits are not what they used to be when I was there," he says, waking up from this reverie of the past. "The world certainly doesn't seem to be very permeated with self-mortification now. People are seeking pleasure. Pleasure," he repeats the word. "Perhaps it will swing back in a few years in reaction to all the self-indulgence."

By this time we have arrived in downtown Tokyo on the Ginza, where we have decided to spend a few hours walking around. We disembark across from a McDonald's hamburger outlet, which immediately catches Brown's attention. It is an absolutely perfect replica of an American McDonald's, except that the writing is in Japanese.

Brown seems both fascinated and repelled by its presence, but agrees to pose in front for a photo with Dick Silberman. They stand on the curb, surrounded by hundreds of Japanese Sunday strollers. I snap a picture.

Then Brown notices that there is a Shakey's Pizza Parlor, a Dairy Queen and a Baskin-Robbins ice-cream stand all across the street.

"Well, they're all here," he says, as we cross the street to the Baskin-Robbins for an ice-cream cone.

Embassy Cocktails

"What's he *really* like?" asks the young and attractive wife of a National Security Council staff member who is accompanying a congressional delegation on a tour of the Far East.

"I mean, my husband and I went to Yale Law School when he was there, and he had a reputation of being so flaky." She laughs, unable to quite find the words to politely express just what it is she means to say about Brown, who has been invited to this cocktail party as "the guest of honor."

"Anyway, I wonder. I really do." She takes another drink from a white-jacketed houseboy who moves about the grand old high-ceilinged reception hall of the American embassy with a small silver tray.

The room is sparsely filled with a few Congressmen, Japanese government officials and a generous helping of foreign service officers dressed like overgrown prep-school boys.

Brown is standing in the center of the room before a large fireplace. A knot of people has gathered around him. The conversation is not electrifying.

"We have many other engagements," he finally says to the chargé d'affaires' wife, who is wearing a long evening gown.

"Oh yes, of course," she says, offering a white-gloved hand to Brown as he strides toward the front door. He departs with a sense of urgency, as if he were on his way to an audience with the emperor. Actually, we are off to the Harumi Dome for the Rolling Coconut Review, a series of concerts by prominent American singers to raise money to save the whales.

"The whales. It's a problem," says Brown, as we get into our chauffeur-driven car outside. "What are we going to save, and what are we not going to save?"

It is raining. We drive through the wet streets of Tokyo without talking.

"Linda Ronstadt thought she might come and sing over here," he finally says. "But I didn't think she should come. She has a concert tour here later on. Anyway, she thought it might be patronizing to come over and teach the Japanese how to save the whales."

The Rolling Coconut Review

Inside the vast auditorium it is sometimes hard to remember that we're in Japan. The people backstage are wearing cowboy hats and "Save the Earth" and "Save the Whale" buttons. A girl in bib overalls, a T-shirt and sandals is singing with a country and western band. But she is Japanese, and the beer can held by a guy standing next to me has Japanese characters all over the label. An audience of thousands of Japanese youths sits out in the darkness beyond the stage, swaying back and forth to the deafeningly loud music. Brown stands three feet to my right. The singer Jackson Browne stands just in front of us talking with Mimi Fariña.

"I think this whole fucking show is great!" says Jackson Browne. "Whoooo-eeeee!" he yelps, and makes a gesture with his hands as if to indicate the top of his head is blowing off.

The music stops. A film of the gray whales migrating along the California coast flickers on a large screen. These leviathans emit strange squeaking, grunting and growling noises as their bulky, graceful bodies turn and dive.

"He sure comes to a lot of these whale events," says a bearded American roadie looking at the Governor, who is now wearing a "Save the Whale" pin, and is seated on a folding chair talking to one of the concert organizers. I cannot help but wonder what Mr. Iwakoshi, president of Nissan Motors, would say if he saw Brown now, immersed in the whale-saving counterculture.

But Brown seems to savor these rapid-fire transitions, perhaps because they attest to his ability to transcend the ordinary stereotypes which seem to trap more mortal men. And yet I wonder in which of these many worlds he feels most at home.

Suddenly, it is Brown's turn to make some remarks. He walks out on the stage into the spotlight. He seems uncharacteristically timid and disoriented by this audience that offers no hint of how they feel about him, or even about saving whales.

"America and Japan have added many things to the planet," he begins. The audience is quiet. "TV's, cars. Both have brought progress and happiness to many people. But as technology progresses, we should also remember that the planets and the oceans must be respected if they are to survive. So, as you enjoy the music, you should think of the many things which will not survive unless man treats them with care. One of those is the whale. And I like to think that the whale is in the image of man himself. As we preserve one, we preserve the other."

There is a ripple of applause as the translator finishes.

"And now, I'd like to introduce another Browne from California," says the Governor. "Jackson Browne!"

"Jackson's gonna knock 'em dead," says Richie Havens from behind me. "It's lucky they got the Governor on first."

There is a tidal wave of applause. It is indeed unusual to be with a crowd for whom Jerry Brown is not the main attraction.

Jackson Browne breaks into his "Here Come Those Tears Again," and the audience begins to clap and scream, yelling in unison, *"Saiko! Saiko! Saiko!"*—which in Japanese literally means "the highest," but which is more colloquially equivalent to "Far out!"

The crowd is on its feet, surging toward the stage.

"Hey, I want to see this," says Brown, moving forward to survey the audience.

"I wonder where these kids really are when it comes to saving whales," he says over the music and roar of the crowd.

"Maybe they just want to hear the music," he murmurs diffidently, and then walks to the rear of the stage.

Chinese Visas

Twenty-four hours have passed since we cabled Peking, and we have not yet received a reply. Brown has left for Nagoya on the famed Bullet Train to visit the Toyota plant. I remain behind with our passports at the hotel, in case the Chinese should choose to respond to our abrupt entreaty. I find myself marveling at Brown's energy. After the frenzied rush of the last few days I am ready to expire; it is a welcome respite to be able to lounge on my bed in this luxurious hotel. Brown continues on, maintaining a constant level of intense activity that seems to leave him neither spent nor irascible.

I am just dozing off when the phone rings. The Chinese have extended an invitation to Brown to visit China tomorrow. They want someone to come to the Chinese embassy immediately for "a friendly chat" and to pick up the visas.

The news stuns me. Brown has done it again on the wing! In twenty-four hours he has succeeded in eliciting a response from people who very often take months and years to answer such requests, and frequently do not answer at all. It is clear that this Governor is a man whom the Chinese have been watching, and whom they see as an important American political figure.

I call Brown on the train, which is now returning from Nagoya. Having checked the airline schedules to and from Peking, it is still not clear to me how this whole trip can be completed in time for Brown to arrive back in California for several important appointments at the end of the week.

I explain what has happened and ask if he is still interested in going.

"Yes," he says, through the static from the train radio telephone. "Why don't you go down and get the visas at the embassy?" He pauses. And then, as if still trying to convince himself that the proposed trip was a sound idea, he adds, "Who knows? Maybe we'll learn something."

"You realize that we would only have a day or so in China."

"Let's see what works out."

It is somewhat disorienting to be suddenly thinking of the new dimension of China in our lives. It is equally disorienting to think of Brown in this new international context. It is not so much that he is a "lightweight" when it comes to international affairs, as some have alleged, but that he is in uncharted waters where there is much to be learned. But these considerations do not seem to deter him.

The embassy of the People's Republic of China is just closing as I arrive late in the afternoon. But I am greeted warmly at the door and immediately ushered upstairs to a small sitting room.

Green tea is served, and an official enters carrying three application forms for our visas. We chat as I fill them out, discussing the possibility of chartering a plane for the return flight. They are unclear about this procedure. I inquire about getting seats on the China Airlines flight to Peking the next day. They tell me that there will be no problem. They are helpful but also appear a little bewildered by this Governor who is in such a hurry to go to China, but knows neither when he will leave nor when he will return.

I hand the official the applications I have filled out with our passports. We sip more tea. Then I decide to make one last call to Brown, who by now is back in Tokyo meeting with the president of Honda at the Bank of Tokyo.

"I just don't know," he says, when I finally get through to him. "I talked to Barzaghi and Davis back in Sacramento. They think the trip is foolish. We'd better discuss it some more. Can you bring our passports, get our luggage and meet here?"

This new twist is almost as stunning as the original news that we had been issued an invitation to China in the first place.

Bring our passports? I think to myself. Jesus! How? They've already taken them and told us to return in the morning!

I return to the sitting room, not sure what to say next. The Chinese sit watching impassively, with distant looks that suggest that they are ready to be further confused by these inscrutable Occidentals.

Groping for words, I begin to explain that some pressing affairs of state have come up in California, and that until further consultations can be held with "the Governor," we will not know whether he will actually be able to visit their country at this time.

"So please give me back the passports," I blurt out, almost too forcefully, fearing lest they have already been taken elsewhere, leaving us the victims of our own carelessly planned plot.

"If you still wish to go to China, please return the passports in the morning," says the official, obviously perplexed by this sudden reversal. He hands me our documents.

"I think it's too jet-setty," says Brown when we meet at the Bank of Tokyo. "I think such a fast trip to China would be too flaky, and I've got to watch that. All this Zen stuff—

and then flying to China for the day. I mean, why are we doing it? What do we expect to accomplish? It's muddy. I think that's what bothers me."

He looks at his watch, which he has steadfastly refused to reset to Japanese time. As is so often the case with Brown, it is not until the eleventh hour, when an issue or problem becomes unavoidable and urgent, that he turns the full focus of his attention toward it.

"It would be different if we could stay awhile," he says. And then, somewhat more hesitatingly, he asks, "Do you think we would see what's-his-name . . . Yes—Hua Kuo-feng?"

I reply that I would assume so, but that I am not certain.

"We couldn't really get back before Friday," says Brown. "I've really got to be there to see Secretary of Agriculture Bergland, and then I've got to go to North Carolina to some Democratic meeting. How offended do you think the Chinese will be? Do you think all this will affect the chances of going later—say, with some larger delegation? Perhaps we could set up some agricultural delegation. Something with a clearly outlined purpose. I wouldn't mind leading such a delegation," he says, brightening a little.

"All right. Let's just get into the car and start driving to the airport. We can discuss it some more as we go. If we are to return to the U.S. as planned, our flight departs in an hour and a half. If we decide to go to China, we'll just turn around."

Governor Brown on the Conveyor Belt

It is 9:15 P.M. Our flight to Los Angeles leaves in fifteen minutes. The China episode is behind us.

We arrive at Tokyo's Haneda airport, which is mobbed with departing passengers. We are standing helplessly amidst crowds of people and piles of luggage, unsure of which long line we should wait in, when a Japanese Air Lines official comes to our assistance. As is so often the case when traveling with Brown, such special assistance seems to be the natural order of things, even though he neither expects it nor demands it.

The official eases us through the crowd via a first-class check-in window, although we are traveling coach. Somehow the official has ended up with Brown's suitcase, while I have his shopping bag full of bric-a-brac presented to him by the various Japanese moguls. He carries his own brief case.

We are spirited past another throng, waiting to get through a security checkpoint, to a long conveyor belt that carries passengers down a hallway. It appears to be nearly half a mile in length.

Somehow the Japanese Air Lines official misses the entrance to the moving ramp, and is peeled loose from our small group. Short of vaulting over the railing, he is doomed to navigate this long hallway on foot—still carrying Brown's suitcase.

So here we are—Brown, myself and Dick Silberman—cruising effortlessly down this automated ramp like figureheads on the prow of a ship, with our faithful Japanese retainer struggling along beside us with the Governor's suitcase on the motionless floorway.

At first, he seems to be trying to sprint ahead of us, as if his strategy is to gain a lead while he is still fresh, realizing that on the final leg of this race, it will be those of us on the ramp who will have the endurance for a strong finish. We have moved only about two hundred feet when an elderly woman in a kimono, straining with two huge suitcases on wheels, heaves into sight on the floor ahead of us. In fifteen seconds we overtake her, like fast-moving traffic in the left lane passing a large truck in low gear.

At this point, the airlines official reaches to help the old woman by grabbing one of her wheeled suitcases with his spare hand. This stops her dead in her tracks. As if by a reflex reaction, she begins to bow to him in a series of prostrations that bring her almost to the floor. He is forced to pause and acknowledge her bowing, thereby losing his slim lead on us. Regaining his composure, the official moves out again, this time encumbered by two suitcases. The old woman begins to break into an awkward half-run.

When they finally succeed in getting abreast of us again, the old woman tries to grab Brown's suitcase from the official, apparently confusing it with her own. Her lungings are like uncontrollable seizures, perhaps motivated by some unfathomable (to us) Japanese prescription of etiquette.

In any event, all that she succeeds in doing is further encumbering the official, who is now breathless and again losing ground in the wake of our invincible onset, like George Washington crossing the Delaware River.

The official looks at us for an instant with a mixture of resignation and pleading as we move effortlessly by. And we, who are equally incapable of doing anything at this moment, find ourselves laughing loudly and hysterically at the absurdity of the situation.

Providentially, the end of the moving ramp approaches. We glide off, still laughing. We have to wait a minute for the official and the old woman, both of whom arrive laughing uncontrollably themselves. The official still clings to the two suitcases. Brown makes no gesture to relieve him, seemingly oblivious to the role his suitcase has played in this comic inter-lude.

Return from Japan

The plane is full. We sit drinking wine and beer at the rear of one of the sections.

A Japanese hostess comes down the aisle, sees Brown and stops at our row of seats. "I hear that you are not married yet," she says with a heavy accent.

"No. I'm not. No. I guess I'm not ready yet."

"Why not?" she giggles, perhaps surprised by her own brazenness.

"Why not? I guess I haven't found the right situation. And why aren't you married?" he asks, turning the tables on a questioner as he so often does.

"I'm not ready yet," she replies, beating an embarrassed retreat.

"Why can't people stay together?" asks Brown, looking away from me into the aisle. "I don't know. Maybe it's too much mobility. Too many tempting possibilities. No linkages. What is the meaning of it all if there is no continuity?

"I had breakfast with Prime Minister Trudeau the other day. I like him. But, you know, this thing with his wife . . . Anyway, we got talking. I told him that I thought people should stick with things. If a person marries a diplomat or a leader, he or she is accepting certain responsibilities that cannot be broken just because someone 'feels like it.' There's something wrong with everyone being so free and mobile—so free and irresponsible that they think they can do anything they like." He pauses. "Well, anyway, I'm not so sure that all this freedom makes people as happy as they think it does."

"Do you think men and women should stay together the way they used to, even though it is extremely difficult and painful?"

He thinks about the question awhile.

"I don't know." And then, as if eschewing any pretense of expertise in the field, he adds, "Well, look at me. I'm not even married. I don't know. I just don't know. Maybe we should all just Carterize ourselves with a wife and children, and . . ." He halts midthought.

"Oh, don't go using that in your book." He laughs as he sees me writing on an air-sickness bag. "I've got to work with Carter. He's an intelligent and fair man. But he's a moralist, not a philosopher, and he really believes in hierarchy." He pauses, as if he knows it is better to say no more, but can't resist one last thought. "I'm not sure Carter properly appreciates the degree of decline in our society."

It is late at night now. People in the cabin are starting to curl up in their seats to sleep. Brown orders another white wine.

The cabin lights go off. There is no one hounding him here. There are no phone calls, no meetings, no decisions to be made. We have nine hours to pass in limbo. Brown seems to enjoy the freedom of conversation that has no object other than . . . other than what? Perhaps it could best be described as a kind of recreational conversation. Where most people like to go to the beach or watch a ball game on TV, Brown likes to talk. He often speaks in homilies, clever riddles and aphorisms suggestive of the Wisdom of Confucius, which tempt interviewers and other political figures to try to make some coherent philosophical system out of the pronouncements which gush forth. But much of what he says is speculative and facetious. It is not easy to construct whole systems from the nonstop bits and pieces of wit, insight, irony and self-mockery which comprise even one day's production of Brown verbiage. He can be serious as well as outrageous.

One night after a few beers and a big dinner, I remember,

he quite comically suggested that he was bored, only had twelve more months of his first term as Governor left and felt like doing "something big." Having ruminated on several almost unmentionable and implausible possibilities, he suggested, "I guess the biggest bang would be to just not run again. Just tell them, 'No more!' and go off and start a pig farm."

The fact that the press often criticizes him for being oblique and contradictory does seem to bother him.

"So often the press just wants to put politicians in quick and easy corners," he says, sipping his wine from a plastic stemmed glass. "They want to know, What's your answer to this? What's your answer to that? It's not easy to say that you don't know, or just to speculate. They think you're being coy and don't believe you.

"I remember a few months ago this Los Angeles *Times* reporter in Washington asked me what I thought of Idi Amin. It was during one of those big Ugandan brouhahas. I told him that I really hadn't thought about it much because I'd had my hands full just dealing with California. I mentioned that after the presidential campaign I no longer had the time to read the *New York Times* and Washington *Post* from front to back.

"Well, he seemed almost offended. He said something about the *Times/Post* having the best African bureau of any paper. Then, later, I got a whole bunch of articles on Africa from his editor in the mail.

"I had this interview with Martin Agronsky. He wanted to know something about whether I saw myself as 'practically principled' or 'principally practical.' I guess he meant, Was I a politician or a visionary? But I don't see how these things are contradictory. I think there really is a difference between an interviewer who tries to pin you down, like Bob Scheer, and one who tries to open you up.

"I really enjoyed myself on my interviews with William Buckley," he says, showing signs of animation. "He's got a sense of humor, although I know some people might think that his program is just a lot of intellectual bullshit. But ideas are important. I don't know if people realize how hard it is to move a whole society with ideas. People seem to have the notion that as Governor or President you can just *do* things—anything. You know, just crank up the legislators and get moving."

"Do you find that having a reporter around influences what you feel you can say?"

"Well, sure. I mean, you have to be aware of it. You could say something and really not think much about it. And then in five years it comes back to haunt you as news," he says in an offhand manner which does not belie the concern he is talking about. "Just look at Carter's remark on lusting in his heart.

"I don't know what it is," he continues, seeming to rein himself in lest he appear a complainer. "But they come out here from New York and Washington, talk for a few hours and then they go back and write something. I think they often see me as flip and arrogant." He pauses again.

"The press," he says, and then drums his fingers on his teeth, thinking about it. "They're an interesting problem. I mean, basically, isn't most of the press just trying to titillate cluttered minds? If a journalist doesn't grab the attention of his reader in the first paragraph, he's lost. He knows that.

"I think members of the press are not too different from politicians. They're ambitious. Their by-lines are important to them. They have a cult of personality. Whether they know it or not, the press are part of the action, but they seem to feel left out. If you try and bring them in, they feel patronized. Maybe I should write a book about the press.

"I suppose that you can say that some way or other everyone is into politics for his ego. How do you get rid of those egos? Do we want to get rid of those egos? I mean, how do you get rid of your selfish desires? I've asked myself that for twenty years. How do you forget yourself and find things to which you can give yourself which are more important? It's that Christian notion. It may sound pompous." He stops talking for a moment, then sighs and says with that Brownian tinge of self-mockery, "I guess I'm a seeker. Of what? Truth or something? Mortification of the flesh? Self-denial?" He laughs.

"I remember in seminary I used to refuse to put salt on my eggs. It was a symbol. Or when I'd get a letter from home, I wouldn't open it up and read it right away. I'd force myself to wait. A little self-denial's good for the soul.

"But maybe we should learn to give rather than deny ourselves. These questions are hard to answer. It would be nice if one could be in politics but not of it. Yes," he says to reaffirm the thought, "to be in the world but not of it."

It's early in the morning now, although still dark outside the aircraft. Almost everyone else in the plane has long since gone to sleep. We are both fatigued. Brown pulls a blanket up to his chin, puts his seat back and soon nods off, head down on his shoulder, mouth slightly open.

Conversations with Brown: the World

AUTHOR: *Were you ever convinced that the Russians were out to conquer the world?*

BROWN: Yes, when I was in grammar school and high school. The sense that Communism was out to destroy Catholicism was fairly well inculcated into my head.

How do you view the Russians and the arms race now?

The world *is* unstable, there are a lot of armaments out there. The Russians have their own power and

ambition. And they should be watched and dealt
with. You can't ignore them. The world has been full
of imperialistic ideological, religious and secular wars
and movements. I don't have the view of the world
that if somehow America disarmed, everything
would be fine. I certainly think the super powers
could reduce their armaments in a mutually agreed
reduction. But the way to do that is to force greater
confrontation between the people involved—military types, industrial types, those who profit from the
armies. Maybe the President has to get to the point
where he can cross-examine the advisors to the advisors of the Chairman of the Communist Party in
Russia.

*This is a tactic that you have frequently used in trying
to find solutions at the state level. Do you think it
would work internationally?*

Yes. The technique of talking to the eighth-level
bureaucrat is something that has to be done in international arms negotiations, since the people at the
top are the prisoners of the perceptions of those
around them.

*Have you been giving more time lately studying or
talking with people about foreign affairs?*

A little more. I mean, I'm not unaware of foreign
issues. I try to see domestic issues in California in the
wider international context because California is a
very international society. If you deal with the problems of this state, you have to deal with the problems
of other states. My trip to Japan was an attempt to
get a Japanese automobile plant to open up here in
California, because it would be sound economically

and environmentally, and because Japan has ties with California. My trips to Canada and Mexico focused on the energy problems of California.

Are there any countries or societies that seem to you to be interesting or hopeful in the world?

Well, I think America is in a unique situation. It has a huge territorial expanse, it's very strong, it's very wealthy, and yet has a great deal of human misery in its midst. I think you can look at other countries to see their pluses and minuses, but I think we have to find our own way.

Do you think we'll have war again in the next five to ten years?

I don't know. I can't predict what's going to go on. I don't know anyone else who can. I think we ought to do everything we can to avoid it. Some would say that means we have to be stronger, and others would say that means we have to be weaker.

What do you think?

Well, I think we have to be strong so as not to create any uncertainty on the part of other countries, but we ought to redirect our energies toward less armaments and more socially constructive investments and activities. And that should be a mutual enterprise, not a unilateral one. To maintain leadership requires more than just weaponry. We should be refining and projecting ideas of where human society ought to be going, at the same time we confront the absurdity of the arms race with the Russians.

BACK IN THE
CAPITOL

Death Penalty

There is a realtors' convention in Sacramento today. All morning long groups of well-dressed and cheerful women, presumably the wives of the convention delegates, troop into the Governor's reception room. Each carries a post card that they have signed. The printed message on the back expresses "shock" that Brown has promised to veto a death penalty bill if it passes the legislature. According to a recent poll, two thirds of the people of California share the convictions of these women.

Jackie gracefully receives the cards at the front desk. Later I see the cards in a large box in the press office, awaiting possible tabulation and final disposition.

The last man to be put to death in the State of California was Charles Aaron Mitchell, aged thirty-seven, a lifelong criminal and police killer. At ten o'clock on the morning of 1967, he was dragged, screaming with fear, into the pale-green gas chamber at San Quentin Prison to his execution. A five-man death team, each receiving $600 in bonus pay, strapped Mitchell to the death chair and then released the cyanide pellets into the flow of acid, sending the fatal gas into the lungs of the bound prisoner.

Edmund G. Brown, Jr., then a young Los Angeles lawyer, was outside of San Quentin on that morning protesting the execution, just as he had protested the execution of Caryl Chessman to his father, the Governor, several years earlier.

"Life is getting cheap," he said at the time of Mitchell's

execution. "It's a horrible thing to snuff out a human life as you would that of a dog. I'm here to protest this barbarity."

The Budget

Several handcarts loaded with hundreds of fat green paperback books are being pushed through the corridors of the Capitol like wheeled pastry trays at an expensive restaurant. It is the Governor's 1165-page, 5-pound-2-ounce, $15.2-billion budget. One reporter, doing some budget analysis of his own, has figured that this makes it worth about $185.4 million an ounce. In any event, the budget calls for the state of California to spend $41.6 million a day, $1.7 million an hour, or $28,910.82 a minute.

The engorged green volume will doubtless be one of the least-read publishing ventures of the year. Its most succinct and readable section is a twenty-line message which precedes the bulk of the budget, written by the Governor himself.

"Limits impose restraints, but also create possibilities," it says. "A society is more than bricks and mortar," he writes in conclusion, "and must commit itself to the human spirit."

Brown is about to hold a press conference, a kind of ceremonial occasion during which he will officially send his budget on to the legislature. He looks handsome and confident in his double-breasted pinstripe suit and polka-dot tie.

"This budget does not call for any new taxes this year, next year or in the foreseeable future, given the continuing strength of the economy," he says almost ebulliently.

What he does not mention is that with inflation up, people are finding themselves in higher tax brackets, so that even without a higher tax rate, state revenues are up 15 percent, leaving Brown sitting on a $2 billion surplus.

Nonetheless, even fiscal conservatives are pleased with the health of the economy in California, and by what Brown himself refers to as his "cheapness."

Financial Disclosure

Today the financial disclosure statements submitted by Brown's staff members are made public. All but a handful report holding no direct or indirect interest in land, other than their homes, or stock in major corporations. Brown himself reports owning his Laurel Canyon house in Los Angeles, worth about $100,000, and some Israel bonds valued at less than $10,000.

Brown and Business

"Oh God! You've just got to see this," says Gray Davis' secretary Dolores, thrusting a magazine at me, and then standing back to watch the expression on my face.

The magazine cover shows a glossy color photo of Brown's head superimposed on the body of a Little Lord Fauntleroy, decked out in a blue sailor suit, ruffled red cravat, white knee socks and black pumps.

The lead article, in *Business West Magazine*, is entitled "A Report Card on Jerry Brown." A subtitle inside reads "Business Rates Brown: C+ for the Governor."

"He leads you to believe he's antibusiness," says one interviewed executive, "when I think he's taken steps which clearly indicate that he is not."

"In the area of fiscal responsibility, he's just absolutely first-rate," says another businessman. Someone in the Governor's office has underlined this quote with a red pencil.

"He's the biggest jerk I ever saw," trumpets another executive. "All he's done so far is talk."

"I talk to my eastern associates," reports yet another businessman, "and they keep asking, 'What's going on in California? Don't people like business out there?'"

Brown has not been unmindful of the mixed reviews he has been getting lately from the business community. After the Dow Chemical Company withdrew its request to locate a large new styrene factory on the Sacramento River, claiming that they were in effect hassled to death by environmental permit procedures, Brown has been evidencing a dramatic interest in placating businessmen. His trip to Japan in search of Japanese industry is an obvious example.

His Secretary of Business and Trade has begun to distribute lapel buttons which read CALIFORNIA MEANS BUSINESS. Newspaper headlines like BROWN'S ATTITUDE CHANGES, TOSSES AWAY NO-GROWTH LABEL have started to appear. Even Eastern columnists like Evans and Novak are reporting to the nation that Brown, "The darling of no-growth environmentalists . . . (is) bragging about California's recent economic growth and expressing hope for more—a sign of evolution of this most fascinating politician."

Union officials like John Henning, the California Labor Federation's executive, who once accused the Brown administration of being loaded with "environmental cultists who are absolute death and destruction to economic growth and the future of this State," seem more mollified.

On the other hand, men like John Zierold, a Sierra Club

lobbyist, have started to attack Brown and "key staff members," whom he alleges "feel that it is not politically wise to get out in front on environmental issues in 1977 and 1978 because of what they perceive to be the political liabilities of doing so."

"Hey, what happened to the 'era of limits,' the 'three-gallon flush' and 'small is beautiful'?" asks one reporter, waiting for Brown to come out of a meeting in his office with the Los Angeles Chamber of Commerce.

Then, just as Brown has thoroughly incited environmentalists by his dalliance with business, he will announce that the Grumman Corporation of Bethpage, Long Island, has been convinced to build a million-dollar solar-heating-unit factory in the San Joaquin Valley. Coming as it does on top of a Brown-backed bill to give homeowners a tax credit of 55 percent—up to a maximum of $3000—for the purchase and installation of these heaters, such announcements throw both sides of the enviro-business struggle into disarray.

No one seems quite sure whether or not there is a new Jerry Brown rising out of all these apparent contradictions, or whether it is just part of the famous "emerging process"—yet another stage in his ever-developing consciousness toward some undefined supreme ultimate.

What does Brown have to say about his own political posture?

"There's no contradiction at all. I don't think carefully planned industry and the environment need be in conflict."

At a recent conference on land-use planning, which featured the late author E. F. Schumacher, Brown almost chastised environmentalists and planners, saying, "Sometimes in government I feel that we have a kind of sensory overload. We have so many mandates and so many ideas that we can't even digest them. We have warehouses full of plans. We have them by the thousands. And they're all master plans. They all build up to the great plan. The trouble is, no one ever reads the great plan.

"I encourage you to get your land ethic together," he told the conference goers, many of whom appeared to believe that

Brown was a supporter of land-use planning by nature of his apparent concern for the environment. "And if it's clarified, a consensus will build and a constituency will mount. And lo and behold, a bill will drop on my desk, flash bulbs will pop, and I will sign it. And a new bureaucracy will be born."

"Is he for it or against it?" one conference participant asked another.

"I don't know."

"Jerry Brown is like one of those crystal balls that hang over the dance floor," says Gray Davis. "He's a man with many facets and interests, and as they become apparent to others, they may think it's a shift in policy. But what is occurring is that different aspects of the man are being revealed. The media gets confused because they focus on one idea at a time, rather than the whole mosaic of leadership that Brown is creating."

An article in a large California daily about the planning conference is headlined the next day: ON LAND-USE PLANNING BROWN MAKES HIS POSITION UNCLEAR.

Appointments

Friends and foes alike agree that one of Brown's strong points has been his appointments, although he has been harshly criticized for taking as long as he often does to fill certain positions. But when he finally gets around to it, one senses that his power of appointment is a prerogative which he has relished and on which he has spent considerable time and imagination. While striving for people with the proper credentials and experience, he also seems to take particular delight in making appointments with shock value.

On several occasions Brown has appointed his adversaries,

as when he put his Democratic gubernatorial challenger Robert Moretti on the Energy Commission or when he appointed Reagan staffer Vern Orr to the Board of Regents of the University of California.

"Sometimes I like to shake things up," he told me after he had nominated his former Secretary of Agriculture, Rose Bird, as Chief Justice of the California Supreme Court. She is the first woman chief justice in the nation, and her nomination engendered much criticism. Of the 225 other judges whom Brown has appointed since his inauguration, 24 have been women, 28 have been black, 27 have been Mexican and Asian Americans and 2 have been native Americans.

Brown seems to enjoy zeroing his attention in on appointments for even the most obscure state board or commission, such as the Advisory Council on Narcotics and Drug Abuse (to which he recently appointed the head of the Haight-Ashbury Free Clinic), the Board of Dental Examiners (to which he appointed the first layman) or the State Bar Board (to which he appointed six non-lawyers for the first time in its forty-nine-year history). Perhaps the classic Brown appointment was that of Robert E. Treuhaft to the Board of Funeral Directors and Embalmers. Treuhaft, who is the husband of author and funeralologist Jessica *(The American Way of Death)* Mitford, immediately became the source of some uneasiness in the profession because of his position against automatic embalming and for inexpensive "burn and scatter" funerals.

Other appointments include cops to serve on an athletic commission, poverty lawyers to serve on a board which oversees collection agencies, a student (who had written a critical thesis on problems in homes for the elderly) to serve on a board overseeing nursing homes, and a woman to sit on the State Boxing Commission.

Brown has also excelled at appointing well-known Californians to other state positions, as he did when he put singer Helen Reddy on the State Parks and Recreation Commission, made poet Gary Snyder the first chairman of his newly established California Arts Council, or appointed anthropologist and the author of *Ishi*, Theodora Kroeber, to the Board of Regents.

"Making appointments is a pastime that Brown takes very seriously," says one of his staff members. "He knows most of these people, particularly in the judiciary, are going to be in our bloodstream for a long time to come. But I think he also enjoys making these appointments. It's one of the few areas where he can act decisively."

"I think I've made some good appointments," Brown tells me. "I've had fun working on them. I look on appointments as a good way to get some new blood into the system."

Death Penalty Veto

The California State Senate passes a death penalty bill today. A few hours later, Brown releases the following statement.

To The Members of the California State Senate:
Statistics can be marshalled and arguments propounded. But at some point, each of us must decide for himself what sort of a future he would want. For me, this would be a society where we do not attempt to use death as a punishment.

Accordingly, I am returning Senate Bill No. 155 without my signature.

Sincerely,
Edmund G. Brown, Jr.

Gray Davis (2)

"I know it's hard to believe," says Gray Davis, as we sit and eat a late lunch in a Mexican restaurant not far from the Capitol. "And I know it may even sound like some kind of self-promotion—that it may not jibe with what many people think."

Gray wears a slight smile—one that I have learned to identify as preceding a remark that he senses will shock. He tends to anticipate the difficulty the listener may have in accepting the statement, even agreeing in advance that what he is about to say may seem implausible. Having thus softened his opposition, he proceeds.

"Yes. Jerry does sometimes think about not running again. Just a few days ago we had a long talk about it. And it was a serious conversation. With Jerry it's not so much a question of surrender as a question of just feeling that maybe it would be nice to spend some time doing something else.

"I hasten to add," he continues—now with a different, almost impish, smile—"that he'll probably run. But the thought does come up. For me as well. I mean . . . I've given a lot of energy to this job. It feels good to see some of our ideas out there happening. But all I have is a shabby apartment, ten suits and a TV that gets two channels. I could see going to work for the Farm Workers or something for a while. Right now I have to wedge time for reexamination and thinking into all these busy days.

"It's not clear what one can really do in the field of politics," he says, eating a taco. "I guess you can reach some people through the administrative arm—just help people get their checks and social services. Get the process going. But mostly I see the Governor's office as an educative position— a chance to talk with people and get them thinking."

Davis' idea is one expressed often by Brown as well. Just as one often sees Davis standing quietly behind Brown in public, so one often finds that ideas originated by Davis and other staff members are inseminated into the public arena by Brown, with whom the idea is ultimately associated.

"I think that we live in a country which, if it hasn't already reached its zenith, is close to it. Perhaps we are already in a state of decline. In any event, we seem to be in a political era of one-term governmental officials. Incumbents seem to get identified with this decline just by being in office, and then the people want to recycle them. People want leaders. But they also seem to resent them. It's a mixture of respect and envy."

Davis' words remind me of a similar sentiment expressed sometime earlier by Brown himself on the subject of the public's rejecting their leaders.

"If politicians would just jump out of the way for a while," Brown said, "and then maybe come back. But they stay long beyond their time. The Greeks had ostracism. An ostracon is the potsherd that's dropped in the pot. If the majority drop it in—then, you're out.

"There was a fellow named Aristides the Just. Aristides was going through the ostracism process, and he stood by as some Athenians came to drop in the potsherd as an indication for him to go into exile. Aristides said, 'Why are you doing that? Haven't I been a good man?' And one Athenian said, 'Look. We're just tired of hearing the name Aristides the Just.'"

A drunk with a week's stubble on his chin and vomit on his shirt has somehow found his way into the empty restaurant. He wobbles over to our table. "Hey, buddy," he says to Davis with slurred speech. "You got a quarter? I ain't got nuthin' to eat."

Davis reaches for his wallet, opens it, extracts a dollar from among an ample collection of brightly colored credit cards, and wordlessly gives it to the man. "Hey, I've got to get back to the office," says Davis, checking his watch.

We walk out onto the sidewalk and pass the Pussycat Theatre, a local porno movie house.

"I don't know," says Davis, looking up at the marquee, thrusting his hands into his trouser pockets, and smiling at a yet unspoken thought.

"I remember when I was running for state treasurer, I had to come up here to Sacramento from L.A. with two aides for some bullshit press conference. The first thing that happened was that they overbooked the flight, so that my two aides got bumped. So I came up alone." He is laughing now, shaking his head and looking at the pavement.

"And then when I finally got up here to the press conference, there was no press. I mean, no one! Just me and no one! So . . . well, I decided to try and call a few stations and see if any of them would make a little tape. One TV station said that they might have a camera crew available in a few hours. So, hell. Here I was with absolutely nothing to do. So I went over and saw *Deep Throat.* I suppose if I'd told the press I was coming to Sacramento to see *Deep Throat,* they all would have come over to a press conference."

Mental Hospitals

"There was this one man who wanted to have his picture taken with Jerry," says a Brown staff intern. "He was one of the mental patients who came up to the Governor's office for the opening of their art show in the reception room. He was very strange-looking, probably badly retarded. He put his arm around Jerry. Jerry just stood there, something he wouldn't have done for anyone else. Very dignified. Kind. I saw a real flash of gentleness there. He had a look in his eyes which made me think that he was not just doing this for the publicity.

" 'You're my hero,' the retarded man said to him. And then Jerry replied, 'You're all heroes.' I really admired him that day."

At Agnew State Mental Hospital in the San Jose area, Brown speaks with a group of people from the Voluntary Action Center and the Junior League, who work in the hospital.

He tells them: "People sit back and wonder why their taxes keep going up—why it is that government keeps getting bigger. And it has gotten bigger. It has taken a dramatic jump forward under the leadership of individuals whose entire philosophy and public utterances suggest the exact opposite. I refer not only to my predecessor, but to President Carter's predecessor.

"So I think we have to ask ourselves—and I'm not raising this as a political question, but as just a way to understand the nature of reality that we all face—Why is it that despite the public philosophy of those in key positions, government gets bigger and bigger, more complex, more involved, and your taxes keep going up?

"The very simple reason is that it takes more than words to put some limit on that growth. There are certain needs and obligations in the community that just have to be taken care of, and if you don't do it—through some volunteer movement, some other arrangement outside of the public sector—then inevitably government will take the task and assume those obligations.

"If you take the mentally ill, the narcotics-abuse programs, the alcohol programs, child-care, nursing homes, hospitals, training activities and you meet every need that can be identified, you would have to double and possibly even triple the existing government activity that we now have at the state, local and federal level.

"Something as straightforward as police activity—how many police can you hire and how many are patrolling the streets? The ratio will never be high enough unless people assume a greater degree of responsibility for their own defense and protection . . .

"There is no substitute for neighborhoods, for mutual-support systems in the private sector. Whether it be neighbors who know each other, who have some responsibility for someone other than themselves and their family—you can't get away from it. The idea that you can put it on government if you want to is going to triple your taxes because then you have to hire a full-time person who doesn't have the commitment involved in it that you would to do that kind of work.

"That's my simple message: that voluntarism is not a luxury, it is a necessity for a civilized society that wants to truly meet its human needs. And we have to expand it in a dramatic way across a broad front of government and human activity. We have to find some way to re-create the spirit of neighborliness and mutual self-support that existed before the mobility and the anonymity and increasing information flow that has been the product of this very prosperous society . . .

"You may think you have more mobility and freedom and liberty—a "do-your-own-thing" kind of ethic—but in reality it comes back in the form of government, taxation, crime and mental confusion . . .

"When I went back to Williams, California, where my great-grandparents came from Germany in the 1850's, I walked into a nursing home. It was a very nice place—people were working hard cleaning and making sure the residents were attended, but I thought to myself, Here's a place where elderly people are sent when they reach a certain age, and are paying $600 to $700 a month for strangers to take care of people that not too many years before would have been upstairs in the bedroom, or on rocking chairs sitting in the living room. It would have been a part of the context of normal life.

"But in order to expand the productivity, the freedom, the mobility, the prosperity, we have segregated, we have specialized, so we have nursing homes for the old, child-care for the young, mental hospitals for those who act in a rather strange way or are different from the rest of us. And schools that start early and keep going till one's mid-twenties, longer if possible.

"We're institutionalizing everybody. And I'd like to de-institutionalize everybody, I'd like to have a community that has a more human spirit to it."

Although it is Thanksgiving Day, pickets stand out in front of the broad avenue that leads up past several wards to the administration building of Napa State Hospital, a state-run mental institution. SACRAMENTO IS THE COO-COO'S NEST reads one placard. SACRAMENTO: YOU JUST BROKE THE CAMEL'S BACK reads another.

Understaffed even during normal times, the hospital has recently been unable even to attract enough qualified M.D.'s and psychiatrists to fill vacant positions. Doctors have been leaving at an alarming rate because of overwork and bad conditions. Some federal funding has even been lost because California's own Department of Health has "decertified" the hospital as unsafe. At the breaking point, the present medical staff has announced that they will resign at the end of next month if the situation is not improved.

Yesterday Brown met in San Francisco with a group of doctors from the hospital. This morning, on the spur of the moment, he decides to spend his Thanksgiving Day at the hospital, talking to those of the medical staff who are willing to either forgo or postpone their own holiday dinners.

It is 10 A.M. as I arrive with my three-year-old son. Brown is already at the hospital, accompanied by Elisabeth Coleman, his press secretary. He looks tired, and mentions having attended a long formal dinner at the Russian consulate the night before. Dr. D. Michael O'Connor, a young psychiatrist and executive director of the hospital, whisks us away in his car to visit some of the wards.

The atmosphere of the hospital, with its well-kept lawns, paths and institutional buildings is akin to that of a college campus. It is a warm, sunny, fall day, and the grounds are dotted with patients. A misshapen man lurches down the side-walk beside us. An older woman with sad blank eyes sits quietly under a tree and stares off into a clump of bushes. Two other patients are crying out to each other across a lawn, where a middle-aged woman with lips that have been carelessly lip-sticked like those of a clown feeds a flock of pigeons while talking to herself.

"This is an acute ward," says Dr. O'Connor, gesturing toward one of the buildings. "You shouldn't bring your child inside."

Elisabeth Coleman takes my son over to watch the woman feeding the birds. We enter the ward.

The halls inside are bare. Our voices echo. Dr. O'Connor pulls out a bunch of keys and opens a door at the end of a corridor.

Loud Musak plays inside. An unshaven man sits on the floor and sucks his thumb. An elderly woman is slouched on a bench by the door, holding a hairbrush.

"How long have you been in here?" Brown asks her. She stares past him without reply, lost in some deep reverie of her own. Her eyes show no sign of recognizing his presence, much less his question. She strokes her cheek with the back of her hairbrush over and over again.

"I hope you have a nice Thanksgiving," he finally says thinly.

"I never thought I'd be talking to you," says Joan Finne-gan, a young R.N., as Brown walks into the staff office. It has glass windows reinforced with wire mesh, and stands in the middle of the ward like a control tower at an airport.

"I'm very disturbed about state mental health care," Ms. Finnegan says nervously to Brown. "With only chemotherapy, there is no way we can really deal with these people. We're overloaded. The staff is demoralized." She seems unsure how to continue.

"If you have any suggestions, I'd like to have them," says Brown, absorbing the scene around him.

We move into a side room where some patients are playing pool. They recognize Brown and are intrigued by his presence here in the bowels of this locked ward. He shakes a few hands, almost as if he were campaigning, takes a cue from one of the patients and tries a shot. He knocks the eightball into a pocket.

"This system has been dysfunctional for a long time," Joan Finnegan is telling me out in the hall as a patient presents a drooping hand to Brown to shake. "But I think the fact that Brown came today shows his interest in grass-roots problems. I'm hopeful," she adds cautiously as we get ready to leave for the next ward.

Once we are outside, a lone reporter from a local Napa radio station approaches Brown.

"The mentally ill are that part of society we have the hardest time dealing with," says Brown into a tape recorder. "It's an outrage. It is a societal problem as well as a state problem. We've got to tie problems with mental health together with other aspects of society. It's just all a product of increasing mobility and anonymity—a failure of social glue. People are found in the streets in bizarre situations, committing crimes. They come here. They're given medication for a while, and then put right back out on the streets. It's a revolving door. But the streets are not a community. I accept a large measure of responsibility for making it better, but I can't do it alone."

"How come black people don't look like God?" a black patient who has been watching the interview suddenly asks Brown.

"How do you know they don't?"

The black patient listens impassively to Brown's response, and then begins laughing.

In Dr. O'Connor's office, about a dozen staff doctors are eating Egg Fluff Donuts from a box and drinking instant coffee from Styrofoam cups. Brown walks in, and they introduce themselves, looking somewhat skeptical of the circumstances that have finally brought their Governor into the midst of their crisis on Thanksgiving.

"I'd just like to get a better picture of where we are," says Brown, sitting down, "where we're going and how we got here."

The doctors need no cue to release the avalanche of problems which confront the hospital.

"We're outnumbered. I have to treat two hundred patients."

"We're buried in paper work and court appearances where we must become the adversary of the patients."

"The penal medical facilities are sending us more and more violent criminals who have supposedly been "rehab-ed." I don't mind working with violent people, but when they're mixed in with my old lady patients and gentle crazy people, it makes me afraid. They rape and steal."

"Each day we are forced to release people who we believe are capable of killing someone."

"We're not complaining about taking care of these people. We just need the staff to do it."

"We feel orphaned by the state. We can't even deliver minimal treatment. We practice defensive psychiatry."

There is an earnestness and strain in the voices of these men and women who appear on the brink of surrender. There is also anger.

"We have one of the most inferior mental health systems in the country. The state must make a commitment."

"I think that we may have to close the hospital down so people will realize what we do here. I don't think you're going to move," says a young psychiatrist, looking right at Brown, "and I don't think the state is going to move."

Brown listens. Then almost thinking out loud, he says, "As each individual in our society gives less, the institutions have to give more. They become substitutes for the family and community."

"Well, we can't give back the patients," retorts a doctor

with contempt, perhaps misunderstanding Brown's comment as a criticism of them.

"All right," says Brown, going on the offensive. "How many of you in this room want to leave?"

Almost every doctor in the room raises his or her hand.

"I think what you have to have is a clear plan about what you want, or you won't have much credibility. Your crunch is a relatively difficult one for the legislators who approve my budget to see."

"We don't want another plan that won't happen," counters a doctor.

"It sounds like another delaying action," protests another. "Tomorrow someone may die. I could lose my license. It's a snake pit. We don't have time to work on a plan. We need help right now."

"Okay," says Brown with a suggestion of challenge in his voice. "Then you should just give up." He pauses and then adds, "But I think you should take a few days. I'm talking about getting something together for next week. I'll put it in my budget next month. We'll get all the decision-makers together here and work it out. It will be interesting."

"God! Life is getting so goddamned interesting," says a staff member who is the only M.D. on duty for almost two thousand patients during the night shift.

"All right. Let's talk about a coherent plan, and I don't think there will be any problem. We need a program with a time frame and a dollar sign."

The doctors are skeptical but appear to want to be convinced that Brown's suggestions will work. They seem to be struggling to extract some almost personal commitment from him.

"We want something with your imprimatur on it," says a psychiatrist.

Brown seems to be holding back from any sweeping promises. I have noticed over the months how he rarely falls into the temptation of overcommiting himself during the emotions of the moment.

"What about R. D. Laing's ideas?" says Brown, momentarily derailing the conversation. It is hard to tell whether he is joking or not.

"That stuff doesn't work on people off the streets of San Francisco who are here for two weeks," says a woman doctor, shaking her head in disbelief. "We don't have the time and money even to do research here."

"Okay," says Brown, returning to the matter at hand. "I'll be back next Friday. I am behind you."

The meeting, which has already lasted over two hours, does not exactly end, but rather disintegrates into small groups of people talking. Several patients look into the meeting room.

"It's a ray of hope, but certainly not sunshine," says Dr. O'Connor, walking outside among his patients.

"Well, what do you think happened here today?" Brown asks several other doctors, standing outside the meeting room under a tree.

"We think you've seen the problem," replies a tall bearded psychiatrist.

"I don't know," says Brown elusively.

Several days later Brown proposes a crash program of $27.7 million to provide 3000 new jobs for California's eleven state hospitals. "I told the Governor that three and a half years of criminal neglect couldn't be put out by a twelfth-hour attempt to spray the atmosphere with greenbacks," says state assemblyman Frank Lanterman, in reaction.

It's almost 2 P.M. Brown walks out toward the parking lot and calls his sister in San Francisco on the radio telephone in his Plymouth to find out what time the Brown family will congregate for Thanksgiving dinner this evening.

"I'll just ride back to the city with Orville and his son," he says to his driver, Dale Rowlee, as he hangs up. "So why don't you head home." Elisabeth Coleman has already left.

He removes his double-breasted blue pinstriped suit jacket and gets into the cab of my pickup with my son, who is munching a cream cheese sandwich.

"I haven't eaten all day," he says as we pull out of the hospital's front gate. "Let's stop at a Burger King. Do you have any money?" The idea seems like a Thanksgiving parody. Providentially, no fast-food places except Denny's (which, for unexplained reasons, Brown declines) are open. As we hit the open freeway, Brown nibbles on a slice of bread from my son's leftover lunch.

In the midst of the holiday traffic, a car full of black children passes us in the left lane. One recognizes Brown. Soon all the children are waving, laughing and pressing their noses against the car windows, making funny faces. Brown waves back, and then lifts my son onto his lap. It is strange to see this man whom I have followed for two years holding this small child.

"Persuasion is very important in all this," says Brown, breaking a silence. "If you don't take time to work with the bureaucrats and officials five levels down, they rebel. It's not true that a Governor can snap his fingers and make things happen all the way down the line. I don't know why people believe that. But I think we'll get some satisfaction at that hospital. We'll get some people from the Department of Health, some legislators, some Department of Finance people out here next week. I'll be back. We'll get everyone together. Some of these people have never met. It'll be an education. They'll erupt and fight, and we'll try to find some answers."

We're heading over the Bay Bridge now, to the city and the San Francisco Zen Center. Brown, who almost never stays in hotels when he is away from the Capitol, often spends nights there. He is always welcome.

B.T.

"Aw, they gave up on me a long time ago. I'm the office rebel," says Brien T. Collins, referred to as "B.T." around the office. He is the Governor's deputy legislative secretary. He leans back in his desk chair, scratches his ribs with the chrome hook which emerges from his right cuff and laughs. He lost an arm and leg in Vietnam.

The phone rings.

"Yeah, babe. Yeah," he says into the receiver he cradles between his ear and shoulder, taking notes with his good hand.

"Oh, I don't remember that one at all," he says, giving me a wink that seems like it might have something to do with women.

"Hey, do I have to come out and organize you guys too?" He laughs with studied nonchalance, lets loose with a string of four-letter epithets and hangs up.

B.T. is a tall man with sandy hair, a pockmarked face and a pronounced limp which, far from being a source of embarrassment for him, seems to provide him with an added quotient of swagger. B.T. is single.

His office walls are covered with signs and memorabilia suggestive of a dormitory room. One yellow and black sign cautions NO RIDING THE HOOK.

Behind his desk is a large California highway patrol target, a man's life-size outline full of bullet holes. Beneath it he has written "This is what happened to the last lobbyist. Wanna try your luck?"

B.T.'s job is to lobby legislators for bills in which the Governor's office takes interest, as well as to clear things like appointments which might relate to a specific legislator's district.

"Okay. Where are we?" he says, shaking his head.

"There's no way to stay on top of all this shit. It's making a fucking old man out of me.

"I got spanked up in the Long Tuan Secret Zone in Nam around the Seven Mountains area," he says, raising his prosthetic hook as evidence. "I had been in five years when I got it in 1967. I even wanted to go back. I can't explain it. It's like talking about sex to nuns. I picked up a live grenade in a confrontation with the dissidents. I got it off by about four feet when it blew.

"Nineteen months in Nam. Nineteen months in the hospital. You see people at their best and at their worst. Pain can really level you. I guess it has helped me just look at those legislators and say, 'Okay, you motherfuckers, here it is!' "

The phone rings again.

"Senator. Hello. B.T. here . . . I just wanted to check with you. The Governor is considering appointing . . ."

"Have I enjoyed working here?" he asks, hanging up. He gives a poor imitation of a hysterical laugh. "Sure. But I'd never fucking admit it."

"How have you found it working with the Governor?"

"Before I worked here, I never would have been able to understand this scene. Here's this guy born with a silver spoon in his mouth, and he's still worried about the taxpayer's dollar. I remember one time we were talking about something, and I said, 'What do you know about this? You never had a job in your life.' He just took it in.

"I wish he had more friends, though," he continues, switching to another vein. "I really value friends. People holding my hand in Vietnam. Me crying. Buddies telling me it would be okay. Lending you a couple of bucks when you're down.

"Jerry's funny. I know he'd rather talk to a bunch of high school kids than all these big shots who always want something. Everyone wants something.

"Sometimes I wonder how I ever got here. I never ran for any political office, and I'm not in this for a career. That's lucky too, because nobody here lasts very long. They just burn out.

"You know what Tony Kline asked me when he interviewed me for this job? He asked if I was married. I told him I wasn't. 'That's lucky,' he said, 'because you wouldn't last long up here.' "

B.T. pauses to light a cigarette.

"How is it working with all these other bachelors?"

"Maybe it's good to have women and children to humanize you and tell you what to do. Sometimes when Jerry has just issued some outrageous statement, some legislator will call me up and say, 'Shit, B.T.! Can't you just take this guy out and get him laid?'

"I think that people who have good relationships with women tend to be less ambitious. There are a lot of guys who have never really been in love. Vietnam taught me how short life can be, and how to find what's good for me. And I know this isn't good for me." He laughs, pounds the desk with his good hand. Then opening a drawer, he reaches in, extracts a nail file with his hook, and commences to clean his nails. He glances up to see my eyes riveted on this unusual manicure.

"It's an odd lot here at the Governor's office. Politics? Friendship? I don't know what it's all about. There's some backbiting. But, I don't think we have that much. And I think there is some real sympathy between the Governor and the people. He even has an effect on me. Sometimes it pisses me off.

"I don't know why people are so loyal to Jerry. It's not fear for their jobs, because he's such a candy ass, he couldn't fire anybody. He expects them just to get the message and walk off and disappear."

He reaches over to pick up the phone.

"Hey, babe," he says to his secretary. "Would you get me some cigarettes if I said please, please, please? . . . You're a sweetheart." He hangs up.

"But hell, actually I don't want to be his friend. I prefer working at a distance. It's just that some people don't have a lot of confidence and want to be stroked all the time. He doesn't understand how to pat someone on the back or take care of the troops. But there are some people who really care about him. Like Lucie, his secretary. She's almost like his mother. But sometimes I just wish he'd go off and get loose. I mean, sometimes even on a Sunday he'll come in with a tie on. Maybe he's been here all night. And then his hair might need washing. What does his mother think when she sees him on TV?" He flips the nail file back into the drawer, and leans back laughing and shaking his head.

"I keep telling Lucie to get him together. I remember one time I told him, in front of a reporter, 'Jerry, what you need is a goddamn woman to kick your ass.'

"He just looked at me. Then later on he asked me, 'Hey, did you say I needed a goddamn woman to kick my ass?'

"Yes."

"And then, deadpan, he said, 'Didn't you see that woman from *Penthouse* magazine who was writing a story standing right here?' "

Senate Death Penalty Override

Today the California State Senate overrides Brown's death penalty veto by a bare two-thirds majority. There is not one vote to spare.

Brown has done no lobbying. He has said that he felt it inappropriate to "twist arms" on an issue of conscience such as this.

The assembly will consider the override in two months.

"It seems to me that the Governor has ignored the fact that murderers are inflicting death as punishment upon the innocent," says an elated pro-death penalty bill sponsor, Senator George Deukmajian, after the vote. "And I believe that the majority of the people of California want a society in which the innocent are not being put to death."

"I am prepared to lock those up who don't conform to society," responds Brown.

Mr. Simpson Dies

Last night Mr. Simpson died at age ninety-six. He was severely burned in the bathtub of his solitary hotel room, too old and stiff to get out when he accidentally turned the hot water on full force.

"I'm gonna fool them all," old Mr. Simpson had said before dying. "I'm a mean son of a bitch. But when I go, I'll go in a lovely way. My ashes will be mixed with those of the sweetest woman who ever lived, Emily, my wife. I've saved them for that, and they'll be spread across the sea. And if there is to be a eulogy, nine words will do. Just say, 'There goes a nuisance that only death could abate.' "

The funeral is this Sunday. On the spur of the moment Brown decides to attend it.

"The men who arrested him for calling governors 'bastards,' and one of those governors himself, paid their respects to the memory of Robert Simpson," reports the Sacramento *Bee* on the funeral. "Mr. Simpson was one whose energy and determination carried him a long time—a person who will certainly be missed."

"It's just a sign that government is subject to the people, and if people want to say something they can," says Brown at the funeral. "I was certainly aware of his presence. He made his presence felt. And I think anytime the machinery of government can be slowed down a bit, even in meager ways, it's a good thing."

Conversations with Brown: a Miscellany

AUTHOR: *Do you enjoy being interviewed as much as you are?*

BROWN: Enough time passes between interviews. Things are always changing. My mind is growing. Interviews provide an occasion for me to focus.

Do you have time to read?

Yes. I usually read before I go to bed. I read and think. At night I often end up putting seemingly unrelated facts together to find meaning.

Are there any particular contemporary writers or thinkers who have deeply influenced you?

I think I learn more from the situations I deal with. I get many ideas from the people I come into contact with—like the British economist E. F. Schumacher, Herman Kahn, Ivan Illich or staff members like Stewart Brand, State Architect Sym Van der Ryn, and Rusty Schweickart, the former astronaut. When I read something or talk to someone, it is often in light of some particular question that I face in my job.

Are you ever going to write a book yourself?

Probably someday. But I am in passage. I am doing what I am doing now and I often don't have the answers.

What is your position on abortion?

Well, I think that the government should not come down with criminal penalties on the side of one group in society. Each woman should make a decision about abortion based on her own conscience and what she believes to be right. You shouldn't be penalized for that decision if you're poor, middle class or rich.

Should the government make funds available for abortion?

I don't think it should carve a special exception out of the Medicaid budget and say abortions will not be funded. We haven't done that for the last few years, and I don't see any reason to change.

Is death something that has figured largely in your life?

Death is obviously something that I have thought about. This is a rather brief tenure that we're all on. Visiting nursing homes for the elderly, hospitals, weighing the death penalty—all those things make you think about death.

Is there anything you want to say about the death penalty?

The only thing to be said about the death penalty is that a society that can comfortably and deliberately kill individuals tends to set a precedent. I see that as one of the most fundamental difficulties with the death penalty. If death by deliberate execution is viable government policy for murderers and people guilty of treason, then it is easier to extend it to other offenses and other purposes. I think that has been a serious problem in history. Therefore anything we can do to make government killing unacceptable is good policy. What the Germans or others have done by way of torturing or killing are obvious gross acts of inhumanity. Any philosophy or set of laws that can make that less acceptable as part of a common culture is worth espousing. I've always thought that if there was one thing I could ever do in government, it would be to make torture and killing less likely.

As Governor, you obviously don't get much chance to work with your hands. What is your attitude toward manual labor?

I've done moderate amounts of labor. I wouldn't call it excessive. When I was in the seminary I waited on tables, washed dishes, swept floors, cleaned toilets, mowed lawns, picked weeds, picked grapes, watered lawns, raked leaves for almost four years. I worked in a can company briefly for a few weeks when I was a kid. But I haven't done that much manual labor in my adult life. I think the idea of manual labor is a good one. The reason I try to go out and visit mental wards, farm workers, farmers and ghettos is that I think the information loop between the chief executive and the most distant recipient of any policies of that chief executive is often very ineffective. I like to measure the abstract statements that are uttered at the legislative or gubernatorial level with the impact down at the street. The idea of people in middle-level or higher-level jobs doing more humble work from time to time would be a good thing. Why can't people be allowed and encouraged to play different roles? It would obviously be good if the top of an organizational structure had to do the work of the middle or the bottom. I haven't seen it occurring much in human history. So I don't know whether it's possible or not. It seems that people want to place people on pedestals, and once people get on pedestals they like to stay there.

Do you think your advisors feel free to tell you you're full of shit when they think you are?

I think they have very little hesitation. I know there are some people that say there are too many yes men around me. But I feel I invite criticism and contrary thinking and I think I get a lot of it. The biggest problem is that lots of times people just don't have any ideas at all.

Do you think we are a society which is overly mobile?

I think people want and need limits and boundaries at the same time as they want freedom. Motion is the medium for much of our culture. Motion. Just pure movement. Going and coming and going. Getting and spending. That absorbs a great deal of activity. Oil is the fuel of mobility, and that's why it's so important. Mobility increases the choices. It's like an undertow, pulling up cultural roots. But it also creates new cultural roots—new configurations of plot and human organization.

If you're reelected Governor in 1978, do you think that you will feel freer to act boldly during the second term?

It would mean a little shot in the arm. Certainly at the end of the third year and into the fourth things get tied into political opposition and the necessity of campaigning. The media tends to polarize, almost to the point of being artificial, trying to find distinctions when perhaps there aren't any. Maybe an election clears that away.

Do you think it's a pretty good or a pretty bad time to be alive in America?

I think it's as good as any other. I have a hard time comparing these things—here I am in my thirty-ninth year . . . How was it different in my twenty-ninth, or my nineteenth? They're all different and they're all incomparable.

Are you looking forward to being forty?

No.

VISITS

Oakland

"Hey, Leroy! Look at me, Leroy!" says a black kid to his friend. "Hey! Lemme show you how I'm goin' to be on the TV."

Both kids start strutting and mugging in front of one of the TV cameramen awaiting the arrival of Governor Brown at Oakland's Prescott Elementary School. Groups of black children, more or less organized into reception committees, stand out on the sidewalk. Brown is already an hour and a half late.

"Hey, mistuh. Is . . . ah . . . the ah . . . what's-his-name? . . . the Governor here?" asks a twelve-year-old black girl, blowing a large pink gum bubble which explodes, to much hilarity, all over her face. A great cacophony is being emitted from the schoolyard, where the children, having been dismissed from class, are waiting for Brown's arrival.

"I think . . . well . . . Everybody says he's a nice man," says Anthony Adams, student council vice-president, who is standing out front wearing a red sash across his chest that reads STUDENT COUNCIL. "I seen him on the TV. Anyway, we had lots more famous people down here before. We had Rochester from *The Jack Benny Show.*"

"Hey, this dude—Brown. Ain't he awful young to be President?" chimes in Michael Williams, president of the student council, who wears his hair braided in corn rows.

" 'Cause Carter can't do nuthin', so *he* oughtta be President," says Anthony. "They been trying to remodel this school forever. But they ain't doin' nuthin'. They just goin' to let it get trashed slow like."

A whole group of kids are gathered around where I stand, all fascinated with the idea of saying something that might make it into the papers or get on TV.

"You know what?" says Anthony, his voice rising above the others. "If it ever happened that I'd be President, I'd make sure we got better teachers. I'd—"

"Sheeeeit, Anthony!" says another kid, drowning him out. "You ain't never goin' to be no President."

"Brown cain't change nuthin' anyways," says Michael.

"No," Anthony almost yells over the other voices. "We still gonna get spaghetti for lunch. Just a pile of grease. And it's cold. It ain't mostly bad. It's real bad! An' we got roaches. Hell, with all the grease they oughtta be big as dogs." The other kids laugh at this soliloquy.

Brown's blue Plymouth is just pulling up the street past Ruby's Beauty School.

"Here he come!" yells Anthony.

"Hey! He be on TV," yells a girl as Brown steps out of the car into the street. He is immediately mobbed by press and well-wishers. Mrs. Howard, the school principal, who is supposed to greet the Governor as he arrives, is completely shut out. She stands awkwardly to the side, wearing what looks to be a new dress, lost and jostled in the crowd. Finally an attentive Brown aide finds her and with great difficulty guides her through the crush.

Then the crowd is moving in a block, as if each person were frozen into an assembled puzzle in motion. Brown gets swept right past Anthony and Michael, who stand in their red chest sashes on the side without saying anything and watch him pass on to the Parents' Room for a meeting.

"It amazes me how much is already being spent to help districts like this," Brown says inside the crowded room. "I often think if we could by-pass a lot of the bureaucracy on the way down—like the courts, police, mental health, schools— and send this help right to the people, we'd be farther ahead. The crazy part is that even though we live in the richest country in the world, we have people living in rundown houses.

We can't change it overnight, but we can try and coordinate
it and get a bigger bang for the buck. It may be a dream. But
we're going to try anyway."

"Lawd God. I just got to shake the hand of my Governor," says an elderly black woman approaching Brown as we
pull up in front of the Little Missionary Chapel in the Oakland
Flatlands. "Thank you, Governor," she says, grabbing one of
Brown's slender hands with a huge black palm. "Keep up the
good work. You got a program! Keep pushin', pushin', pushin'!"

"Hey, tell him how we ain't got no curbs and drains," a
woman standing behind her says loudly.

We move on down the block past a series of wood-frame
houses that have been boarded up and abandoned.

"You're in the wrong army," Brown suddenly says to a
young black man leaning against a street sign in Army uniform.

"Yeah?" says the kid, looking dumfounded, and then
reluctantly offering his hand for Brown to shake.

"You know, we got an army here in California, too. You
ought to join our army," counters Brown. He is referring to the
California National Guard, in which he is to subsequently
initiate a project, the Inner City National Guard, where re-
cruits will receive job training and placement as part of enlist-
ment.

We pass on down the block, leaving the kid in our wake
staring after us in stupefaction.

"Mr. Governor! You're too much," yells a dude in curlers
across the street as he slaps his thigh. "Hey, my man," he jives,
"when am I goin' to get my forty acres and a mule?"

Brown looks over across the street. Then everyone in the
group stops and looks over. The man who has just called out
to Brown suddenly shrinks back, overcome by a sudden embarrassment at all the attention.

"Come on over," says Brown with a laugh.

The man in curlers wears a black velveteen shirt slit to the
navel. He drapes one arm around his friend, and they both turn

their backs to the Governor. They are laughing, and appear to be trying to disappear like ostriches from the limelight into which the remark suddenly cast them.

It is incredibly hot in the small living room of this stucco house. The curtains are drawn. People are smoking. Every folding chair in the room is occupied. Everybody, with the exception of one couple, is black.

Brown emerges with a cup of coffee from the kitchen, where he has been on the phone to Sacramento. "How'd I get the only cup of coffee?" he asks, looking around at the others in the room.

The Committee for an All-Oakland Organization is having a discussion meeting to which they have invited the Governor.

At first no one in the room speaks. Just as the awkward silence grows embarrassing, an older man sitting on a couch draped with a bedspread leads off: "If we can't get these vacant abandoned houses rehabilitated, we can't get them back on the tax rolls and revitalize this city."

The one white man in the room joins in, switching subjects as though anything anyone could say was fair game. "Why are all the judges letting the felons back on the streets?" he asks, resisting the temptation to address Brown alone. "Too many judges represent the criminal element. Let's put these professional criminals in the prison. It's gotten to the point where *we* are living in the jail, with the criminals owning the streets." Heads nod in agreement.

The discussion goes on for an hour or so. It jumps from subject to subject. Everything that is bothering the people in the room cascades out without logical sequence. It is as though this is some kind of political encounter group in which the job of Brown is to remain silent and listen like a therapist.

Red-lining, federal and state funding for this and that, regulations, bills, laws—it's a large snarl. At one moment the discussion revolves around a legal detail. The next moment it soars off to some wild abstraction.

Brown is weary but he stays with it, asking questions until he extracts some sense. But the problems are so complicated that one can see how a Governor could become totally consumed in the issues of this one small area.

People have difficulty distinguishing between matters which can be handled locally, by the state or by the federal government. They are bursting with problems, complaints, grievances that come forth in this small room like a torrent of small disconnected particles that defy any ordering into a coherent picture.

I am just wondering how any man can maintain a sense of political possibility when confronted daily with this mountain of seemingly unsolvable dilemmas, when Brown breaks in.

"We can only do a certain amount at the state level," he says, rubbing his eyes. "The stronger you all get, block by block, the better. It's not as though there is one person who can ride in on a white horse and solve everything that's wrong here, and everywhere else across the country. What we've got essentially is a society of problems. It's going to be a long haul. We'll just take it step by step, remembering that we're all just floating on top of this turbulent social experience. The stronger you get, the stronger I get. I just want you to remember that."

The people in the room clap politely. They seem drawn to Brown, but at the same time reflective, perhaps disappointed, to find that now at last, having gotten to the state's top executive, there is still no immediate solution to those things amiss in their lives.

Regents' Meeting

"Never has education been more irrelevant to more kids," says Brown, attending a meeting of the Regents of the University of California.

"I suggest that these pillars of progress and bastions of expertise have failed the society in many ways," he continues, roundly annoying university officialdom, who view Brown's occasional forays into their affairs with grim tolerance.

"The university is a very powerful institution. It can do more, and has to do more," he says, criticizing a nationwide survey of scholars who have given the University of California's schools of education and law high ratings. "Being at the top of the list is maybe not a sign of success but failure . . . It's just not enough to be number one in the face of the injustices and despair throughout the state . . . The Regents should be a forum of criticism and examination for the University. We have great law schools, yet there is something fundamentally wrong with the way our legal system is functioning."

"If the Governor came every month, we might get something done," notes the one student Regent.

"All I want to do is to get the dialogue going," Brown says later, when I ask him why he attended. "It's all a part of questioning the effectiveness of our educational system," he adds, bringing to mind his by now well-known remark, "I question whether we can teach mothers macramé when Johnny still can't read."

Brown has often found himself at cross-purposes with the traditional practices of the University of California, and has used his prerogative as Governor to appoint to the Board of Regents several people whose views are unorthodox.

One such new appointee, the seventy-three-year-old British-born psychiatrist, author, thinker and dolphin devotee,

Gregory Bateson, recently wrote a letter to the chairman of the board in which he said that most of the educational efforts of the University were, "a building of sand [in which] 90%, or even 98% of them [the students] go into various sorts of activities which will perpetuate our way of life, and on the whole aggravate its pathologies, its greed, its hatred of nature and its hatred of intellect."

"The Regents' meetings are so boring, I thought Bateson might liven them up," says Brown.

Comments like this have enraged some, provoking *New York Times* columnist Anthony Lewis to charge that "they smell of anti-intellectualism . . . All it needs is a sentence about pointy-headed professors who can't park their bikes straight."

"I don't think it is so much that Jerry is down on academics," says Gray Davis, ever one to bolster Brown's spontaneous statements with reasonable elaboration. "He is just questioning the disproportionate salaries they command. One thing that also distresses me about the university is that rather than serving as a leveler in society, it tends to serve the middle classes. We should be using public money to minimize the disparity between high and low, not to augment it.

"Jerry's always asking how salaries can be higher for administrators than teachers when the basic mission of the university is to teach. I think he feels that the universities are getting isolated from the average man, and that the educational establishment is being taken over by a class of people whose members only communicate with one another."

Squad Car Patrol

Tonight Brown ends up unannounced in Santa Ana, Orange County, where he spends the night riding shotgun in a police squad car. It is yet another in a rash of "drop-ins," which have ended him up on different occasions sleeping in a San Francisco slum and a mental hospital.

"I think we're going to have to lock up a lot more people," he says, with his usual glibness, after his night on the beat. "Police are working around the clock. I don't see any reason why judges can't work at night, too."

"If you ask me, I think Jerry gets bored sitting around the office," says one staff member. "You know, he's kicking around here on the weekends working when most people have gone home. I think he just wants to get out and have a little excitement. And since he doesn't really know how to cut loose from his work, he takes an excursion and makes recreation out of work. It's like the field trips we used to take from school."

Out Dancing

When Governor Brown leaves his office, he is usually accompanied by one of his drivers, who are members of the California Highway Patrol. These security people are very pleasant low-key professional men. But if there is one thing that makes them uneasy, it is the nighttime sorties Brown makes, both with friends and alone, to local Sacramento cowboy bars and cafés. One driver recounts a trip to a small bar in which a man was murdered the night after Brown had made an appearance.

Another night spot Brown has visited is the Artistico Reno Club, a Mexican café on the outskirts of Sacramento, near the railroad tracks. It lies just down the street from the grain-storage tanks of the Globe Mills, and across the street from the Indian Thrift Shop and a large sign which reads MARISCO'S FOOD ANYTIME—TO GO.

There is a trailer parked in the front parking lot of the Reno Club on which someone has written with an unsteady hand SHILINSKY'S TACO STAND—making one wonder if the great American melting pot is now turning out Jewish-Mexicans here in Sacramento. Above the entranceway someone has written HOY, with a magic marker on a piece of cardboard.

It is dark inside. There is a Mexican band playing on a stage that is faced off with plastic brick veneer. Dim red globe lamps cast the only light on the tables and dance floor (which is simulated hardwood-pattern linoleum). Large grainy blowups of various Latino song stylists adorn the walls. It is smoky. There is a pool table by the jukebox, and a long bar patronized almost exclusively by Mexicans. The bartender barely speaks English.

Brown and Wilson Clark, an environmental advisor, had just returned from a Western Governors' Conference in Denver on a Sunday night.

"We were just out cruising, looking for something to do," says Gigi Coe, a friend of Wilson Clark's. "We went out to the Virgin Sturgeon"—a decaying barge restaurant on the Sacramento River which serves good hamburgers and often has country music—"and met some friends who wanted to go to the Club Reno. If there is one group whose heart Brown has won, it's the Mexicans. He's like Kennedy for them. And they went wild when we arrived.

"We sat down, and then the women started trooping over, asking to dance with the Governor. They'd ask me and this other woman very politely, not quite sure what our relationship with Jerry was . . . Well, goddammit! Jerry took off his coat, rolled up his sleeves and kicked the jams out. He's a pretty good dancer, and he really went out there and boogied. Everyone was dancing up a storm.

"Dale, the security man and driver, was going crazy. The Club Reno is in what they call a 'marginal neighborhood.' Dale was examining every molecule of the place. He was really concerned. He said to Jerry, 'Listen, Governor. I'm not worried about the 99 percent of the people. It's just the other 1 percent.'

"But Jerry didn't seem to care. Finally, Dale called some other guys in. You know, people in the club were juiced—but they were all really friendly. They'd come over to our table and say hello. One guy was having trouble with a welfare check. Another guy had a Polaroid camera, and of course everyone wanted a picture of themselves with the Governor. Jerry seemed to be really enjoying himself. Then someone shone a spotlight on him while he was dancing. He didn't dig that at all. He just walked off the floor very quietly. I don't think we left much before two A.M."

Space Day

A large backdrop behind the speaker's platform at the California Museum of Science and Industry in Los Angeles shows a color view of earth as seen from outer space. It is encaptioned CALIFORNIA IN THE SPACE AGE: AN ERA OF POSSIBILITIES.

The large auditorium is dark. Slides of the NASA Space Shuttle, to be test-launched for the first time tomorrow, flash on a screen. The room is filled with over a thousand scientists, aerospace executives and space enthusiasts. Space Day has been decreed by Governor Brown. Many of his closest staff, like Stewart Brand, Jacques Barzaghi and former astronaut Rusty Schweickart, who is now a Brown advisor on science and aerospace, have been working feverishly on this day for weeks.

"The earth map is drenched in the blood of a thousand —a million—conflicts in recorded history," says Brown from the podium, looking down at the audience, past the rocket ships and models of air contraptions hanging from the ceiling. "But when we look at the earth and the human species from a hundred miles up, we cannot help but sense the oneness of humankind."

As usual, he speaks without a prepared text, wondering out loud what the effects of the closing frontiers on earth will do to the "psychology of the people."

"This is a rather limited piece of material we all live on," he says. "As the frontiers close down, and people begin to turn on themselves, that jeopardizes the democratic fabric itself."

Brown seems to be trying out some new ideas on the audience as he thinks them up.

"But I don't think the frontier is closed," he continues. "It's just beginning to open up in space."

"I'm absolutely lost in admiration of Governor Brown's talk," says Carl Sagan, also one of the speakers. Cornell astronomer, a handsome, insouciant man, he is America's foremost academic popularizer of space travel.

"It is gratifying to get this kind of support for private business in this state," says Robert Anderson, also a speaker, President of Rockwell International, a prime contractor for the space shuttle. The watchword of Mr. Anderson's company is "Space: Down-to-Earth Benefits."

"A space program can create new wealth," says Brown. "And out of this wealth comes a higher standard of living, a boom to California's business and job market. It's imperative that instead of sinking back into the past, this state move into the future."

THE NEWLY SPACED OUT BROWN COMES AS A SHOCK head-

lines the *New York Times*. HE'S GONE BONKERS ON SPACE headlines the San Francisco *Chronicle* snidely.

"What's happened to last year's 'era of limits' and 'small
is beautiful'?" asks one reporter, echoing a familiar refrain as
he surveys the bevy of high-price P.R. booths that the various
California aerospace firms have set up around the auditorium.

"Well," says Brown, showing his customary relish for
contradictions, "even an 'era of limits' has limits. In space,
bigger is better. The 'era of possibilities' does not change my
feelings about the 'era of limits.'"

"I almost didn't come," says Jacques Barzaghi, who has
been working hard on the organization of this event for some
time. "It's like when you've been cooking all day for a party,
then when you finally are ready to serve the exquisite meal, you
don't feel like eating."

"We have to go all the way in all directions," Jacques
Cousteau is saying now from the podium, speaking of the
possibilities for monitoring the oceans from outer space. "In
the bottom of my heart, I know that in spite of the problems,
technology will still be the way to solve our problems."

Just outside the pressroom, I run into a familiar-looking
figure. "What do you think of Governor Brown?" I ask Timo-
thy Leary, who has dropped into Space Day. His face is sunburned, nose peeling. He has on white tennis shoes without
socks, a green bandanna around an open-necked checked shirt
and light cotton surfer pants. He wears his gray hair longish,
in the manner of the English upper classes, which makes him
look a little like an aging yacht-club commodore after too many
years of too many drinks with lunch.

"I didn't dig his limits-to-growth period," says Leary,
without any inquiries as to whom his questioner might be. "It
was senile," he says, giving a kind of zany cackling laugh. "But
I like his youthful vigor here at Space Day. This is a historic
moment, with this Governor throwing his weight behind the
exploration of space."

He drains a Styrofoam cup of coffee he is holding, and
throws it into a wastebasket.

"Well, we can say this about him. He was the first hippie Governor. He brought us all that inner space. So now I suppose it's only appropriate that he take us into outer space."

"Are you interested in outer space?" I ask.

"Am I interested in outer space?" he repeats, laughing. "I'm interested in all high altitudes and far-out experiences as a senior space cadet."

Just at this minute, a space movie in the main auditorium is announced over the loudspeaker system. Leary jumps to his feet as if he had just heard the trumpet of Gabriel and runs toward the auditorium.

Brown is sitting in the front row in his black and white checkered suit. Hands folded. He seems very reserved today. I cannot help but notice how much more pronounced is the gray around his temples than it was when I first saw him in person a year and a half ago.

Today there is a play within the play. At this precise moment, the California State Assembly is debating the final stage of overriding Brown's veto of the death penalty. The senate has already voted to do so. Last count, the assembly was one vote short of following suit.

Some see the possibility of the override as a serious rebuke to Brown. Others claim that Brown would just as soon see an override at this moment, even though he opposes the death penalty, rather than have to rerun for the governorship in 1978 alongside an inevitable initiative on the ballot.

After a break for lunch in an adjacent rose garden, Brown returns to the hall. He is surrounded by a knot of people, asking questions, presenting gifts, gawking.

"I come from the Astronomical Society of the Pacific," says one man, who gives Brown two bumper stickers that read BLACK HOLES ARE OUT OF SIGHT and ASTRONOMERS DO IT AT NIGHT.

The lights dim. *Space: Impact on California and the World* is the afternoon's first topic. Brown sits in the dark, listening and watching.

"That's the latest I have," a reporter is saying with some

exasperation into a phone in the pressroom. "Brown is sitting out there in the auditorium. It's hard to get to him. He's playing this game that he's not concerned about the assembly outcome. He says that what's happening here is much more important."

"I'm worried in a larger sense," says Elisabeth Coleman, Brown's press secretary, looking exhausted. She is curled up in a stuffed chair, without her shoes on, in the Governor's staff room. "I think he's going to get hurt for his stand on the death penalty. I just heard a lot of people . . . You know—they read about that three-year-old girl the other day who was killed and thrown in a ditch, and they just want revenge."

Back in the auditorium, Space Day proceeds: "Space settlements . . . Outer-space solar collectors . . . Visions of the high frontier . . . Retrieval of asteroids for natural resources . . . Communications satellites." Technical, serious discussions. This is no collection of futurists or science fiction buffs. It is industry and science.

Brown is still sitting up front, seemingly glad to be rendered inaccessible by the seated crowd, silent around him.

I pass Elisabeth again in the hallway. "They've voted fifty-four to twenty-six for override," she says.

"Are you going to tell the Governor?"

"Yes, of course," she says, hurrying toward the auditorium, where there is a color slide on the screen showing a map of California, encaptioned "California Space Program Participants."

She walks down the aisle to where Brown sits with Jacques Cousteau. "They voted for override," she whispers in his ear.

"Well, I don't want any cameras—anything," he says curtly. "It's not important," he adds, in a way that suggests that because he has long since made his decision and closed his own mind, he wishes the press would stop bothering him.

But the press is bunching now, just to the left of the speaker's platform.

"What's happening?" a TV anchorman asks another reporter. "Is he going to make a statement?"

"I don't know."

Brown just sits in the darkened room, looking away from this gathering storm.

Finally Gray Davis walks over to talk with him. Some of the audience is beginning to be distracted from the speaker, aware that something is up.

Then one TV crew—all modesty overcome by the urgent sense of getting the story—breaks loose from the pack and walks out in front of the crowd to where Brown is sitting.

"Please. Please," he says at once firmly and respectfully. "There is a speaker talking."

The TV crew shows little inclination to retreat.

"Please wait until this is over. Then I will make a statement," says Brown, forced to relent.

"He'll be out in ten minutes or so," says Gray Davis, walking to where the other members of the press stand, watching to see what fate befalls the TV crew. "Why don't you guys go into the next room and get set up. I'll bring him in."

The press trudges off. Davis rolls his eyes upward, intimating that this is not a most relished moment.

Finally Brown leaves his seat, trying to attract as little attention as possible. He comes over to where I still sit.

"Where am I supposed to go?" he asks, heaving a sigh.

We walk back to the next room. As he comes through the door, the klieg lights go on, and a plethora of microphones are thrust forward.

"What is your reaction, Governor, to . . .?" Several media voices all chorus at once with questions.

"In view of the fact that the legislature and the people have voted for it by a two-thirds margin . . . Everyone has their own conscience," he says, subdued, not quite speaking in complete sentences.

"As long as it is a valid law, I will carry out my responsibilities to uphold it," he says. "Yes, I'm disappointed. I hope the day will come when society will not use death as a punishment."

Someone asks a question about NASA and Space Day. His spirits rise only slightly in response.

"I'm sorry to have kept you all waiting," he finally says, almost numbly. Then he walks back into the darkened auditorium alone.

The Chinese and Linda Ronstadt

The Governor's car, with Dale Rowlee at the wheel, works its way through rush-hour traffic, down the Bayshore freeway toward San Francisco International Airport. Brown and I sit in the back seat, returning from a tantalizingly brief and very stiff meeting at Stanford University, with a delegation from the Chinese People's Institute of Foreign Affairs.

"That was an awfully short meeting," he says, reflecting back on the encounter with this group of Chinese diplomats who have been visiting the United States and Canada. "It's too bad we were late. We really didn't have time to talk." He pauses, his eye caught by some story in the evening paper on the seat beside him.

"Hey, didn't they say that they were taking the train to L.A. tomorrow?" he asks, looking up with a renewed burst of enthusiasm. "Maybe we could set something up and go on the train with them."

"Here's your call, Governor," says Dale, handing Brown the radio telephone receiver.

"Hi . . . Who's this?" asks Brown into the receiver. "This

is Jerry. Tell Linda Jerry's calling." Pause. "Hi. What's up tonight?" Pause. "Oh yeah? Well, why don't I call you from the L.A. airport when I get in?" Pause. "Good. See you."

"Hey," he says to me, again directing his attention toward the Chinese. "It's Friday night, and I'm free until Monday. Why don't you fly down to L.A. tomorrow, and we'll get on that train with them and talk. We'll see what we can arrange. We'll drive up to Santa Barbara and ride back a few hours with them to L.A."

We arrive at the airport, almost late. We breeze through a checkpoint behind an airport pickup truck that has been waiting to guide us out onto the runway to the waiting plane. The plane is about to leave. He's out of the car with nothing more than his brief case, and up the ramp with the wind blowing his hair and tie.

"Okay. Great. Call me in the morning," he yells down just before he disappears on board. "Let's do it. Let's just do it. It will be interesting."

It is Saturday morning. I call the number Brown has given me in Malibu.

"Hello," says a sleepy female voice.

"Is Jerry there?"

"Just a sec."

"Hi. What's happening?" says Brown a moment later, his voice in a lower early morning register.

"Did I wake you up?"

"No, no, not really."

"What about our rendezvous with the Chinese?"

"Let's go. Come on down and we'll drive to Santa Barbara and meet the train. I'll have a car pick you up at L.A. International."

Wayne Waddell is waiting at the L.A. airport in the blue Plymouth when my plane taxis in from San Francisco the next morning. We drive north up the coast with thousands of other Los Angelenos heading to the beaches for a Saturday outing.

An hour later, Wayne turns left at a sign near a large supermarket, which says MALIBU BEACH COLONY.

"We're going in to see Linda Ronstadt," says Wayne to the gate guard, who waves us through.

It is sunny and warm, with a soft breeze blowing in off the ocean. I knock on the door. Brown answers. "Come in. Come in," he says casually, as if inviting me into his own house. He is jacketless with suit pants and a tie on and holds a *Wall Street Journal.*

We walk to the back of the house into a cheerful sunroom with large windows looking out to the beach and the Pacific Ocean. There are several chaise longues, a guitar on a couch, some audio equipment on the floor and a few half-finished glasses of white wine on the coffee table, evidently left over from the night before. Vases of bright flowers are everywhere in the house. Two small children play out in the courtyard.

Linda bounces in, wearing a jersey top and short shorts. She has bare feet, tanned legs, and her black hair is tied up.

"Hi. Want some coffee?" she asks cheerfully, and then disappears into the kitchen, from whence issue sounds of grinding beans and the clatter of cups and saucers.

Brown is sprawled out on a couch. He calls Amtrak for a schedule. Then he dials Gray Davis in Sacramento to talk about sending a certain state representative to Alaska on an energy fact-finding trip.

"We were trying to decide whether or not it would be appropriate for Linda to come with us on the train," says Brown, hanging up. He is smiling, half asking and half stating. "What do you think the Chinese would make of it?" He pauses. I'm intrigued by the idea of Linda Ronstadt in short shorts and bare feet frisking around a private train car of Mao-suited Chinese comrades—doubtless inducing one of the century's major cultural collisons.

"Maybe it's a little weird," says Brown—as if even the slightest hesitation in response from me was enough to convince him that mixing one's private life and diplomacy with members of a Communist government was not an astute move.

"No, I think it would be a little incongruous," he says to Linda, having gained conviction, as he often does, by considering the problem out loud.

Linda wrinkles up her nose at the idea of her exclusion, but smiles understandingly, then heads back to the kitchen for the coffee. Brown returns to the phone.

At one time or another, Brown has been linked, at least in the public mind, with any number of young women stars. He often visits singer Helen Reddy and her husband, Jerry Wald. For a while he seemed interested in singer and Nashville star Ronee Blakley. Joni Mitchell is another singer who has often performed at benefits and events Brown has organized, and with whom he has been associated. And in spite of his frequent protestations against what he calls "Malibu chic," here he is in the house of country/rock singer Linda Ronstadt.

Although the nature of his relationships with these women remains obscure, his public identification with them did win him *Rolling Stone* magazine's "Groupie of the Year Award."

Linda returns with a tray. As we sip our coffee we talk about China—about leisure, culture, sex, music. Linda is curious, wondering what the Chinese might make of a person and musician such as herself.

"Do you think they will ever invite any bands to China on some sort of a cultural-exchange program?" she asks, simultaneously realizing the incongruity of her idea. She smiles and almost defensively adds, "I know that the Russians invited the Nitty Gritty Dirt Band over."

"It's coming. It's coming," says Brown, smiling that special smile of relish he reserves for ideas and events which at once intrigue him and are clearly beyond the pale of present possibility. "We're going to work on it."

Linda lets out a quick squeal of delight at the idea. "I wonder what a Chinese would make of such a concert."

I mention that the Chinese do not at present seem to be too interested in songs about heartbreak and desire with the big boogie beat.

"Well, let's get going," says Brown, rising. "Why don't you drive up with us to the Santa Barbara station?" he says to Linda, while dialing another of his endless telephonic communications. "Then we can meet you later tonight at the reception for the Chinese at the Beverly Wilshire Hotel."

Linda jumps up, smiling, and busies herself with some domestic chore in preparation for our departure.

The drive north up the California coast to Santa Barbara takes about two hours. It is relaxed and pleasant. It is odd to be in the passing lane, gliding by station wagons full of families on their way to the beach. Some cast a brief glance into our anonymous-looking car, then return their attentions to their own affairs, unaware that they are being passed by the Governor and Linda Ronstadt.

Linda whispers something into Brown's ear.

"Wayne, can we pull into that Texaco station for a minute?"

We swing in, unnoticed. "I should just put a bag over my head," jokes Linda, as she opens the door and runs into the women's room.

"You know," says Brown, as we pull back onto the highway, "I sort of respect the way the Chinese toe the line. That's real power—having so many people all working together. We used to have this prescription in the Jesuits of 'Acting according to the gospels as if we were one.' We have our gospel, and they have their political lines." He reflects a moment on this. Then he asks, "Do the Chinese like to get philosophical in an eclectic way? What I mean is, What would they think of these types of comparisons?"

I suggest that they might find this type of analogy invidious.

"It's too bad Linda can't come on the train," he adds, pondering our forthcoming adventure. "But I've got to keep things straight. Can't mix everything up." And then on a more questioning note, he adds, "I don't think the Chinese would understand, do you?"

Somehow our conversation gets on the subject of people's motivation for doing things.

"Are you ambitious?" I ask Brown.

He looks comically pensive, as though he were doing a spoof of someone thinking through a serious matter.

Linda leans forward with a big grin on her face, grabs his left hand and looks right into his eyes as if this were going to be some magic moment of truth.

"Ye-e-e-e-e-s-s?" she probes, laughing in anticipation of whatever sage answer may be forthcoming.

"Ambitious?" repeats Brown coyly. "Maybe."

Another pause. Linda is still staring at him playfully.

"But I'd say I was more of a seeker," he says. Linda puts her hand warmly on his knee, as one might put an arm around a small child who had answered a threatening question without artifice.

"How do the Chinese handle role identification in terms of the difference between being male and female? Is there any of the confusion we have here?" asks Linda.

I reply that the Chinese seem to place far less emphasis on sexual identity, and in general seem to define themselves more through work and politics than sex.

"I think all that Freud business is bullshit," offers Brown gratuitously. "It's not a question of repression, it's a question of how to redirect people's energy."

"Work is really important to me," says Linda. "I mean, I'm willing to give up . . . ummmmm . . ." she laughs, without completing the thought. Then, trying to launch herself on a slightly different line of reasoning, she says, "It really is easy for me to understand how someone would want to spend most of their time with their work. My work is very important to me."

Just at this point we pull up to the railroad tracks in Santa Barbara. The train is twenty minutes late, so we wait in the parking lot in the hot car, drinking fruit juice and eating candy bars.

The train pulls into the station just as a group of teen-age girls on their way home from camp arrive on the scene. "I just can't believe it!" exclaims one of them. "It's him!"

They crowd around, laughing and joking with Brown. The Chinese curiously peer out the windows of their private train car at the sight of this American leader among the American "masses."

Inside the train, the Chinese are in shirt-sleeves, feet up on the seats, taking it easy. The car is filled with cigarette smoke.

Brown walks to the front of the car and sits with Ambassador Hao Teh-ch'ing, President of the Chinese People's Institute of Foreign Affairs. With almost no warm-up, Brown launches into a monologue on his current pet project, the space shuttle, and the possibilities it presents for communications and collection of solar energy that can be beamed via microwaves back to earth.

The Chinese sit impassively, listening, not quite sure why this all is happening and what it's all about. The fact that the Governor of California, about whom they are well versed, should want to board a train and ride with them would normally suggest to the Chinese that they were about to be asked for something, or that some important subject was going to be broached. In Brown's case, the motivation seems to be just curiosity and a fascination with the idea of going to China at some point. He is talking almost aimlessly—the way a musician might vamp chords waiting for a theme or melody to emerge.

"We could take stuff from the moon and catapult it beyond the moon's gravity, as material out of which we could make space colonies," he says.

The translators are having a little trouble with the space lingo. But when the translation comes to the word "colony" in Chinese, Ambassador Hao comes briefly to life. Next to the words "capitalism" and "imperialism," the word "colony" ranks relatively high on the Chinese blacklist of phenomena.

"But there's no one out there in space," says Ambassador Hao finally, laughing, apparently unable to get his mind off of terra firma and into outer space with this unpredictable young Governor before him.

"Some people think that by the year two thousa
there are too many people here on earth, people will jus
to escape to one of these space colonies," says Brown, pr
on.

I can feel the Chinese thinking to themselves, Whe
going to get to the point? This doesn't have even a re
connection to the problems of liberating Taiwan!

Hao rolls with laughter. The other Chinese, who
slowly bunched up around the four seats occupied by B
and the ambassador, smile tentatively. They drink green
Coke and Fresca, and look back and forth at one anoth
if to check and see if any of their comrades have been ab
extract the real significance of this encounter.

"This is a highly imaginative and innovative solutio
says Ambassador Hao, perhaps wondering how class stru
will manifest itself in outer space.

"This is going to happen in my lifetime," adds Bro
quickly, as if to banish the reservoir of Communist skeptici
he senses around him over this interplanetary escapism.

"Does China have any nuclear power plants?" he ask

"No," replies Ambassador Hao, "not yet."

"I think the problem of nuclear waste may be one of t
ultimate problems we can't solve," says Brown. "We should
least try and use nondepletable energy sources like the su
wind and bio-mass first."

"Well, if mankind can go to outer space, why can't w
solve the problem of nuclear waste?" asks Hao.

Then, with no plausible bridge, the Chinese switch th
conversation to the "inevitability of war between the supe
powers," a current Chinese theme. It is as though, having
allowed Brown to discuss his favorite subjects, the Chinese
have now decided to discuss their favorite subjects. Ambassador Hao lets go with a diatribe against the Russians.

"Can you ask the Soviet Socialist imperialists not to expand?" asks Hao.

"Why not?" parries Brown.

"Because they want to control the world," says Hao, roar-

ing with laughter, as if the Russians' passion for expansion were self-evident. "They are more imperialist than the worst imperialists! Just like when a person has a lot of money, he will want more and more. There is no limit."

"I still haven't heard a structural reason why the Soviets must expand. What are they looking for? What do they need?" asks Brown.

"Their only purpose is to enslave the people of the whole world and to gather all of the wealth," says Hao. "Millionaires are not satisfied and want to make more money and become billionaires . . . Outwardly the Russians are strong; but inwardly they are weak. Their wild ambitions to dominate the world will never change. If they were to unleash a war, they would be defeated. The Chinese people are very optimistic."

"So am I," says Brown, starting in on his second cup of coffee, and beginning to look a bit bored. He puts his feet up on the seat opposite, beside Ambassador Hao, who is wearing slippers.

"Take your shoes off," Ambassador Hao says, slapping Brown's black wing tips, and laughing. "This is a free discussion.

"If relations between our two countries are normalized, we are in a more favorable position to counter the Polar Bear. So I hope that farsighted American politicans will deal with this issue from a long-range viewpoint," says Hao, looking pointedly at Brown. "China has a saying that if you only see the seed and overlook the melon, then you're short-sighted."

Brown nods while he removes his shoes.

"America owes us a political debt. You have no grounds whatsoever and are not justified in your position either before the Chinese people or before the people of the world."

Brown is looking right at Ambassador Hao, but registers no reaction as to where he stands on these issues.

"We are friends," adds Hao, backing off just a little. "So I am not using diplomatic jargon, and I'm putting my views to you candidly."

Soon we are pulling into L.A.'s Union Station.

"Where is your baggage?" Ambassador Hao asks Brown.

"I don't have any," he replies.

"Oh. Someone is taking it for you?"

"No."

"Did you send it ahead?"

"No. I believe in traveling light," says Brown.

"Oh yes. I see," says the ambassador, dropping the matter.

I walk out through the station with a young man who is in charge of the American desk of the Institute of Foreign Affairs in Peking.

"Where is the Governor's secretary?" he asks, turning, and almost whispering into my ear.

"He doesn't have one with him today," I reply. "He often travels alone."

The comrade furrows his brow with puzzlement. "Where is the security guard?" he asks, as if he were hoping to solve this riddle by coming at it from a slightly different angle.

I explain that Brown rarely has a security guard with him when he travels, except for the police officers who chauffeur him in his state car.

My companion nods, seeming both to have trouble digesting this information and reluctant to continue the probe.

"I wonder if Linda is going to be able to find us," says Brown as we walk into the lobby of the Beverly Wilshire Hotel in Beverly Hills. The hotel is festooned for the occasion with Chinese and American flags hanging side by side in the front courtyard, where Mercedes, Cadillacs and Rolls Royces are dispatching their charges.

"Maybe she's already here," I suggest as we walk into the bar. We are early for the reception. Brown orders a bottle of mineral water.

"No," he says with conviction, looking at his watch.

"How do you know?"

"Because I know." He smiles. "She's always late."

We walk to the elevator and head upstairs to the roof-garden reception for the Chinese. It is a lovely warm evening.

Waitresses in white and black uniforms move incongruously among the Chinese guests in their Mao suits, serving elegantly prepared trays of shrimp and caviar. Since only a few of the Chinese speak fluent English, there is very little interchange between them and the guest list of prominent and wealthy Los Angelenos, which includes Brown's mother and father, former Governor Pat Brown and his wife, Bernice.

Suddenly Linda Ronstadt appears on the rooftop, wearing a white dress. She pauses for a moment until she spots Brown, who is standing with his mother and father in the middle of this unusual assemblage. He looks a trifle apprehensive—as if he had not yet figured out just how to keep all the planets in the developing solar system of this reception from imploding.

With a large grin on her face, Linda walks over to where he stands.

"Mother, Dad—this is Linda Ronstadt," says Brown.

"Oh, Linda," says Brown's mother warmly, taking both of Linda's hands in hers. "We've read so much about you."

"Hi, hi," says Pat expansively. Then, having surveyed this lovely and talented woman brought to the reception by his son, he says to no one in particular, "Don't you think it's just awful, this crap about Anita Bryant, Jerry and the gay thing in *New West Magazine?*"—He refers to a recent article entitled "Will Anita Bryant's Crusade Smear Jerry Brown's Campaign?"— "It just makes me sick. Just sick." He speaks with a sense of indignation which seems to be reinforced by the living proof of his son's masculine prowess before him.

"That's just *New West,*" says Brown, obviously not thrilled with the theme of the discussion. "They're just doing what they do best—trying to sell magazines."

There is a pause. The five of us stand motionless.

"They should go and get themselves published in China for a while and see how they like that," says Brown, giving an unconvincing chuckle and glancing over toward a group from the Chinese delegation who are looking out over the sparkling lights of Beverly Hills and Hollywood.

"Well, it just makes me so goddamned mad," says Pat, unable to resist another comment. He turns to Linda, clearing his throat. "Why don't you bring our son by some time? We never see him."

"Aw, come on. That's not true," says the younger Brown, just as his father wheels around with a smile to greet some arriving acquaintance with an effusion of good will.

"There he goes," says Brown, shaking his head. "Back into the crowd to pump some hands and gather some more votes."

The party moves downstairs to the elegantly decorated hotel apartment of Mrs. Howard Ahmanson, where we are served a dinner of prosciutto, cannelloni, green salad and spumoni in her antique-furnished dining room.

I strike up a conversation with my dinner partner, one of the ranking Chinese members of the visiting delegation. We discuss the recent political events in China, involving the downfall of Chairman Mao's widow, Chiang Ch'ing, and the "gang of four." He is intelligent and candid.

Suddenly during dessert, my dinner partner leans over and asks, "What is 'date'?"

Describing it as a sweet dried fruit, I give him the Chinese name.

"No, no," he retorts firmly. "What is *date*? Like, 'Governor Brown has *date*,'" he says, accentuating the word date.

"Oh, I see," I reply, unable to suppress a smile. He turns around and casts a sidelong glance at Linda, who is sitting beside Brown at the next table.

"Well," I begin, "a date is someone of the opposite sex whom you invite out for dinner or the movies if you're not married. Brown's actually the youngest Governor in the United States. Linda is a well-known singer and a friend of his," I say, painfully aware of the gaping holes in the comprehensiveness of my explanation.

"Does she sing folk song?" asks my dinner partner, searching for some toehold of understanding.

"Yes. And rock and roll," I reply.

"Ah yes. Rock and roll," he says, terminating the discussion.

It's almost midnight, and I have to get back to San Francisco. Brown and Linda offer to take me to the airport to catch a late flight.

"Come on," says Linda, opening the door to her Porsche. "Three can get in. Here. You drive. I'll sit on Jerry's lap."

We cram in, slam the doors and pull away from the hotel.

"Are you both comfortable?" I ask, noticing that Linda is hunched up under the roof on Brown's lap.

"Oh yes," she purrs, giving Brown a warm hug around the neck.

Conversations with Brown: Privacy, Marriage and the Future

AUTHOR: *How much of their private lives do you feel politicians ought to reveal to the public?*

BROWN: Politics is a part of life, but not life itself. Politicians have an obligation to give a fair amount of time to the job. But I do not believe they are obliged to explain every conscious and unconscious theme that may run through their minds.

What sorts of questions really annoy you?

Questions about why I believe a particular thing,
what I'm going to do in ten years, what I do when
I'm not working at the office, what are my religious
views.

Do you think it's just none of other people's business?

Well, I have a hard time putting limits on what
people have a right to know. My concern is this: To
the extent that I totally publicize not only the official
part of my existence but also thoughts and my private fears and desires, I lose something that is important to me. I don't think it is necessary to probe into
the innermost life of a candidate for a voter to make
an important political choice. It may be of interest
to biographers as time goes on, but political choices
require an understanding of what a person's political
program is, what the individual is doing in an official
way, what his major themes are, what philosophies
he espouses. To try to probe into a person's religion,
his reading habits, his aesthetic sense, the life of his
unconscious mind is really destructive.

*Yet you've answered a lot of questions like that, even
here.*

Right. I've answered some. But those kinds of what-
do-you-do-when-you're-not-being-Governor questions are very ambitious . . . (He laughs.)

*Why do you think people are so fascinated with these
questions?*

I guess they're trying to grope themselves—to find
out what life means and what they should do. A

public figure is not only an official functionary, but also to some extent an exemplar of the culture, and since the culture itself is in a period of transition, people are groping to understand the future, themselves and where they're going. Unpredictability creates insecurity. So they want to know from public figures where things are going. I'm not sure they would have been so interested twenty or thirty years ago. There's more media today. Communication is a larger part of the gross national product than it used to be. There are more writers, there are more television reporters, there is more scrutiny since the explosion of college degrees, since Freud and books on the ego, the subjective, on subconscious motivation. So you put all that together, and it's natural that this surfaces in the public dialogue. I would be surprised if in Lincoln's campaign many of the questions that are now put to politicians were asked. They probably weren't that important. I'm not sure that people cared about George Washington's religious beliefs or what he did when he wasn't being President.

Do you think that the fixation on personalities which seems to be so rampant now is distracting from more important issues?

Just as people can get interested in personalities, people can manufacture personalities and private lives that will conform to people's dreams and hopes just to please the public. It can become psychopathic. You just manufacture feelings and a private life that will mirror the expectations of the electorate.

You've spoken a lot about the breakdown of churches, institutions and the family. Is it possible for a man or woman who has a family to perform the kinds of tasks you're performing?

I think it would be difficult but probably not impossible, but it would take a very special relationship. It just takes time and some space away from the public. But there's no doubt that the more a person gives to the job and to the problems of society, the more absorbing it is and complex and exciting and frustrating and emotionally absorbing. And to take that path just takes more and more psychic energy. It is possible to limit one's commitment to the job and the ideal. It's a question of where I want to draw the limits, or when. And that's really a changing factor depending upon where I am.

That's pretty vague.

Well, I mean what more is there to say? One can go home at five o'clock and just forget it. It's really hard to take the problems of society seriously and then forget about them at five or seven or eight.

So you think there's inevitably a conflict, say, between one's private life and family and the demands of state.

There can be, and there certainly has been for me. I do think about it and I think about whether I want to get as absorbed in the job as I am. Just being governor does tend to absorb a part of one's consciousness, and that tends to limit one's options—but it opens up many other options. Anyone in a demanding job has a certain involvement or commitment. The same positive qualities are found in my job as are found for artists, entertainers, businessmen, trial lawyers, athletes, writers, architects—anyone involved in engrossing, complex, stimulating activity. To be good at it takes a tremendous amount of time, and many people can resolve that investment of professional time and apparently do very well. But I have friends and time to do the things I want to do.

I remember speaking to one of my Cabinet Secretaries one night as we finished working at eleven. He'd just called his wife. When he got off the phone he just turned to me and said, "Governor, if you want to stay in this work, don't ever get married."

It strikes me as ironic that it was so few years ago that not being married was an incredible liability for a politician.

The emotional involvement of a job like being Governor or Senator or President puts a lot of pressure on a relationship. That's obvious from looking at the divorces and state of the marriages of those in public life.

What does the high divorce rate tell you?

That modern relationships and families are fairly complicated.

Do you think more so than before?

The family's important because it's a basic building block of the society. And to the extent that it weakens, to that extent the state will become more intrusive by trying to fulfill its functions.

Do you look forward to having a family at some point in your life?

Yes, I do.

Have you ever thought that you might just drift away, marry and have a family?

I've thought about it. So far the right occasion hasn't quite presented itself.

Are material goods important to you?

I spend most of my time working. I don't have a great deal of time for concerning myself with choices among competing material goods.

Do you enjoy buying things? . . . When's the last time you bought something?

I can't remember. It might be interesting to go out to buy things—but it's also very interesting to try to put together a mental hospital when it's in a state of decline. What is more interesting? Governors are not chosen for long periods of time. There are important questions. There's a great deal to do. I don't think governors are elected to indulge themselves and spend their time with their credit cards. They can do that before or after they get the job. One only has a certain amount of psychic energy, and if one directs it to accumulating goods and services, then he has less energy for evaluating ideas and focusing on the interactions of government. I just spent the morning at a mental hospital, so the questions in my mind are: What is possible for people who go there? How much will it cost? Do we have the administrative capacity to carry it out? Can we attract doctors? Can we create an esprit de corps? Can we inspire confidence? Will the people be interested in it? Will the legislators be interested in it? Will it really make a better society? After that it's hard to say, "Well now, what about a new car? a stereo set? or a television?"

Do you find yourself making a distinction—which I think is very well demarcated in most Americans' lives —between leisure and work, holidays and job?

Not too much. I don't have any sense of when the day begins or when the day ends. But there are certain ceremonies I'd like to see more deeply recognized like Thanksgiving, Christmas or Easter. I think it is important to have days when you celebrate. I'd like to see more of that kind of leisure time.

Do you find yourself fascinated with power?

It's a word I don't use very often.

But you have a lot of power, insofar as any man does.

I don't think I have been interested in it. I don't know. The word doesn't . . .

I mean, aren't you conscious of yourself as you move in and around political power?

No. Not as much as you'd think. I mean, I can't say I don't ever think about power, because I think of new things every day. In fact, you raise the question in a fashion that makes me think about it in a way I've never thought about it before.

I think a lot of people aspire to high political offices because the power is appealing to them.

I don't know what that means exactly. I mean, how much of government is just ceremony and how much of what a Governor does has an impact? How much is a Governor cutting a ribbon that would have been cut anyway and how much is he actually changing the social and political process?

Power implies something that would not have happened but for the Governor. If everything is going to happen anyway, how do you define that as power? It isn't clear to me what things occur because of my action and what things would occur anyway. I'm not saying there isn't power there, but I'd have to take a specific example and see what it is. That gets into the question of achievement and what has been done—what can be done.

What that your administration has done do you consider significant?

Well, I'd want to think about that. I'm usually thinking about what I should be doing next year. People ask me that question, and I'm never totally satisfied with the answer. But I think bringing the Governor and state government a little closer to the people has been important. Bringing into the state government people who are interested, open and in touch with some of the emerging perceptions and concerns of California that have been left unrecognized in the last decade. I think this gives hope for more response from the government. And by communicating with people and meeting with them, they influence me and I influence them. By communicating simply and clearly both by example and word I have been able to make the government mechanism more a part of the people that government is supposed to serve. I'm not saying that each constituency is satisfied, but the connecting loop between the government and the people in California is working much better now than I think it worked before. One can list concrete legislative actions and administrative decisions. But more than that, government is a live process with people working on problems. The rate of getting an idea from the mental ward—or the school, or the farm—back to the state for response, and then finally back into the system—the rate of completing that circle—is faster, and the whole system more responsive.

A student down at Cal Tech asked me the same question the other day. So I asked him what he thought a Governor could do that he would classify as significant. He couldn't answer and changed the subject.

Is the idea of being President at all intimidating?

Sometimes, in the sense that the problems I deal with on the state level are not that immediately earthshaking. What I'm dealing with can usually be postponed. The immediate crisis is often more a crisis in the media than anything else. I would think with the Presidency there would be times like recession and depression, wars, disasters of one kind or another, where there were far more serious consequences. So to that extent it is a more awe-inspiring job.

Do you think you would enjoy being President?

I try not to think about those things too much.

Surely you must still think about the Presidency.

Sure, it's a consideration. But it's just one of the many considerations which go into making a decision. It's the one which the media seems to be most interested in. One journalist from New York told me recently when he came out to interview me that they are "going to force me to run" . . . I guess just by continuing to mention me as a match for Carter. I don't even like to talk about it. Basically, when I am making a decision I consider a whole host of more important considerations such as whether or not an idea is a good one, who supports it, who will benefit from it, what are my convictions about it, and what are the chances that it can happen.

Why don't you just say to the media what you have said to me: "Obviously the Presidency is a consideration, but just one among many"?

Oh no! Then all you'd have in the paper the next day is a headline which says "Brown Admits He Is Thinking About Presidency." All the rest of what I said would be lost. Then everyone would come out of the woodwork and say, "Brown should promise to commit himself to California or not run again for the Governorship," or "Brown shouldn't use the Governorship as a stepping stone." It wouldn't work.

Do you think you are crisis-oriented as some people have suggested?

No, not really, although it goes against the conventional wisdom. But I think I often use a crisis as a takeoff point to find a solution for the broader issues.

How do you take defeat?

I don't know.

I mean, let's say you were defeated for Governor in 1978.

Well, I was defeated for the Presidency in 1976.

No, but that really was a victory in defeat.

Defeat is the next thing to learn. I learn certain things in victory and I learn certain things in defeat. We're defeated and we win every day.

You mean defeat wouldn't be a terrible blow to you?

I think there would be a month or two where it would probably have some impact. I don't know if it would be any longer than that. I'd have to think about it. Life is so full in every moment that whether I'm defeated, or don't run or finish with this program and go on to the next . . . it's all going to change. I've done very few things in my life that have lasted longer than a few years.

Did you ever fancy that life would be as interesting if you went down to a smaller level rather than a larger level from being Governor?

Well, obviously that's going to happen. It's just a matter of time. I want to be ready for it.

What will happen in the interim?

I can't imagine being Governor for . . . at the most two terms.

What else would you want to do?

Well, I've thought about that.

You have?

I have. That's one of the reasons I haven't announced for Governor.

Well, what are some of the things you've thought about?

I'm trying to find a way not to run, but I can't.

What do you mean you can't find a way?

I can't find anything I'd rather do. I'm trying to imagine what else I would do.

Have you been able to imagine anything?

No.

EPILOGUE:
CARTER
VS.
BROWN

Introducing the President

It is dusk as Brown's blue Plymouth pulls out of the underground garage of the Los Angeles Century Plaza Hotel. We are on our way to the airport to meet President Carter, who is arriving momentarily on Air Force One for a thousand-dollar-a-plate fund-raising dinner.

Brown sits in the front seat with his driver. Gray Davis and I sit in the back seat. A pair of the Governor's black socks are draped over the headrest of the front seat to dry—an apparent last-minute effort to ready Brown sartorially for a trip to the East Coast in the morning.

"Everyone in Washington has been so uptight about Jerry introducing the President," a Brown aide has told me this morning. "They wanted Lou Wasserman, who is the organizer of the dinner and head of Universal Studios and MCA to introduce Carter. Wasserman is a big poobah who gives money to Democrats. But finally they just compromised and decided that Wasserman would introduce Jerry, and that Jerry would introduce Carter. It's all so silly. The Carter people are too paranoid even to let Jerry talk."

When Brown himself was asked several days ago whether or not he intended to go to the dinner (of which only 7½ percent of the proceeds will trickle back into the coffers of California Democrats), he replied, "Do I have any choice? I think it's what you call a command performance. But Nietzsche has a saying, *'Amor fati.'* That means 'Love Your Fate.' So, I will go with joy and exhilaration."

In anticipation of Carter's arrival, thousands of pickets

have assembled outside the Century Plaza Hotel. There are farmers on tractors, protesting the reinstitution of the Land Reclamation Act, which would divide up large tracts of publicly irrigated land into 160-acre family farms. There are people protesting Carter's flirtations with the PLO, some Nazis, some gay-rights advocates, a group protesting the neutron bomb and a large contingent marching under a banner: DON'T GIVE OUR CANAL TO A DICTATOR.

It is a veritable smorgasbord of dissent. The protesters march past the hotel in a large circle. Brown is curious, his interest probably all the more piqued by the fact that the pickets are waiting for another man.

"No, no. I want to go right through them. I want to see them," Brown says to his driver, just as he is about to make a turn and circumvent the throng.

As the Plymouth turns into the street toward the crowd, Brown rolls down his window. A group of protesters spot him. A cheer goes up. Several motorcycle cops, suddenly realizing that the Governor of California is behind them in the middle of the crowd, fire up their bikes and begin to blaze a trail.

"What's it all mean?" asks Brown humorously, pulling his head back inside the Plymouth. "It's like a festival. People seem friendly."

We are waved through a gate by a group of police, and pull into a special part of Los Angeles International Airport, behind a string of black Cadillac limousines parked next to a platoon of motorcycle police and ambulances. A helicopter circles overhead, scouring the adjacent areas with a searchlight. The parking area is crawling with secret service agents wearing hearing aid–like earphones. Radios and walkie-talkies are crackling everywhere. Two men walk with guard dogs. Hundreds of people move about their task with grim urgency. Even given that Brown is only a Governor, whereas Carter is President, the difference between the way in which these two men travel is stunning. I had not encountered such security consciousness since stumbling on the Reagan presidential campaign one day at the Portland Airport.

"It's all incredible," says Brown, looking around in the failing light at the scene around us. "All of it for one man."

"Do you think you could manage to stay out of this security vise if you ever became President?"

"I'm sure we could end run it. I mean, I often just drive my car around alone on the weekends. People don't notice you if you don't have all this." He gestures at the warlike activity around us.

"I think you have to *want* to get out of all this to really do it," adds Davis. "You have to want to keep things more spontaneous. Carter is always such a fanatic about being on time and having everything organized that it's easy for this whole security establishment to get in on every move."

"Let's wander around," says Brown, as if he felt the need to exhibit some spontaneous impulses right now.

We walk away from the area where the dignitaries and press are assembling and head out toward the gate through which we have just passed.

"Okay, mister. Let's keep off on the side," says a policeman in the half light, pushing Brown out of the way of an incoming limousine without recognizing him.

"Have you been doing this for long?" Brown asks him.

"We've done 'em all since Eisenhower," says the policeman gruffly, as if it were unbecoming for a man with such serious responsibilities to answer questions from the masses at a time like this.

A woman who stands on the other side of the chain-link fence with a group of well-wishers suddenly spots Brown and takes a flash photo of him with her Instamatic. Brown's face is momentarily illuminated before the policeman, who does an almost cartoonlike double take.

Then, suddenly, Brown is walking out the gate that this policeman has been guarding so zealously.

"Here. Why don't you stand with me and get someone

else to take a picture?" he says to the smiling woman with the Instamatic.

The policeman is not clear what the proper approach should be, now that one of the people whom he is supposed to be guarding has defected to the wrong side of the fence. But before he can galvanize himself to any course of action, Brown is back on the dignitary side of the fence and striding off toward the reception area.

"Where's the landing area? . . . Whose limousines are these? . . . What's the meaning of life? . . . Where is this President?" Brown asks comically.

"Can you imagine putting up with this all day?" asks Davis, looking at Brown, shaking his head and laughing.

Air Force One is landing now. It taxis in. The ramp goes up. The TV lights go on. The door opens. And suddenly there's Carter in that familiar presidential pose—standing at the top of the ramp, frozen in place for a moment while the cameras grind, waving with one hand like a beauty queen from a parade float.

The President steps down and works his way through the waiting line of dignitaries, which Brown has joined with no apparent enthusiasm, save the awareness that his absence would be taken by all as an act of lèse majesté. Carter carries his own valise, as if it were a prop in a play. He self-consciously puts it in the trunk of his waiting limousine. Up since dawn, with stops already made today in Des Moines, Omaha and Denver, Carter looks tired. His face is puffy and his skin has an unhealthy pale mottled look. He looks as if he had aged since the campaign of a year ago.

When the official greeting is over, Brown, who is supposed to ride back to the hotel with Carter, seems to consciously cut loose and walk away from the presidential entourage, as if he did not wish to associate himself too thoroughly with it.

Carter gets into his limousine with the Los Angeles mayor, Tom Bradley. California's Democratic Senator, Alan

Cranston, gets in on the other side. Brown, who is watching out of the corner of his eye, turns to put a little more distance between himself and what appears to be shaping up as a slur of some magnitude.

"What's up?" I ask Brown, as he moves away.

"I don't know," he says, shrugging.

Just then, one of the doors of Carter's limousine bursts open. Senator Cranston steps out quickly. A presidential aide calls out, "The Governor! Where's the Governor?"

I hasten over to Brown, who by now is out of earshot of the limousine. He turns, sees that he is being summoned, walks back, and seconds later is speeding off to the dinner with the President at the head of the motorcade.

"I sense that Carter is not overjoyed by Jerry's presence," says Gray Davis, as we return in Brown's car to the hotel. "But I think he does try hard to keep things cordial. I know from other visits to Washington and Plains that it really drives Carter and his staff crazy when they want to find Jerry for something and he has wandered off talking with someone else. I think that's one of the major differences between Jerry and Carter. Carter is quite rigid and tries to keep large numbers of issues on the front burner at once. Jerry tends to take things more one at a time and focus in on something with all his attention. He tries to bring a lot of people into the process until he has a real solution. I think that's what he did with the Agricultural Labor Relations Board that settled the Farm Workers/Growers problem."

Back at the Century Plaza the pickets have grown in numbers and are chanting, "Carter, Carter, you can't hide. We all know that you're inside." Carter's huge motorcade has gone into the hotel through the rear entrance.

Inside, the lobby is boiling with a homogenized blend of secret-service agents, stars and wealthy L.A. denizens on their way to the banquet in tuxedos and evening gowns, and a large contingent of celebrity hounds in search of prey.

It is at this point that I realize I do not have any of the correct press credentials to get into the banquet. Having been with Brown all afternoon, I have missed the last possible deadline to apply. Security is tight. Special press passes, which are worn around the neck like dog licenses, have been issued to correspondents only after a security check has been run.

I find myself standing at the head of an escalator leading to the hotel's grand ballroom with a large group of autograph seekers. I have been politely but firmly barred from entry by two secret-service men. I stand forlornly for about ten minutes, watching the likes of Paul Newman, Joanne Woodward, Helen Reddy, Jane Fonda, John Denver and Burt Reynolds—engraved invitations in hand—glide effortlessly down to dinner.

Just as I am about to give up, Brown himself comes down the stairs. I ask him if he thinks he might be able to oil me past the two agents.

"Sure, sure," he says, as if he welcomes the challenge. Then, handing me his own invitation, he says, "This ought to do. I guess I'm not going to need it to get in."

Turning to the secret-service agents, he says, "Sure—I'll vouch for this guy. There's no problem, is there?"

The secret-service men seem momentarily nonplused. Before they have regained their senses, we have both slipped down the escalator to the ballroom.

At the bottom, Brown is immediately pounced on by a reporter with microphone in hand. "You seemed to be standing alone out there with the President. How would you compare your reception to Carter's?" he asks.

"That question is just media hype." With no further answer, Brown walks away toward the side of the large rotunda in which a predinner stand-up cocktail party is raging. He stands alone now. Whereas he radiates great confidence and élan once engaged in a group, there is a suggestion of awkwardness and vulnerability about him at this moment, as if he is not quite sure how to deport himself while on public display, at the same time that he is the center of no one's attention. Like a skilled host, Gray Davis responsibly moves his conversation over and incorporates Brown. The moment passes.

Slowly the thousand guests work their way into the banquet room. Whereas Brown is seated out in front at one of the tables, Carter has still not materialized.

"In a minute, the President will come out and visit each and every one of you at your tables," says Lou Wasserman from the podium, after struggling for several minutes to get the attention of the crowd. And then, as if he were introducing a new act in Las Vegas, he suddenly picks up the tempo and says, "And now, your friend and mine—the Governor of California, Jerry Brown!"

There is applause. The room rises as Brown works his way to the podium. Then there is a hush. People seem more curious about what Brown will say by way of introducing Carter than about what Carter might say himself.

"I am supposed to keep talking until the President comes in. So, if I stop in midsentence, you'll understand."

There is patchy, confused applause and a few attenuated laughs after this strange opener, which at once seems to acknowledge the respect due the highest office in the land and make fun of it.

Having established a mood of ambiguity with these initial remarks, Brown proceeds in a more conventional vein. "We have a leader of our party who has taken on the difficult tasks of projects which have been unattended for decades . . . The spirit which pervades Washington is one of confidence . . . I know from my own limited experience that things can get pretty tough . . ."

He continues on soberly for several minutes. Then suddenly he stops, turns toward the back of the stage from whence Carter is presumably to emerge and asks, like the emcee for a third-rate talent show, "Is he here yet?" Pause. "No?" Pause. "Well, in that case I'll have to go into phase two of my talk."

The audience is laughing now, albeit nervously, because most people in the room know that "phase two" is exactly that part of Brown's introduction that the Carter people had hoped to avoid.

"Are there any questions?" Brown is asking the audience with a smile, like a professor winding up a lecture a few minutes early. Some people look around, unclear just how to respond. "No? We're going to be here awhile, what else can we talk about?" Pause. "This is the first fund-raiser I've come to for some time, and I'm not even getting any of the funds."

"I can't believe it!" says a Brown-watcher, Richard Reeves, standing in the press section and clapping his forehead with his hand. "I've heard Presidents introduced a thousand ways, but never anything like this! This man is incredible! Actually, I came all the way across the country just for this introduction."

Suddenly, as if to resolve the situation on neutral terms, the band starts pounding out "Happy Days Are Here Again." Brown, wordless now, stands behind the podium, incongruously emblazoned with the presidential seal, clapping in cadence with the musical interlude.

Finally Carter emerges. While Brown wears a dark double-breasted business suit and long tie, Carter is dressed in a tuxedo and black tie. He waves to the crowd, greets Brown, then chats perfunctorily with him for an instant. Brown leaves the stage as Carter takes out a sheaf of notes and begins talking.

"I got a personal handwritten letter from you, Governor Jerry Brown," says Carter with a broad smile. "I decided to come anyway." Applause. "As you know, we formed a partnership way back in the campaign, and we have been moving toward the same goal for a long time." Applause.

"I was hoping that you would meet my goal—to raise enough money to have my brother Billy come out and speak next year," he continues, looking right out into the audience. "Billy brings me a lot of good publicity, as you well know. I wish we could have gone along with my plans to involve him in the government." Laughter. "I had it all arranged. I was going to reorganize the CIA and the FBI together, but Billy said he wouldn't head up any agency that he couldn't spell, so that fell through." Laughter.

Whereas Brown's introduction seemed bizarre, Carter's speech seems commonplace and bland. Having warmed his audience up with a few standard formula jokes, he moves into the hard stuff: poverty, defense, nuclear energy, governmental organization, unemployment, human rights, oil, foreign policy, Israel, open government.

It is a grocery-list speech, sincere but lusterless, and there are few laughs once the jokes are over. Behind me, members of the press corps begin chatting with one another.

Finally the speech ends, and as Carter begins his two-hour dirge of shaking hands with every guest in the room (something I cannot imagine Brown doing), I walk back to where Jody Powell is standing at the rear of the press section. He is looking handsome in his black tuxedo, with his bow tie rakishly absent.

"Do you think Carter feels any uneasiness about being introduced by Governor Brown, since everyone seems to be squaring them off as rivals?" I ask him.

"Not a bit." His reply is chilly. "Brown's introduced him several times before. It's no big deal."

"Is that a straight answer?" I ask.

"As straight as the question." Powell throws an empty cigarette package on the floor and turns to someone else. He is obviously not eager to pursue this line of questioning.

A moment later I recount this scene to Richard Reeves, who has flown out with the Carter entourage on Air Force One.

"I'm not sure about Carter himself," he says, smiling. "But most of his staff are terrified of Brown. Just terrified."

About the Author

Born in New York City in 1940, ORVILLE SCHELL has lived in California and the Far East since his graduation from Harvard. A student of Chinese language and culture, he is the coeditor of the first three volumes of *The China Reader* and coauthor of *Modern China*. His two most recent books are *The Town That Fought to Save Itself* and *In the People's Republic,* a remarkable account of eight weeks spent living and working in China. He lives on a ranch in Northern California.